Frederika Macdonald

The Iliad of the East

A selection of legends drawn from Valmiki's Sanskrit poem, the Ramayana

Frederika Macdonald

The Iliad of the East
A selection of legends drawn from Valmiki's Sanskrit poem, the Ramayana

ISBN/EAN: 9783337153069

Printed in Europe, USA, Canada, Australia, Japan

Cover: Foto ©Thomas Meinert / pixelio.de

More available books at **www.hansebooks.com**

THE

ILIAD OF THE EAST:

*A SELECTION OF LEGENDS
DRAWN FROM VALMĪKI'S SANSKRIT POEM,*

THE RĀMĀYANA.

BY
FREDERIKA RICHARDSON,
AUTHOR OF "XAVIER AND I."

London and New York:
MACMILLAN AND CO.
1870.

LONDON:
R. CLAY, SONS, AND TAYLOR, PRINTERS,
BREAD STREET HILL.

PREFACE.

OF the two great epic poems of India, the Rāmāyana and the Maha-bharata, the former is generally supposed to have claims to the greatest antiquity. The title of the work is derived from two Sanskrit words—*Rāma* and *ayana*, signifying the adventures of Rāma; the Prince whose virtuous career is therein recorded, being Rama Chandra, the hero of the Kshatriya or warrior caste,—as distinctive from Parasu-Rāma, the champion of the Brahmans, and Bala-Rāma, the brother of Krishna, the Hercules of Hindu mythology.

Rāma Chandra, like his two illustrious namesakes, is supposed to be an Avatar, *i.e.* an incarnation, of Vishnu, who at the request of mortals and immortals consented to pass through this lower phase of existence that mankind might be delivered from the oppression of the demon Rāvana, whose life Brahma had secured against all save a human hand; but whilst the hero passes through his many struggles and afflictions in utter ignorance, or forgetfulness, of his divine nature, he appears for the most part as a courageous and devoted man, and is seldom withdrawn from our warmer sympathies by any display of supernatural endowments.

It is probable, even, that the story of Rāma's birth owes somewhat of its miraculous character to the passage of the primary legend through the hands of the Brahmans; who would naturally be more disposed to attribute Rāma's virtue to some special condescension on the part of a celestial being, than to admit that any member of an inferior caste could rise to so high a state of perfection. "It is certainly likely," says Professor Williams in his interesting essay on Indian Epic Poetry, "that at some remote period, probably not long after the settlement of the Aryan races in the plains of the Ganges, a body of invaders, headed by a bold leader, and aided by the barbarous hill-tribes, may have attempted to force their way into the peninsula of India as far as Ceylon. The heroic exploits of the chief would naturally become the theme of song, and the hero himself would be deified; the wild mountaineers and foresters of the Vindhya and neighbouring hills who assisted him would be poetically converted into monkeys, and the powerful and savage Aborigines into many-headed ogres and blood-lapping demons; these songs would be the property of the Kshatriya, or fighting caste, whose deeds they celebrated, but the ambitious Brahmans, who aimed at religious and intellectual supremacy, would soon see the policy of collecting the rude ballads which they could not suppress, and moulding them to their own purpose." (Indian Epic Poetry, p. 9.)

Professor Max Müller[1] also gives it as his opinion that some actual military expedition gave rise to the legend of the Rāmāyana; and he compares this struggle to the war against Persia, which did so much to elevate the Greek character, by demonstrating the superiority of valour and discipline over brute-force.

The Rāmāyana comprises in all some twenty-four thousand verses, or *slokas*—the Sanskrit word for the peculiar metre supposed to have been invented, in a moment of inspiration, by the Poet Valmīki, and subsequently accepted by Hindu writers as the proper form of expression for heroic poetry.[2] The

[1] History of Ancient Sanscrit Literature, p. 17.
[2] Assuming that the Valmīki-sloka owes its origin to the author or authors of the Rāmāyana, we should here have proof that the poem was anterior to the Maha-Bharata, where the same metre occurs:— on the other hand, this would exclude the Rāmāyana from the Vedic

poem is further divided into six books, which are as follow:

The Adi-Kanda,—which commences with the introductory episode of Valmīki's call to be a poet; then proceeds to the story of Rāma's birth, of his childhood and early youth, of his marriage with Sītā, and concludes with a somewhat important episode, viz. the triumph of the youthful warrior over Parasu-Rāma, which incident alone suffices to show that the primary author or authors of the poem did not belong to the Brahmanic caste.

The Ayōdhyā-Kanda,—which tells of Dasaratha's wish to share the government with his son Rāma; of Kaikeyī, the jealous stepmother's plot to procure the young prince's banishment; of Rāma's ready submission, and of the departure into exile of Rāma, Sītā, and Lakshmana, the devoted brother of the hero; of Dasaratha's death, and of Bharata's vain attempts to persuade his brother Rāma to ascend the throne, until the term of his exile had expired.

The Aranya-Kanda,—which treats of Rāma's residence in the forest Dandaka; of the offence given to Sūrpanakhā, the sister of Rāvana; of Rāvana's

period, where the Valmīki-sloka is unknown, though in the Sutras there are Anushtubh and more Trishtubh-slokas.

abduction of Sītā; of Rāma's search for the traitor, and his alliance with Sugrīva, brother to the King of the monkey tribes.

The Kiskindhya-Kanda,—where Sugrīva relates the ill-treatment he has met with at the hands of his brother, Bālin, and where Rāma slays this unjust monarch and gives the rule to Sugrīva, who in his gratitude sends forth his subjects to scour the country in search of Sītā. The company of monkeys under the command of Hanuman, Son of the Wind, learn from an old vulture that Rāvana has taken his captive to the isle of Lankā, and encamp accordingly on the sea-coast.

The Sundara-Kanda,—in which we read of the marvellous adventures of Hanuman, who leaps across the sea, and after many vicissitudes discovers Sītā. The faithful ambassador returning to fetch Rāma, the hero and his allies are sorely put to it, to know how they are to cross the sea, when the Spirit of the Ocean appears to them, and bids them construct a mole; which is done, under the superintendence of Nala, son of Visvakarman, the architect of the pleasant heavens where dwell the gods.

The Yuddha-Kanda,—which contains a full account of the struggle; of the valour of both armies, and the fierce heroism of Rāvana; finally of Rāma's triumph and the death of his adversary; of the vindication of Sītā's purity, and—the allotted time having expired—of the exiles' joyous return to their native city.

There is a seventh book sometimes appended to the Rāmāyana, entitled the *Uttara-Kanda*, which records the apotheosis of Rāma, but it is a comparatively modern addition, and conceived in a spirit quite at variance with the rest of the poem.

As may be well imagined, of these twenty-four thousand slokas, there are many hundreds that might be abstracted without in any way damaging the work's entireness. There are countless repetitions, besides digressions which occupy sometimes the best part of a volume. Above all, passages abound at nearly every page, which, though not impure in themselves, are calculated to offend the nicer refinement of our time. In spite of these drawbacks, the Rāmāyana is so rich in poetic beauty and genuine humour,—reveals at the same time so high a moral standard, and a spirit of such large and tender humanity, that it seems strange it should have remained so long unrecognized by English lovers of literature. Translations in Italian and French have appeared, and Schlegel has translated the three first books into Latin; but up to the time of the commencement of this work, the excellent but necessarily very condensed summary given in Professor Williams' essay, to which I have referred, and some fragments translated here and there, by an admirer of Indian literature, was all that was available to the English reader. I am told indeed that a translation of the poem was undertaken by Messrs. Carey and Marchmont in 1806, and the first three volumes actually printed at Serampore; but unhappily the vessel conveying them was lost at sea, and only a few specimen copies, that had been previously despatched, arrived in this country. Of these, one is to be had at the reading-room of the British Museum; this translation, however, only carrying the reader through the best part of the Aranya-Kanda,—that is to say, about half through Valmīki's production.

It would of course require a Sanskrit scholar of no ordinary proficiency to render the Rāmāyana literally into English; and whilst an immense service would thereby be rendered our literature, it is scarcely probable that such a work would become generally popular, both on account of the unwieldy dimensions of the poem, and of the other disadvantages I have mentioned. My object in this present work has been to give a readable and familiar form to these Eastern stories; certainly as well deserving of general appreciation as the legends of Grecian and Scandinavian mythology. As regards the plan and facts of the story, I have been careful of course strictly to follow the original; and it has been my endeavour to comprehend in this small volume all the most striking and noteworthy incidents recorded by the inspired Brahman. I have told these facts in my own language, rather than in that of my guide, the French translator, Mons. Fauche, firstly, because not being able to refer to the original Sanskrit I have no opportunity of deciding how far he has himself been textually faithful to Valmīki; and secondly, because such frequent and lengthy omissions would have been necessary to compress into moderate volume any general idea of the narrative, that the most remarkable passages, from a poetical point of view, would have been eliminated, and a quite erroneous impression as to the style and literary value of the original produced.

Then, as to the title I have chosen;—I am far from wishing to uphold the somewhat daring theory, advanced by Monsieur Fauche, that Homer, during his voyages with his captain and disciple, Mentes, probably fell in with some Phœnician merchants who, together with Indian wares, brought also the legends current in that distant land, which undoubtedly the youthful Melesigenes never visited himself, or later, in his days of blindness, he had delighted to picture in his poetry, the richness of landscape, and the fulness of sunlight, in that country whence he drew inspiration. Fascinating and ingenious as this suggestion is, I dare not for a moment presume that it was this chance encounter, and no war against Ilium, nor the legend of any such war, that furnished the poet with that skeleton of facts to which his genius gave a soul.

Nor would I ask you to admit the somewhat less presumptuous assertion, that the epic poems of Greece and India found their source in one and the same historical incident.

But the analogy between the two works is striking enough, and the differences are sufficiently characteristic, to make the comparison interesting and instructive. Thus, in both instances, we have a wife carried off from her lawful lord, and an expedition undertaken to recover her and punish the ravisher. But, on the one hand, we have the beautiful but abandoned Helen; on the other, the chaste and devoted Sītā, whose childlike and yet heroic character is one of the most charming sketches of womanhood I know.

Again, whilst we admire the valour of the Grecian warriors, there clashes with this feeling an involuntary repugnance at their bloodthirstiness, which no note calling our attention to the different code of the so-called "heroic" age can do away with. But in the Yuddhākanda we have side by side with deeds of daring the generous forbearance towards a weary or wounded adversary, and the fair and honourable warfare which, one would think, must at all times have been essential to true heroism.

Stories of slaughter being monotonous as well as unattractive, I have chosen less incidents from the Yuddhākanda than from the other volumes; but the kind reception of the deserter Vibhīshana contrasted with the murder of Dolon by Ulysses and Diomed, after they had lured him to give them the information they desired, and the funeral honours paid to the dead Rāvana, compared to the dragging of Hector's corpse at Achilles' chariot wheel, are sufficient to show the different standards revealed, severally, by the two poems.

To conclude, I cannot but break through my rule, for once, to translate literally the panegyric with which the author himself winds up the story :—

"He shall be delivered from sin, the man who, in the world, can keep in his ears this tale of the Raghuide of indefatigable deeds.

"He shall have sons, if he desire sons; he shall have riches, if he long for riches; *he* who in the world hearkens whilst they read what Rāma did.

"The young girl who desires a husband shall obtain this husband to delight her soul; has she beloved ones journeying in a strange land, it shall be given her soon to have them restored her.

"Those who in the world listen to this poem, composed by Valmīki himself, shall acquire every gift, the object of their desire, just as they may have wished!"

Reader! need I excuse myself further, for having drawn your attention to a work of such altogether unusual efficiency?

April 1870.

NOTE.—I take this opportunity of gratefully acknowledging the valuable assistance I have received from the eminent Sanskrit scholar, Dr. Haas, to whom I owe the system I have followed in rendering the names of the personages of our history into English.

The Sanskrit alphabet not being equivalent to our own, there exists the most perplexing diversity, the same word having six or seven orthographies, as employed by different authors: for what homology of method may exist in this work I am indebted to the learned gentleman I have named.

CONTENTS.

CHAPTER I.
HOW VALMIKI RECEIVED THE GIFT OF POESY 1

CHAPTER II.
THE STORY OF RISHYASRINGA 12

CHAPTER III.
THE DESCENT OF THE GANGĀ 30

CHAPTER IV.
THE PENANCE OF VISVĀMITRA 51

CHAPTER V.
DASARATHA'S FAULT 76

CHAPTER VI.
THE INTERVIEW BETWEEN SĪTĀ AND ANASŪYĀ 90

CHAPTER VII.

SŪRPANAKHĀ 101

CHAPTER VIII.

RĀVANA'S CRIME 116

CHAPTER IX.

THE DEATH OF JATĀYU 145

CHAPTER X.

RĀMA ALLIES HIMSELF WITH THE ORANG-OUTANG, SUGRĪVA . 156

CHAPTER XI.

THE LOVE OF INDRA 179

CHAPTER XII.

THE ANCIENT VULTURE SAMPĀTI 186

CHAPTER XIII.

THE ADVENTURES OF HANUMAN, SON OF THE WIND . . . 197

CHAPTER XIV.

NALA BUILDS A MOLE ACROSS THE SEA 241

CHAPTER XV.

RĀMA AND LAKSHMANA, WOUNDED BY INDRAJIT, ARE RELEASED FROM THEIR TRANCE BY GARUDA, KING OF BIRDS. 255

CHAPTER XVI.

THE DEATH OF KHUMBUKARNA . . . 269

CHAPTER XVII.

THE LAST COMBAT—LAKSHMANA WOUNDED . 284

CHAPTER XVIII.

THE LAST COMBAT (CONTINUED).—DEATH OF RĀVANA . 294

CHAPTER XIX.

THE REUNION OF SĪTĀ AND RĀMA 301

NOTES 311

THE ILIAD OF THE EAST.

CHAPTER I.

HOW VALMĪKI RECEIVED THE GIFT OF POESY.

EIGHTEEN hundred years before the Christian era [1] a devout and learned Brahman, named Valmīki, withdrew from the habitations of men, and took up his abode in the wild and solitary forest. No contempt nor aversion for his fellows led him to abandon their society. Nor did he, after the manner of those times, hope by macerations and self-inflicted penances to obtain some special boon from Brahma, some dignity in this world, or some assurance of happiness in the future state. What he sought was an unobscured vision, an unbiassed conscience, an impartial judgment.

Standing near to, and on a level with it, a man does not perceive the true features of a country: that which is near obscures what is distant, or gives an erroneous impression of its importance; but if he climb a moun-

CHAP. I.
Valmīki takes up his abode in the forest

[1] *Vide* Note 1.

CHAP. I. tain, and look down on the whole scene, all things retain their just and relative proportions.

Thus did Valmīki, from a distance, survey all life, that, having learnt to know living creatures better, he might be able to serve them more.

The forest where he dwelt was like a marvellous temple reared by the hand of Nature. The trunks of the lofty tamarind and mango trees were as the columns which upheld the roof of foliage, where birds of a thousand dazzling hues flashed to and fro, like gems that had taken to themselves wings: the ground was richly strewn with flowering shrubs, that entwined their gorgeous blossoms, and wrought them into fantastic patterns: the air was heavy, as with perfumed incense; and in the shady nooks and glens myriads of guilty creatures found sanctuary.

The manner of his life there.

For many years, the Brahman lived in these lonely wilds, dividing his time between contemplation, and the observance of those sacred rites, which are reverent words of greeting spoken to the universal Father, who is at once the source of life and its sustainer.

The simple inhabitants of the woods soon abandoned their terror of the harmless anchorite; he in whose heart dwelt the love of universal nature, whose sole nourishment consisted of roots and berries, and to whom the passion of anger was unknown, became for them a *guru*[1] and a friend, to whom they had recourse whenever they needed counsel or sympathy. Even the timid gazelles, who came in flocks, in the cool of even, to the borders of the stream to quench their

[1] *Guru*—master, teacher.

thirst, and offer to Brahma their thanksgiving for the gift of lustrous waters, at his approach, would merely raise to his face their large, grave eyes, pleading: "We are at our prayers: forgive us if, just now, we do not wish you good-evening, dear Valmīki!"

CHAP. I.

Often, when the cool night had hushed the feverish pulses of the day, would the thoughtful Hermit pace the narrow pathways of the wood, pondering on disunion, and cruelty, and sin, and on the best method of banishing them for ever from a world whose natural beauty they deface. Then the glow-worm would extenuate itself, to shed forth a brilliant light, "Lest," he whispered, "the kindly *guru* tread unawares on some serpent or poisonous plant!"

The thoughts which possessed him.

The tigers and other beasts of prey would creep stealthily out of sight.

"Valmīki would chide us," they said, "if he knew that we were about to destroy life. But what are we to do? We do not find roots and berries agree with us."

At the sound of his footsteps the flower would open her corolla, and ask, half sleepily, half tenderly:

"Are you ill, Valmīki, that you are so restless? There is a healing virtue in my root; pluck me, if you will, O saintly anchorite!"

But the Hermit answered:

"I am not ill, dear little sister! It is the thought of the evil that is in the world, which keeps me wakeful."

At length, one evening when the pensive anchorite sat at the entrance of his hut, reflecting as usual on

Nārada is sent to the Hermit.

CHAP. I. the method of rendering man noble and generous and pure, Nārada, the messenger of the gods, appeared to him. When he saw the knit brows and the earnest gaze of the Hermit, he smiled, and said to him:

"By the contemplation of the glorious Immortals, on whose raiment is no speck of dust, and whose heads are crowned with garlands of undying flowers ; by the recital of the deeds wrought by their invincible might ; by the history of their bounteous gifts and heroic lives, the soul of man must be elevated. Is not this so, Valmiki ?"

"Nay," answered the Hermit, sadly; "I once thought this, but I was in error ! Man is not immortal—he is not strong, nor rich, nor joyous ; his garments—ay, and his soul too—need to be cleansed often from defilement. How then shall he be incited to great actions by the achievements of the gods ? Gazing on the sun, does he learn how to shine ; or on the ocean, to engulph great rocks ? He says of such deeds, truly, they are great, but they were not wrought by *men !*"

"How then shall he be ennobled ?" asked Nārada.

Valmiki explains that man needs an example of human virtue to stir his emulation.

The Brahman was silent for a while, reflecting deeply ; then he answered :

"Were it possible to hold up in his sight one clothed like himself in mortal flesh ; poor and weak, and tried by suffering even as he is, who has yet done generously and well ; who has upheld truth and justice, endured sorrow without bitterness, controlled his passions, and dealt kindly by all living creatures : then truly had he a pattern whereby to shape his life—an example to stir his emulation, and fire him with the thought: 'Shall not I attain to this heroism? Am not I also a man?'"

"Ay," answered the god, "you say truly! But can there a man be found whose life displays, indeed, this unblemished virtue? In all the three worlds, is there such an one?"

"I, who honour Mankind, would fain think so," answered the Hermit, meekly. "It is true that it has not been vouchsafed me to meet with one thus perfect in mind and deed, but Humanity is great, and counts many heroes."

At that, the messenger of the gods smiled his approval.

"You do well," he answered, "to *believe in man;* that is a faith conducive to high and generous deeds. Yes; there exists, indeed, a Hero who has clearly shown that the human load of suffering and weakness is powerless to impede the upward growth of him who raises his soul above dishonour, and whose glowing deeds must kindle men's self-respect, and show them, as in a mirror, the noble stature to which it befits them to attain.

"Rāma, the son of Dasaratha, is the name of this illustrious Hero. By respect for his father's promise unwittingly given to Kaikeyī, his treacherous stepmother, this young prince, the heir to the throne, abandoned the court, and the fair town of Ayōdhyā, and wandered forth into exile. In the solitary forest, with Lakshmana, his brother, and his wife, the lovely young Sītā, he led a contented existence, banishing all resentment from the minds of his companions, as well as from his own. The innocent guests of the wood he avoided injuring or alarming; but when the blameless anchorites implored protection against the evil Rākshasas, the enemies of gods and of men, he armed himself in their defence. During this war, Rāvana, the king of the Rākshasas, having artfully disguised himself as a hermit, entered the dwelling of Rāma and carried off the beautiful Sītā, in spite of her supplications for mercy. Indignant at this outrage, the birds and beasts of the forest, one and all, promised to succour this Rāma, who had ever shown a tender regard for their safety. Even his terrible grief for the loss of his beloved Sītā did not render the Hero indifferent to the wrongs of others. In his pursuit of Rāvana, having encountered the mournful ape, Sugrīva, whom the unjust suspicions of Bāli pursued from place to place, he espoused the cause of the innocent monkey; and when the unnatural Bāli was about to murder his younger brother, he slew this unjust monarch of apes, and gave the empire into the hands of Sugrīva. Thus he won the devoted attachment of these agile lords of the forest. Hanuman, the prime minister of Sugrīva, the daring son of the Wind, having traversed at one bound the seething and turbulent ocean, discovered Sītā, confined in the Island of Lankā. ' Thus was Rāma recompensed for not having disdained the affection of inferior creatures. Having marched with Lakshmana, and Sugrīva, and the whole army of apes, the magnanimous Dasarathide slew the Rākshasa in battle, and gave to his vanquished enemy the obsequies befitting a king. Then, the fourteen years of exile to which the promise had bound him having expired, he returned, with his joyous Sītā, to the happy town of Ayōdhyā. There sharing the empire with Bharata, the son of Kaikeyī, who had nobly reigned in his absence, the illustrious Rāma seeks to ensure the happiness of his people by a wise and merciful government. An obedient son, a loyal brother, a chaste spouse, a faithful ally, a fearless yet a merciful enemy, disdainful of none, but filled with kindly consideration for all living creatures, tell me, O saintly anchorite! does not this kingly Rāma wear a crown of transplendent virtues?"

CHAP. I

Then Valmīki, transported with gladness, exclaimed: "This is the man I have sought, whose story shall bring to the hearer the knowledge of Truth and of Virtue!"

Valmīki exclaims that here is the perfect man he has sought.

"And now," continued Nārada, "can there a bard be found worthy to hymn the life of this hero—his patience, his chastity, his valour, and his tender respect of life? In all the three worlds, is there such an one?"

Then the head of the humble anchorite was bowed mournfully on his breast.

"Alas!" he answered, "I know not such an one!"

"Yet," returned Nārada, "he lives, this poet, who shall give to the noble deeds of Rāma the wings of harmony, that they may brood over the souls of men; keeping nobleness and generosity and purity ever in their sight! I charge you, Valmīki, by your love for

CHAP. I.

Charged by the god to discover a poet able to sing the story of Rāma, Valmīki is troubled.

man, that you rest not until you have discovered this inspired bard!"

With that the divine envoy returned to his celestial home.

The Hermit was sore troubled by his last words. "How shall I discover this highly gifted poet in these solitary wilds?" he asked himself. "Surely my Disciple, Bharadvāja, is not he?"

And with that he turned an inquiring gaze on his Disciple. Now Bharadvāja was an excellent young man, but of a simple and mild demeanour; the fire of Poesy looked not forth from out his eyes.

More and more perplexed, haunted by the words— "I charge you, by your love for man, that you rest not until you have discovered this inspired bard!" —Valmīki arose, and sought the little lake Tamasâ. whose waves are limpid and transparent as is the soul of a Brahman.

"To be clean and pure is to attain great wisdom," said the Hermit, thoughtfully; "in these fresh waters will I lave the body that has been put under my dominion; and may the One Divine Spirit, in whose hand lies my soul, so cleanse it also that no earthly defilement may dim its perceptions!"

He prepares to bathe in the lake Tamasâ, when he sees two herons of rare beauty.

So saying, the saintly Anchorite prepared himself reverently for those ablutions which to the Brahman's mind have so holy a significance.

Whilst he yet lingered on the brink, he beheld, on the opposite shore of the lake, two herons of surpassingly beautiful plumage. It was the season when an ineffable tremor thrills all Nature, and when she responds with passion to Love's whispered invitation.

There is, at this time, more beauty in the world: all living things are radiant with ardour; the colours of the trees and flowers are of a richer dye; the insects wrap themselves in fire, and all birds break forth into song!

"We thank Thee, O Supreme Author of life!" exclaimed these herons of marvellous plumage, "for the gift of lustrous waters; for the wings which give us empire over the realms of air; but, above all, we thank Thee for the mysterious transports of love, which make us find all bliss, each in the other!"

But even whilst these harmless birds expressed thus joyously their thanksgiving, the arrow of some pitiless hunter hissed through the startled air, and, piercing the poor breast of one of the winged lovers, destroyed the life that had just reached the supreme moment of delight! Then the dolorous shrieks of the bereaved heron, who beheld his innocent mate stretched there dabbled in blood, saddened the shores of the lake Tamasâ; saddened, too, the heart of the kindly Hermit.

"O cruel hunter!" he cried; "mayst thou attain no glory in the eternal revolution of years, since thou hast not feared to strike this heron in the delirious moment of love!"

As the bubbling springs gush from the breast of Prithivî,[1] so leapt the words from his heart; and as the sound of flowing waters mellows itself into

One of the birds being slain by a hunter, Valmîki deplores the deed.

[1] *Prithivî*—goddess of the soil.

CHAP. I.

He is struck by the melodious sound of his own words.

harmony, so did his grief for the desolate bird sing itself into measure; swaying his thoughts to and fro, with a musical, dreamy movement, as the breeze blows forward and back the boughs of the sad Casserina. The rhythm of his lamentation rang in his ears whilst he bathed in the limpid waters; and even when he quitted the crystal lake, the enchanting measure still haunted him. Against his will he kept repeating it over and over, until, sorely puzzled and distressed, he fancied that some charm had bewitched him. Perceiving that his Disciple was regarding him with astonished eyes:

"Tell me, my son," he asked, very humbly, "is there not a strange melody in the words you hear me repeating over to myself?"

"I cannot say," answered his Disciple. For Bharadvāja, though an excellent young man, had not received the gift of Poesy.

Brahma visits the Hermit, and bids him tell what preoccupies him.

That day Brahma himself, the magnanimous ancestor of worlds, came to visit the meek Anchorite. Having reverently bowed himself to the earth, Valmīki, his hands clasped above his head, as is befitting in the presence of one worthy of honour, begged the most illustrious of gods to inform him of his pleasure.

Then Brahma said: "The fame of your great wisdom and sanctity has reached me, O Hermit! I would hear you speak of virtue and knowledge, and of the grave contemplations that have absorbed your mind during your habitation in this forest."

Valmīki thought to tell his illustrious guest of the way to encourage man to become noble, and generous, and pure. But his rebellious tongue, instead of obeying his will, once more repeated the musical words in which he had deplored the death of the heron.

Valmiki can find no words save those of his lament for the heron.

Abashed and covered with confusion, the humble Anchorite trembled before the most ancient of gods.

"He will think I mean to mock him!" he said to himself, mournfully.

But the eternal Brahma smiled, and said : " Happy art thou, Valmīki, who hast found favour in the sight of the ardent goddess of eloquence ! The divine quality of pity has drawn to thee the burning kiss of the capricious Saraswati ! Up, then, O man ! who hast tasted an immortal's love, speak forth the Divine breath which inspires thee ! Sing to the listening ages the wondrous history of Rāma, whose ineffable beauty shall not fade till the stars grow dim in heaven."

Brahma says he has earned the favour of the goddess of harmony, and bids him sing the deeds of Rāma.

. . . Thus did Valmīki, in whose heart dwelt the love of universal nature, receive the divine gift of Poesy, in exchange for *tears of pity !*

CHAPTER II.

THE STORY OF RISHYASRINGA.[1]

*IN the consideration of Nature, we should keep two thoughts present to our minds: first, that we have before us no merely interesting subject for investigation, but the *Mother* from whence we proceed, and of whose very body we are made; whence it follows that we are, in a certain sense, indulging in contemplation rather than observation; that the laws we are seeking to discover, the life we are striving to trace through its various evolutions and changes of form, are the same laws which regulate our own being, and the process of development which we also are bound to follow. Secondly, we should recollect that there is nothing visible and sensible which does not symbolize something immaterial and spiritual; so that we have here to establish, not merely the physical resemblance between our own life and that of Nature, but to read the special secret, of our inner being which lies here, written in hieroglyphic characters: thus may we frequently learn by sudden revelation, as it were,

[1] Recounted by the sage Sumantra, in the ears of Dasaratha, father of Rāma.

more than long hours spent in analysis of our sensations and ideas will disclose.

Overhead, the serene unbroken azure, and the sun laughing in his golden splendour; underfoot, the arid dust, the shrivelled grass, the yellow leaf, the dead flower; can there be a more pitiful sight? What makes the special horror of the drought is this contrast: death and decay *in the centre of sunshine!* The earth is cut off from all communication with heaven; that is why her beauty fades. Let the grey cloud-messengers, with their filmy wings, float down to her and whisper her, that the sky thinks of her with tearful longings, and straightway she will revive and smile.

In the midst of prosperity the heart of man is parched and arid also, without the kindly dews of sympathy; and if the supernal message of love fall not on him from the skies, the sweetly perfumed blossoms die, ere ever they have rent through the bud.

Once upon a time, in the country of the Angas, there was a sore dearth for want of rain. The sufferings of the earth-mother were shared by all living creatures; the gasping land was too feeble to bring forth fruit or herb, so the animals died, and the men grew wan from hunger. Lomapāda, king of the Angas, having vainly implored the succour of Vishnu, the penetrating spirit, whose essence thrills all being, and in whose sight all life is precious, grew weary of the burthen of existence.

"Eternal Spirit!"[1] he moaned, flinging himself on the earth, "life is too grievous; let me die."

[1] *Vide* Note 1.

CHAP. II.
King Lomapāda laments himself.

"In Thy sight, the light of eternity masters the shadows of time, Thy love embraces the infinite ; and destiny, which is Thy will, works for the good of the universe! I know Thou art just. I would not reverse Thy decrees, Thou who alone art, and in whom all that is, exists. But *I* am the prisoner of time, and these days are altogether evil ; as far as my vision extends, is nothing, save pain and sorrow. Alas ! my heart is that of a *man;* it comprehends nought, save the grief of its fellows ! And I am king of this people ; mutely their eyes hang on me, as on the face of their father ! How can I bear this, and live ? All their sufferings are felt by me ; the weight of their accumulated misery is bowing me down to the ground ! O Brahm ![1] if there be no succour, call me back to Thy bosom ; and let me return to unconsciousness!"

He calls his councillors together.

Having breathed forth this supplication, the monarch arose, and summoned to his presence his ministers and courtiers, and all the Brahmans and holy men in his domain who devoted their lives to prayer.

"Can none of you," he asked, "suggest how this curse may be removed from the land? I am resolved to put an end to my life, if I cannot assuage my people's distress!"

Then a holy Brahman stepped forth from the council. His life had been pure and tranquil ; so that his soul reflected the Divine Will, as a still lake gives back the blue of heaven.

"Listen, O king," he said. "In the deepest shades

[1] *Vide* Note I.

THE STORY OF VIBHÁNDAKA.

of the forest dwells a hermit, named Vibhándaka. Long ago he left this city, his heart full of bitterness and morose hatred for men, because amongst them he had found crime and folly. He despised pleasure too, and scorned beauty; for once he had been deceived by both. Taking with him his infant son, Rishyasringa, he chose a cave, in the wildest glen of the wood, to be this young child's nursery.

A Brahmin tells how the morose Vibhándaka has brought up his son in the wilds of the forest.

"'I give thee, my son,' he said, 'the savage beasts of prey for comrades; from them thou wilt learn less cruelty and wickedness than from thy fellows! Thou shalt hear the parrot shriek, the jackal howl, the lynx mewl, and the hyæna screech, but thou shalt be spared the discordant voice of man! Here, amid reptiles and venomous insects, thou shalt yet live in ignorance of what is most vile and loathsome in Nature! Exposed to the caprices of heaven, a thousand dangers attending thy every footstep, thy life a series of hardships, afflictions, and perils, thou shalt know more peace and security than in the crowded city. Grow then; and, if it be possible, lose the base nature Brahm has laid on thee; and ignore that thou art that vile and miserable creature,—a man!'

"Thus has Rishyasringa grown from childhood to youth and heard no human voice, and looked on no human face save that of his father. Dreading the irascible hermit, the hunter who passes that way, or the pious anchorite who chances on the solitary cave, steals away with silent haste; even the prowling beasts of the forest avoid it; for the immortals having promised to grant Vibhándaka what boon he would.

He tells how Vibhándaka having the power to curse, the avern is avoided by all.

CHAP II.

He counsels to fetch this young recluse, and promises the drought shall cease.

None seem disposed to go on this errand.

as a recompense for his austere life, he craved the *power to curse.*

"And now, Rishyasringa has become a man; and in his heart all manner of generous and noble qualities are in danger of death, as are the fruits of this starving land. The gods have chosen this youth to be the achiever of noble deeds, and the father of a gallant race; and it is thou, O King Lomapāda! who shalt rescue him from the rule of this bitter ascetic; who shalt fling open the doors of his heart, that his brethren may make it their home; who shalt teach him the noble ardour of love, by giving him thy daughter Kāntā to wife! Thou shalt give this hero to the world; and in return the grateful clouds will pour their treasures of rain at thy feet, that thy thirsty land may revive!"

When he heard that, Lomapāda sprang from his throne, and asked his ministers and courtiers:

"Which of you will, forthwith, set out in search of this young hermit?"

At first there was a stir among them; and each said to his neighbour:

"This is an honourable mission; it well befits one so illustrious as yourself!"

But none came forward and said, "I will go."

At length a kinsman of Lomapāda, and the most valiant prince among the Angas, stepped forth and said:

"Tell me, O saintly Brahman! has this Vibhāndaka indeed received from the immortals the power to curse?"

"Yes," answered the holy man; "the gods promised to grant him what he would: thus he obtained from them this terrible boon."

Then all the company exchanged dismayed glances; there was no more talk of going to fetch Rishyasringa.

But Lomapāda looked from one to another, eagerly. "None offers himself for this mission?" he exclaimed. "Alas! and my people dying around me!"

However, when a few days had elapsed, the sorrowful monarch once more summoned his ministers to his presence.

"I have thought of a plan," he said, "by which we may bring this young man hither, and yet avoid the curse of the terrible Vibhāndaka. Do you still refuse me your aid?"

The king suggests a plan to rescue Rishyasringa.

Then the courtiers, reddening with shame, answered him:

"Never did we refuse you our aid, O Lomapāda! We are your slaves, and at your word will risk our lives, or even incur the terrible curse of Vibhāndaka!"

Under their breath they murmured:

"Is he once more going to ask us to undertake this perilous enterprise? Why should the arrival of Rishyasringa remove this curse from our land?"

"Hearken," said Lomapāda: "this youth has spent all his life in the woods; he has seen only the blameless animals and birds, the reptiles and ferocious beasts, and his father, whom hatred for his kind has transformed into a savage! How shall it be, think you, when Rishyasringa beholds, for the first time, the

c

lovely countenance of woman? Though ignorant of the name of love, he cannot be a stranger to the fire of passion. Experience may not have shown him how to think, but nature has taught him how to feel. As through the dimness of night the ocean swells towards the moon, so is the blind heart of youth drawn by the beauty of woman; it knows not, nor stays to ask, wherefore.

"Fit me out, then, a spacious vessel; plant it with trees and shrubs, with mosses and flowers and ferns, so that it may seem like a blooming island, and let the most lovely maidens in my kingdom embark on it, disguised in the dress of anchorites, that seeing them in this familiar garb Rishyasringa may have no misgivings. Then let the wind and the floating river drift these charming young messengers near to the solitary hermitage; and in the absence of Vibhāndaka, let them lure this youthful savage on board their delicious vessel. Or I greatly err, or my little maidens will soon return, bringing me the willing captive you dared not go to seek! See that my orders are obeyed without delay, that the clouds may once more pour down their generous rains to rejoice the hearts of all creatures!"

When the ministers heard the project of Lomapāda, they were delighted beyond measure; and at once set about organizing the expedition. Now that it had devolved on others to fetch the young hermit, they were quite convinced that it was of the highest importance that the Brahman's advice should be conscientiously obeyed.

So the young maidens embarked on the vessel that was like a blooming island, and the wind and the floating river soon drifted them near to the solitary hermitage.

The messengers chosen by Lomapáda.

Now, latterly, Vibhāndaka had avoided, as much as possible, the society of his son. Truth to tell, he knew he was a dangerous companion; he was of such an irascible temper, and the habit of cursing had so grown upon him, that he frequently uttered the most withering invectives, half inadvertently. To avoid any irretrievable mistake of this sort, he kept out of Rishyasringa's way. It was his custom to seize his hermit's staff, at early dawn, and sally forth into the woods; and he would wander about until the fever of his malice was worn out, and his baneful energy exhausted.

Thus Rishyasringa was often left many days by himself; that is to say, quite alone: his heart was no companion to him, for it was only peopled by vague desires.

One evening that there were many sighs in the young man's breast, and that his head was heavy, he knew not why, he strolled forth into the glen in search of sweet roots and berries. It was that marvellous hour which closes the tropical day, when Light becomes an Illusion, and ecstatic Nature beholds the vision of her expired Lord. The greyness of twilight is not there: Mystery casts off the shade and clothes itself in radiance. The natural order is reversed: Reality assumes vagueness, whilst the Dream becomes irrefutable!

CHAP. II.

At the same time there is nothing to apprehend. This enchantment is altogether lovely: the weird, the grotesque, the fantastic even, have no part in it. Touched by this nebulous splendour, all colours are rarefied, not dimmed; all forms rendered ethereal, not distorted nor effaced.

Under the stately plantain, and the sweetly perfumed mango, passed the dreamy Rishyasringa. Overhead he heard the hushed twittering of birds, as they nestled close to each other under their canopy of leaves. On either side of the narrow path Vibhāndaka had torn out of the flowery wood, stretching into the heart of the silent forest, he saw the long grass and the feathery ferns, kissed here and there by this translucent light; and springing up every now and again, the prickly cactus, with its blood-red flowers, and the jessamine with its wreaths of snow, and other blossoms of soft and brilliant hues, that seemed to be whispering somewhat to their glossy leaves;—he had not dared to step on one side and wander amid this beauty; he felt that it concealed a secret; felt, too, that he was the only being here who did not understand nor share in it!

He was very sad.

Presently a shower of dates, that came rattling on him from a palm-tree above, roused him from his reverie; looking up, he perceived perched on the topmost bough a squirrel, who, in confusion, had wrapped its face in its bushy tail; but two bright black eyes gleamed through the fringing shade anxiously.

"Oh dear," it said, penitently, "I'm *so* sorry! the

branch I sprang from shook itself, and so the fruit fell. I assure you it shook itself. Don't curse me, noble son of Vibhāndaka!"

"Curse thee, thou foolish little squirrel?" said the young hermit, with a mournful smile; "I would rather bless thee, if the power were mine!"

A little further on he came upon a solitary gazelle. It stood in the shadow of a Casserina fir, the saddest of forest trees.

There were large tears in its eyes.

"Alas!" it moaned, "my harmless companion, who would not even crop the young flowers that craved for life!—yet, because she bounded across his path, the cruel Hermit slew her with his malediction! Ah me! and I am left alone!"

Then Rishyasringa had essayed to comfort the mournful beast, saying:

"I too am solitary; let us weep together!"

But at sight of him it started and prepared for flight.

"Do not fear me," pleaded the youth; "for worlds I would not do thee ill!"

"You are the son of Vibhāndaka!" was the answer.

"Nay," said Rishyasringa, meekly; "thou and I have one Father, to whom we both owe life. We are brothers; oh, do not fear me!"

But with the words, "*You are the son of Vibhāndaka,*" the timid gazelle had fled.

Then bitterly, and with tears, the lonely Rishyasringa flung his arms up into the empty air:

"Wherefore, O Brahm!" he cried, "hast thou drawn me from the void, and dowered me with sense and conscience, and this carefully constructed frame? Creation's scheme were perfect but for me! I see the marvellous unbroken thread of life binding together all that is by sympathy and interchange of service; I only—I, in whose identity the various powers and efficiencies of nature would seem to meet—am without the circle!

"Behold, in me is the power of song; but there are none to hearken to my lay! Strength have I, but there is nought to conquer; skill—but wherefore should I toil? Thoughts which have wings flock to my mind, but whither should they fly? Stars and flowers and pearls are mine, but whom should they enchant? Desires have I, but they find no goal;—fire, but it eats into my life; a heart which hungers after love, but starves!"

Even as he spoke, on the air came floating to him, gradually, slowly, as sail the swans a-down the sacred river, a breath that grew into a whisper, a whisper that broke into a song, a song that woke the jealous birds up in their nests, that roused the echoes from their sleep, and won from them a very fond response! Then to the astonished eyes of the young recluse appeared, bounding towards him through the wood, a company of wondrous anchorites, whose countenances were radiant as the sun, and whose forms seemed more than mortal!

Smiling and singing—gems sparkling beneath their homely garments, their silver nūpura [1] ringing out the time of their footsteps—they danced nearer to

---

[1] *Nūpura*—anklet worn by Indian women.

him, and nearer. The air crept round, and wrapt them in perfumes; the trees showered down on them blossoms; the caressing flowers kissed softly their feet. The wind played with the folds of their raiment; stirred them—then shivered with dread!

Rishyasringa trembled more than the wind.

In the acacia-tree the kokila, the most amorous of birds, softly, softly warbled its pain.

Rishyasringa dared not even sigh; but his pain was more than the kokila's.

Opposite the young hermit they paused; they ceased singing; they surrounded him; they looked into his face with their large dreamy eyes; they looked into his face and smiled!

Rishyasringa smiled too—and trembled.

"Who are you?" they asked. "Do you dwell alone in this forest? O beautiful youth! tell us your name, and why you dwell in this desolate forest."

He answered:

"I am Rishyasringa, the son of Vibhāndaka. I know no world save this forest. You say true, it is desolate; and yet——"

Then he broke forth, eagerly:

"Nay, it is not desolate, oh believe me! not *very* desolate! If you would linger here a while, graceful strangers, I would show you that it is not unlovely. My hermitage is near at hand; it is a cavern in the rock; the walls are glistening with silver ore, and creeping shrubs hang their green tracery before its mouth. No venomous reptiles nor beasts of prey approach it. In this glade are sweet roots and berries

He invites them to visit his hermitage.

and luscious fruits, which I will gather for you; and close by is a river where your reverences can bathe: the overhanging trees shelter it from the sun, and its waters are pure and cool. If you love flowers, there are many here of brilliant colours, and of the sweetest perfume; and there are birds too; the kokila sings ever in the acacia-tree. Oh, believe me, it is an excellent forest, and not desolate!"

At his breathless words they laughed merrily; and their voices were like running water. Rishyasringa laughed too; he knew not why.

"Show us your hermitage, gentle youth!" they cried; and some of them twined their round, young arms through his; and one laid her soft, warm cheek upon his shoulder, and whispered: "Show us your hermitage, Rishyasringa!"

So he led them to the cavern in the rock, and gave them sweet roots and berries and luscious fruits; he brought them water too to wash their feet; and offered them the eight things of the Arghya,[1] according to the rites of hospitality.

From time to time the youth and these lovely maidens exchanged wistful glances, and smiled one on the other.

But the blooming messengers of Lomapāda were not without uneasiness.

Uneasy lest Vibhāndaka should return, they dare not linger.

"If Vibhāndaka should return," they thought; "surely he would blight our beauty with his potent curse, and distort our forms, as did the angry Marut to the daughters of the King Kusanābha."[2]

So after a while they sprang to their feet, and said:

[1] *Vide* Note 2.   [2] *Vide* Note 3.

"Farewell, Rishyasringa, and thank you for your hospitality."

"Farewell?" exclaimed the youth; "and you would leave me? O lovely strangers, I beseech you stay with me!"

"And Vibhāndaka?" they said.

Then Rishyasringa thought: "My churlish father would surely do them some ill turn!"

"You are right," he said. "Alas! farewell!" and with that he bowed his head down upon his hands.

"When they are gone, I shall die," he thought.

"Nay but, Rishyasringa," said the damsels, "shall we not see you more? Will not you visit us also in our hermitage? Do you not love us, gentle youth, that you ask not where we may be found?"

They encourage the youth to seek for their "hermitage."

He looked up at them, half in wonder, half in hope:

"I have seen," he said, "the bright stars rain down from heaven; for a moment there was light—afterwards the blackness was more intense. Were it not madness to seek to trace such stars?"

"Nay," they laughed, "not if they lay gleaming at one's feet! Our hermitage is so near that, if you seek, you cannot fail to find it."

And with that, waving their hands to him and saying, one by one, "Farewell, Rishyasringa!" they passed out of the cavern.

When Vibhāndaka returned to the hermitage, his son came not forward as usual to greet him; nor did he bring him water for his feet, nor offer him the

The return of Vibhāndaka.

CHAP. II.

Rishyas-ringa tells his "dream."

eight things of the Arghya, as the laws of etiquette require.

"How now?" asked the Hermit; "of what are you thinking, Rishyasringa? and why do you sit there, with clasped hands and vaguely wistful eyes. A youth trained as you have been to a solitary life, guarded from the storms of passion and the deceits of love, can have no amorous dreams to poison and befool his mind! Since such follies are unknown to you, what means this languor, so unbefitting the demeanour of a virtuous ascetic?"

Rishyasringa answered: "I had a dream. I thought that, being in the wood, I met a company of young anchorites; they were surely saints of most distinguished virtue, for their countenances were radiant as the sun, and their forms seemed of more than mortal beauty. They entered this cavern, and it was filled with light; at their touch my pulses started, and for pain I could have wept, but when I looked into their large, soft eyes, it became delight; and though I suffered still, it was from excess of joy! At length they rose, and waving their hands to me, they said, one by one, 'Farewell, Rishyasringa,' and faded from my sight. Then all grew dark."

As he listened to the youth's story, Vibhāndaka's lip curled scornfully. He said to himself: "The fumes of sensual desire have bewildered the boy's brain! So it is; without temptation man becomes impure, and loses his innocence in the midst of ignorances!"

"Listen," he said, harshly: "there is what looks like beauty, and what is disease; what seems a promise, and what means despair; what wears the garb of sunlight, and is as foul as sin. See you have no more such dreams, Rishyasringa! Your saintly anchorites were demons beyond a doubt!"

And with that, the surly Vibhāndaka stretched him on his couch of leaves, and fell asleep.

Rishyasringa could not sleep.

"They certainly were not demons," he said.

Early on the morrow, as soon as Vibhāndaka had left the hermitage, the young recluse started forth in search of the graceful strangers.

The kokila, the most amorous of birds, was singing in the acacia-tree, but he could not find them;—the flowers were glistening with dew; the air was full of perfumes; the trees softened the garish sunlight; in the arms of the Casserina fir a little breeze was sighing, —and yet, he could not find them!

He flung himself down upon the grass.

"They are gone," he said, "and for me remains nothing but to die."

But it was not to be so. He heard a rustling amid the bushes, and all around him the air quivered mirthfully; the roses laughed, until their blooming petals floated in tinted showers to the earth; the airy grass trembled with glee; the saucy little beetles, peeping out from it with their jewelled eyes, chuckled with delight; and from behind the trees, and from the centre of the shrubs, and as it were from the very bosom of the ground, sprang the blooming anchorites, smiling on him, and singing.

"Did you think that we had left you, Rishyasringa?"

CHAP. II.

They lead him to their vessel: then the rain begins to fall.

And the echoes repeated, "Had left you, Rishyasringa."

"Yes," he replied. And then the youthful maidens, and Rishyasringa, and the echoes laughed together for joy.

"Come," they said, "let us show you *our* hermitage!" and so, some holding his hands, and some singing and dancing around him, they led him to the vessel which was like a blooming island.

As he stepped on board, far away, over the city of the Angas, a fleecy cloud spread its swan-like wings, and the generous rain began to fall and refresh the thirsty land!

* * * * *

When Vibhāndaka returned, he found the hermitage deserted.

"Rishyasringa!" he cried; but there was no response. Then seizing his hermit's staff, he rushed back into the wood, shouting, "Rishyasringa! Rishyasringa!" The frightened echoes gave back his shout, pleading: "You see we are as zealous in the matter as yourself!" All living things kept out of the infuriated Hermit's path as he strode along, tearing up the shade with his piercing eyes, and questioning the distance.

At length, having reached the outskirts of the forest, he met one, driving a herd of cows speckled with different colours, and of the most unusual beauty.

"Whose are these wondrous cows?" he asked, in spite of his wrath, transported with admiration.

"Rishyasringa's," replied the herdsman.

At that Vibhāndaka abated his pace, and walked

on wondering. Presently he met a troop of lordly elephants, whose ornaments were of gold and ivory.

"Whose are these lordly elephants?" he asked, amazed.

"Rishyasringa's," answered he in whose charge they were.

Utterly bewildered, the recluse stood there, in the road, his hand to his head. After a while, one passed him driving a chariot, all inlaid with gems, and drawn by four horses swift as the wind, and haughty as the waves of ocean.

"And whose is this noble chariot?" he asked.

"Rishyasringa's," was the answer. "To-day this youth weds the lovely Kāntā, the daughter of the King Lomapāda. By the counsels of a saintly Brahman this illustrious monarch has rescued Rishyasringa from the hands of his savage father, the enemy of all living creatures!" and with that the charioteer drove on, and left the Hermit standing there alone.

But having seen the wondrous cows, and lordly elephants, and noble chariot, Vibhāndaka reflected that this was probably the work of Destiny. So he returned tranquilly to his hermitage.

At sight of the new possessions of his son, Vibhān-daka's wrath is appeased.

CHAPTER III.

THE DESCENT OF THE GANGĀ.

I.

Himālaya, king of all mountains

HIMĀLAYA, the king among mountains, and the dark and lofty Vindhya, stand scowling one on the other, and exchanging looks of defiance.

"I am the king among mountains!" cries sternly the proud Himālaya. "The clouds have robed me in purple, and crowned my forehead with snowflakes! I tower up into heaven, rending the azure veil which conceals the home of the immortals. The secrets of the three worlds are known to me; I overlook the whole earth, and from the sighing ocean the dark-winged vapours ascend and whisper to me their griefs; I am in the confidence of the stars, and know the story of their loves; I know, too, why some of them fall out of heaven."

The sullen Vindhya wraps his misty cloak around him: "I am weary of this lumbersome giant!" he mutters. "He impedes my view, and robs me of the sunlight; his ill-bred boastings offend me." Under his breath he adds, "But for this shapeless monster *I* had been king amongst mountains!"

2.

The ancient Himālaya is the wealthiest of monarchs: he has treasures of gold and of silver; caverns whose roofs are of diamonds, and whose floors are studded with emeralds. He has, too, a daughter, who is a star in the heaven of beauty.

Brighter than sapphire or diamond that flashes and gleams in the sunlight; wilder than youthful zephyrs born in the season of rain, thrilled with the songs of the kokila, and laden with the perfume of flowers; more dreamy than the pallid lotus, who shrinks from the sun's caresses, but at night flings back her petals, that the pale and amorous Sōma[1] may feast on her unveiled beauty; sweeter and lovelier far was the laughing and tremulous Gangā, the peerless daughter of Mēnā, the child of the old Himālaya!

The beautiful Gangā is child of the old Himālaya.

3.

Up in heaven the stars have grown restless; the earth has decked her in flowers; the clouds delay their ascent; they brood near, they break into weeping. They weep, and die of their love for the beauteous Gangā!

The Sun himself grows pale.

"I am not cruel, O Gangā!" murmurs the love-sick Sun; "my passion is ardent and wild as the love of the radiant Indra;[2] but its fervour need not affright thee!

"Do not fear me, O youthful maiden! O beloved, do not fear me! Let my kiss stray amid thy tresses,

Gangā is beloved by all living.

---

[1] *Sōma*—the moon. [2] *Indra*—god of the firmament.

that wildly float into ripples; it shall not scorch these wavelets; O Gangā, it shall not burn thee!

"Let my beams just lie on thy bosom, thy bosom that swells and that flutters! O child, they shall wander there gently, like a mother's hand which caresses. Beloved, they shall not harm thee!"

4.

The young and dreamy Gangā flings her arms round the old Himālaya.

"I would know what love is!" she whispers. "Find me a suitor, my father."

The ancient monarch answers: "You must find one yourself, my child; I am too old to be hunting for suitors!"

5.

One day the great Himālaya was absorbed in weighty reflections.

The fumes of his grave meditations mounted up to his brain, and wrapped him in a mantle of vapour.

Having solved at length some problem of unusual abstruseness, the mists round him were rarefied; then he perceived, standing near, three Strangers of majestic appearance.

6.

The immortals visit the old Himālaya.

Their countenances were of an azure hue, like the early flower of the Nymphæa; their eyes were large and clear, and their gaze never faltered nor drooped; their heads were crowned with wreaths of blooming flowers; and they stood upright, there in the midst of the air.

The ancient Himālaya was a monarch of experience and wisdom : he knew that the eyes of men grow weak through the tears they have shed; that their feet are nailed to the ground ; that if they weave them garlands, the flowers hasten to wither.

"These strangers are the deathless gods!" he muttered.

7.

The noble and bland Himālaya flung at the feet of these visitors his diadem of glistening snowflakes.

"What is your pleasure, O heroes?" he inquired with eager courtesy. "I have treasures of gold and of silver ; caverns whose roofs are of diamonds, and whose floors are studded with emeralds : I have, too, a Daughter, who is accounted a star in the heaven of beauty"

"Give us this peerless Daughter to wife," they answered.

The gods as Gangā in marriage.

"So be it!" replied the urbane Himālaya.

Then the immortals laughed aloud in their gladness ; as for the ancient monarch, he resumed his weighty reflections.

8.

"O youthful and tremulous maiden, whose dreams are haunted by wonder, whose heart is fluttered by whispers, awake,—it is Love who awaits you !

"O graceful daughter of Mēnā, O nymph with the

CHAP. III.

long floating tresses, awake,—it is Love who awaits you! Leave, oh leave your couch mid the rushes, languid daughter of Mēnā! Bind not your showers of hair; come arrayed in its floating wavelets; stay not to shake from your fingers the spray of glistening waters; pause not to lay on one side your garland of weeds and of lilies. Come, O child, O beloved! forsake your couch mid the rushes. Fanciful, dripping, and bright, come; it is Love who awaits you!

"Hearken, O child, O beloved! The stars grew dim in our kingdom; sun and moon were smothered by clouds; the gandharvas[1] had no voice for the song; the apsaras[2] had no heart for the dance; the souls of the gods were oppressed.

"Hearken, O child, O beloved! we have come from heaven to seek you; for heaven is not heaven without Love!

"Then awake, O child, O beloved! Leave your couch mid the rushes, fanciful, dripping, and bright —come; it is Love who awaits you."

9.

Thus sang the enamoured immortals in the ears of the languid Gangā.

Then, her eyes still heavy with sleep, the dreamy and youthful maiden arose from her couch mid the rushes, and fanciful, dripping, and bright, came forward to meet the immortals.

*   *   *   *   *   *

[1] *Gandharvas*—celestial musicians.
[2] *Apsaras*—celestial dancing girls.

10.

In this same wood of Velā, where the sullen Vindhya and the arrogant Himālaya exchange looks of defiance, the devout monarch Sagara, the magnanimous ancestor of Rāma, celebrated, at the time of full moon, a great and solemn aswamédha.[1]

Rishis and Brahmans and saintly anchorites, and all the noblest of those who murmur prayers under their breath, came from far and near to be present at this great sacrifice.

But lo, when all was prepared—when the sacred wood was piled, and the torch that yearned to consume it flamed in the hands of the priest—a serpent, under the form of Ananta,[2] rose from the midst of the ground, and seizing the sacred horse, the victim promised to Brahma, disappeared with it, swallowed up by the yawning earth.

Surprise fell on the monarch Sagara; as for the Rishis and Brahmans and saintly anchorites, they were filled with hot indignation.

11.

"O monarch of the powerful countenance," they said, "you do well to gaze thus aghast!

"Here is a story of shame that shall roll down the river of time, refusing to sink out of sight, uneffaced by the gathering years!

"Here is a pleasing jest for the winds to tell one another, whilst the trees of the forest listen, and their branches quiver with mirth!

[1] *Aswamédha*—sacrifice.   [2] *Ananta*—king of snakes.

CHAP. III.

"Here is a tale for the parrot and shrieking macaw to repeat; to scream at the top of their voices, and convulse all nature with laughter!

"Far and near the people shall say: 'Show us this precious Sagara, this arrogant ruler of men, who was put to scorn by a serpent! Show us this valiant king, whose victim promised to Brahma was stolen from under his eyes!'"

Then the brow of the monarch grew red as the bolts of the flaming Indra.

"What would you have me do?" asked this furious Tiger of Men.[1]

12.

"There are sixty thousand heroes who call Sagara father. Summon my sons forthwith!" shouted this enraged ruler of men.

The Sagarides are charged to find the thief.

Then these sixty thousand princes came in haste, and found their magnanimous parent lying with his face in the dust, howling and biting the dust like an elephant struck by the hunter.

They joined hands round him, and reverently performed a pradakshina.[2] Then they asked what had shaken the balance of his equable humour.

"Slay me this ravisher of the horse!" moaned forth the prostrate monarch.

"We will!" replied in one breath the sixty thousand heroes. At that the relieved Sagara rolled no more in the dust.

[1] *Tiger of Men—vide* Note 1.
[2] *Pradakshina—vide* Note 2.

13.

"Nor Rakshasa,[1] nor Naga,[2]" said this sapient ruler of men, "has thus deranged my sacrifice; they had not dared to face this company of holy men! Some divine being it is who has perpetrated this baseness. Search him out, though the gloomy Tartarus lend him its sightless blackness; search him out, though the azure gates roll back to afford him a refuge.

"My sons, fear not his rank; this deed annuls his divinity. Gods and men alike must obey the dictates of justice; gods and men alike, if they violate the immutable law, have against them the universe and the uncreated Lord of existence!"

14.

The sixty thousand sons of Sagara explored the land far and wide; with lances, pick-axes, and clubs they threw up the earth and examined it, but nowhere could these indefatigable heroes discover a trace of their enemy.

But broken by axes and spades, hewed and hacked and wofully injured, her innocent bosom gashed and mangled, the harmless goddess Prithivī mutely appealed to Heaven. A dolorous cry mounted up from serpents and lizards and beetles, and myriads of living creatures whom the furious zeal of the heroes had wounded and maimed.

15.

Then all the living creatures whom the gentle Prithivī shelters, and the gandharvas, who are tender

[1] *Rakshasas*—demons.   [2] *Nāgās*—snake gods.

to all things, and the lower gods, whose hearts are open to pity, ran to the supreme Giver of life, their eyes overflowing with tears.

"Eternal Brahm," they sobbed, "deign to help us! Thou hast given us being; it is thy Essence which quickens our blood! Art thou deaf to the voice of thy children, who even now lie in thy Bosom? O Sea! art thou cold to thy rivers flowing out from thine innermost heart? O Heaven! art thou dead to thy stars which shine and glisten in thee? O infinite Existence, dost thou scorn thy Breath which has made us?

"These pitiless sons of Sagara are rending the breast of the earth; one by one we are smitten and perish; one by one these ruthless avengers rob us of that thou hast given!"

16.

Then the eternal Fount of Existence answered them, gravely smiling:

"From the vast ocean of life ascend the formless vapours; in the breast of the air they meet, they embrace and unite into clouds.

"Heavily brood they in space, then break into glistening raindrops, that rush down to the earth to perform there their destined journey.

"But either in streamlet or river, soon, or after long windings, all return to the ocean when their allotted task is accomplished.

"Ponder this well, and perceive that all works together for harmony.

"These noisy sons of Sagara are but the servants of Destiny. Vasudeva Kapila¹ has taken this horse— he whose eyes see the fruit of events, who beholds the whole workings of time, who effects, too, the welfare of all.

"Man follows the bent of his will; subdues, or is led, by his passions; respects life, or ruthlessly snaps it; bows to the law of his conscience, or wilfully lives in rebellion.

"He says to himself, 'I am free!' He says true. He *is* free to grow noble; he is free, too, to work his undoing. But let him act as he will, he is a tool in the great hand of Destiny, used to perfect the fabric of life!

"There are sons of the night, and their portion is blackness; there are sons of the dawn, and the daylight is theirs: *both* are workers for Destiny; from the labour of both issues harmony!

"Out of evil comes good, but not for the doer of evil; he has earned for himself sorrow: that he did *freely!* He has worked for the good of the universe: that he did *blindly*, in obedience to the hidden pleasure of Destiny.

"Out of evil comes good: these Sagarides who destroy life shall have their own lives taken from them; but from this act of theirs shall follow a blessing: the bountiful, fecund, young Gangā shall bring her fresh bubbling waters to rejoice the hearts of all creatures!"

---

¹ *Vasudeva Kapila*—other name for Vishnu.

<small>CHAP. III.</small>

<small>*Brahm replies that all events tend to the good of the universe.*</small>

17.

CHAP. III.

From the august Presence the suppliants withdrew very sadly.

"We are not Vasudeva Kapila," they murmured; "we see not the fruit of events; we behold not the whole workings of time—we, who must die!

"Since *we* must die, what to us is the descent of the Gangā?"

They were reptiles and small creeping creatures who spoke thus.

18.

Meanwhile the sons of Sagara returned to their illustrious parent. They joined hands round this sapient ruler of men, and affectionately performed a pradakshina.

"O Elephant among Kings!" they said, "we have dug up the whole face of the earth, but nowhere have we discovered a trace of this ravisher of the horse.

"What would you have us do next? Speak, O Lion of Men, we burn to accomplish your pleasure!"

19.

The heroes' search being fruitless, Sagara bids them seek the thief in Tartarus.

After a few moments' reflection the monarch of the powerful countenance replied:

"The god who has troubled my sacrifice has fled to the infernal regions; that is my firm conviction.

"Follow him thither, O heroes! and when you have slain the thief, capture the sacred horse. With my grandson, the valiant Ansumat, I will await you here." And so the Sagarides once more commenced their diggings.

They encounter the elephants who support the world.

20.

Throwing up the earth on the northern coast, they presently discovered the lordly elephant, Virūpāksha; who, together with his three brethren, sustains the globe, with its forests and mountains, its cities and villages.

If, in momentary weariness, the monstrous elephant stir his head, then the world shakes, with its forests and mountains, its cities and villages.

21.

O Virūpāksha, what a burthen is thine! The forest with its lofty trees and monstrous animals? The mountain with its mines and quarries? Truly thou art heavily laden!

But the cities and villages, and all the sin and the sorrow, and the heavy hearts of men and women which they contain? O Virūpāksha, over-burthened Virūpāksha, what marvel if at times thy head droop with fatigue?

22.

The courteous princes performed a pradakshina round the lordly elephant, and began to dig towards the south. Soon they discovered another colossal elephant, the sublime Mahāpadma; they greatly admired the large animal, and danced round him a pradakshina.

Towards the west they found a third elephant; the

CHAP. III. robust Saumanas. They saluted him with a pradakshina, and asked him how he did.

They then arrived at the side of the Himālaya, and saw another elephant, the magnanimous Himapāndura. They reverently touched this king of animals, and gave to him, as to the others, the honour of a pradakshina.[1]

23.

Having reached Tartarus, they see the horse, and Vishnu beside it.

Having thus torn up the whole earth, these dauntless heroes perceived the sacred horse, stolen that day of full moon in the peaceful wood of Velā, grazing here at liberty.

By the side of the unconscious quadruped was Vasudeva Kapila.

Then the sixty thousand Sagarides shouted with one voice: "Halt, thou ravisher of the horse! Knowest thou why we have thus rent the earth? It is that we may have the joy of looking on thee!"

At that Vasudeva Kapila turned, and looked at these heroes.

24.

Cold and still grew their hearts, that once had bounded so gladly; thus the antelope lies, struck by the hunter's arrow.

The heroes are reduced to ashes by the gaze of Vishnu.

Vague and dark stared their eyes, whose vision had been as the eagle's; thus looks the paling moon when Rahu[2] devours her radiance.

As the icicle melts at the dawn; as the lotus dies in the drought; as the grass of the prairie shrinks,

[1] Literally translated.   [2] *Rahu—vide* Note 3.

scorched by the hot breath of Indra, so these men of vigour and youth paled 'neath the fixed gaze of Vishnu; paled, and sickened, and died, and fell like reeds in the tempest! Paled, and sickened, and died, and lay at the feet of the god, a heap of formless cinders; the toy of the mocking winds!

Chap. III.

25.

The illustrious ruler of men, the anxious monarch Sagara, called to him the youthful Ansumat, whose limbs were like young fir-trees.

"Thy uncles are long in coming," he said to the youthful warrior; "my son, go in search of thy uncles and bid them return here swiftly. My heart misgives me, Ansumat; bid them return *very* swiftly."

And so the valiant young warrior went forth to seek for his uncles.

Sagara sends Ansumat to look for his uncles.

26.

The lordly Virūpāksha, the magnanimous Mahāpadma, the robust Saumanas, the sublime Himapāndura, all greeted the nephew of sixty thousand uncles, and gave him news of his relatives.

But when the indefatigable youth reached the infernal regions, and beheld the state of his uncles, he fell on his face on the ground, uttering the most dolorous shrieks.

27.

Having bemoaned with tears and loud wailings the fate of these illustrious Sagarides, Ansumat looked round him anxiously for water, with which to lave the

He finds their remains, and bemoans their fate.

CHAP. III.

Seeking water to give them funeral honours, he is called by Garuda.

cinders of these unfortunate heroes; for unless cleansed by lustrous waters, the dead are not admitted into Paradise, the defilement of earthly passions rendering them unfit for the celestial abode.

28.

As he sought far and near for some purifying stream or fountain, the youthful hero heard himself called by his name.

Looking round, Ansumat perceived, perched on the topmost bow of an acacia-tree, Garuda, the king of all birds.

The winged monarch sat there, swaying himself to and fro, and loudly calling "Ansumat!"

The grandson of Sagara was glad to see him, for this illustrious fowl was the maternal uncle of these sixty thousand heroes who had become ashes.

29.

"Do not afflict yourself, most illustrious of men!" said this magnanimous bird. "These Sagarides shall be glorified in the three worlds. Though I am their maternal uncle, I do not deplore their fate.

The king of birds tells him the ashes of the Sagarides shall not be cleansed till the Gangā comes to earth.

"Meanwhile capture the sacred horse, and lead it back to Sagara; and give him this message from me: 'Thy sons cannot enter Paradise till purified by the ceremony of lustrous waters; but this shall not take place until the Gangā shall quit the celestial regions, and bring her sparkling wavelets to rejoice the inhabitants of the world.'"

Then Ansumat returned to Sagara, and told him word for word all that the sapient fowl had said.

30.

For the space of one thousand years the afflicted monarch Sagara strove vainly to find some means of inducing the beautiful Gangā to abandon the home of the gods.

And after his death, Ansumat sought, by penances and fastings, to gain the favour of Heaven, and the pity of the gentle Gangā.

And after Ansumat, Dilīpa, son to the nephew of sixty thousand uncles, laboured vainly to discover a plan to purify these unhappy Sagarides.

At length Bhagīratha, the magnanimous son of Dilīpa, abandoning his throne and the city, embraced the career of an anchorite on the wild slopes of the old Himālaya.

The penances gone through to earn the descent of the Gangā.

31.

Clad in a garment of skins, his head bared to the humours of heaven; keeping his passions in check; subsisting only on roots, alike tortured by heat and by cold, did the saintly anchorite importune the aid of the gods by the spectacle of his self-imposed sufferings.

At the close of one thousand years Brahma, the merciful guardian of men, appeared to him.

"Cease these inhuman macerations!" said the god. "What is your request, Bhagīratha? Would you rise to the caste of a Rishi, or even that of a Brahman? Do you desire a son? Tell me what is your wish, O Bull among saintly anchorites!"

Brahma asks Bhagīratha what is his request.

32.

Then the emaciated anchorite answered:

CHAP. III.

"To be called 'Rishi' or 'Brahman' is accounted an honour among men; but I had much honour, Brahma, and I abandoned it!

"To hear a child's voice lisp the word 'father' is unquestionably the crown of tenderness and pride; but I, Brahma, have dwelt in this wilderness a thousand years, and have no love to be crowned by this ineffable gift! Not to obtain an honourable title have I left my country and my throne; not to gain lineage have I turned my back on family and friends."

"For what then?" asked Brahma.

"That these sixty thousand heroes might at length enter upon their bliss," replied this worthy ancestor of Rāma. "That the Gangā might bring her purifying waters here below!"

Having heard "the descent of the Gangā," he advises the ascetic to appeal to Siva.

"Your request is a hard one," answered Brahma; "for if the Gangā were to fall on the earth, her turbulent waters would overwhelm the world! Yet such a penitence as yours should not prove unavailing. Implore the aid of Siva: the lord of all creatures, in whose sight life is precious, may perchance devise a means of performing this difficult task."

With that Brahma returned to heaven.

33.

After a hundred years Siva promises his aid.

For another hundred years the saintly Bhagīrath continued his self-macerations.

At the close of that time, Mahādeva[1] appeared to this king of ascetics, and said:

"I am content, O most virtuous of men! I will

[1] *Mahādeva*—another name for Siva.

sustain this river of purifying waters. I will, too, induce this Bride of the immortals to quit her celestial home."

34.

Then the glorious and generous immortal climbed the brow of the old Himālaya, and called to the fanciful Gangā, the queen amongst beautiful rivers:

Siva calls to Gangā.

"O child of the old Himālaya, whom the arms of Prithivī once cradled, this breast where then thou didst slumber is parched with a feverish thirst,— therefore, descend!

"The little flowers are withered; the leaves of the lotus have shrunk; the troops of gazelles are weary, they find no stream to refresh them; the storks and herons are dying; the swans have abandoned the country; the men are feeble and sickly; the dead lie imprisoned in Tartarus, uncleansed by lustrous waters, —therefore, descend!

"O Gangā, Bride of the heavens! thy home is full of delight; the air is heavy with perfumes; the mirthful apsaras flit joyously hither and thither; the strains of the dreamy gandharvas thrill every ear with rapture. The light here is golden, yet soft; the shade here is languid, yet warm; and the gods who dwell here are happy!

"O Gangā, daughter of Mēnā, who sprang from the breast of Prithivī! the earth is the dwelling of sorrow; the air is laden with sighs; in flight from want or from danger, all creatures are restless and wandering; the sound of weeping is frequent;

CHAP. III.

the music of laughter is rare; the light is scorching and ardent; the shade is gloomy and chill; and the men who dwell there are mournful;—therefore, descend!"

35.

Rushing from heaven the Gangā is received on the head of Siva.

Then the large heart of the Gangā started and throbbed in her bosom; and, without pause or reflection, the generous queen of all rivers rushed from the home of the gods in a burst of impetuous passion, singing, "I come, O beloved! Doubly beloved for thy sorrow!"

Stepping forward, the generous Siva, in whose sight life is precious, received the great rush of waters, and upheld on his forehead the impulsive daughter of Mēnā, that in her generous fervour she might not overwhelm the earth.

36.

Here, on the forehead of Siva, troublous, immense, rapid, for the space of one year the impatient Gangā remained, between earth and heaven.

After a year the god lets down a tress of his hair, by which she escapes to earth.

Then the cautious Mahādeva let down one tress of his hair; and by this channel the impassioned daughter of Mēnā rushed down to the arms of Prithivī!

37.

The gods, the Rishis and Brahmans, the Asuras, the Siddhas and Nāgas, and all the hosts of earth and of heaven, came to witness this marvellous sight—the joyous descent of the Gangā!

The spray of glistening foam leapt up to the azure vault, as sprang from the head of Siva this child of the old Himālaya, singing: "I come, O beloved! Doubly beloved for thy sorrow!"

The air was filled with flashes, and the waves shouted and roared; in their joy they bounded and leapt, they rushed the one at the other, they dashed themselves into fragments, and fell like diamonds and fire-flies! The dolphins and reptiles and fishes, and all that live in the waters, were tossed merrily hither and thither by the laughing and frolicsome River.

38.

The saintly King Bhagīratha, in his chariot of gold and ivory, put himself at the head of the Gangā, to direct and guide her footsteps.

Singing and dancing, and laughing, and scattering jewels on all sides, the obedient Gangā followed, kissing the trace of his chariot, and babbling words of endearment.

As the Gangā passes, the land revives, and men are purified.

As the smiling River passed, the flowers unfolded their petals, the storks and herons revived, and the swans, like fluttering clouds, came back to embellish the land.

Then those whom a curse had smitten, at the touch of these glistening waters were freed from the malediction, and restored to virtue and fame.

39.

Bhagīratha directing his steps to the sea, the docile Gangā followed. From thence he led her into the

CHAP. III.
Bhagīratha leads the river to Tartarus, and laves the ashes of the Sagarides.

bowels of the earth, into the gloomy regions of Tartarus.

There, having performed the ceremony of lustrous waters in honour of his sixty thousand ancestors, he beheld the illustrious Sagarides, clothed in ethereal purity, ascend with rapturous joy to the home of the deathless gods.

40.

Brahma, having seen with approval this devout and magnanimous hero *thus washing all these ancestors*,[1] came himself to visit the monarch, and spoke to him, gravely smiling:

"So long, O saintly Bhagīratha, as the sun and the wind shall continue, the hearts of all living creatures shall cherish and honour thy name.

"So long as the eternal sea shall kiss the gentle Prithivī, so long in the restful kingdom shall the Sagarides bless thee gratefully.

Brahma blesses the hero, and calls Gangā after him, Bhagīrathī.

"This queenly bride of the gods now kisses thy feet with devotion, is babbling to thee her love, the docile love of a daughter; henceforth men shall call her Bhagīrathī; for she prays thee to call her thy daughter!

"And now, O Lion of Men! by the constant view of these waters, cleanse thy soul from all stain, and clothe it in limpid purity!

"Farewell! I return to Paradise!"

[1] Literally translated.

CHAPTER IV.

THE PENANCE OF VISVĀMITRA.

VISVĀMITRA was truly said to be an elephant among kings! He was of lordly stature, of an imperious and hasty temper, and of unexceptionable lineage, having descended directly from Brahma himself. These kingly qualities naturally gained him celebrity in the three worlds, and secured the tranquillity of his reign and the happiness of his people.

At length, however, he wearied of the blessings of peace, and felt that for the maintenance of his health and spirits something less insipid than this unbroken tranquillity was absolutely necessary. And, on the strength of this, let us not conclude that he was of a specially restless and intemperate disposition. We read, in the translation of Monsieur Fauche: "Or Visvāmitra gouverna ce globe en roi qui semblait une incarnation de la justice, *plusieurs myriades d'années.*" To put it at its meanest figure, let us say *one* myriad, instead of several;—after ten thousand years, is it surprising if he required a thorough change?

Now, to a king desirous of the large excitement of war, two things are primarily necessary: an army

CHAP. IV.

Visvāmitra longs for the excitement of war.

to fight for him, and an enemy to be fought with. Generally speaking, the latter is more readily found than the former. But in this instance that was not the case. In these extensive domains it was easy to gather together a formidable army, but Visvāmitra was so prosperous a man that every one regarded him with the most enthusiastic friendship.

No enemy presenting himself, Visvāmitra put himself at the head of his troops and marched forth in search of one.

Over hill and dale, through the heart of sombrous forests and the narrow streets of crowded cities, marched the innumerable host, always on the lookout for perilous adventures and dangerous exploits, that might render the monarch's name illustrious in the three worlds. None such, however, came in their way. As a rule, if you want to avoid adventures, go forth in search of them; destiny likes to attack people when they are off their guard, and prefers an unarmed victim.

After a time the king and his army came to the hermitage of the eminent saint, Vasishtha. The tall trees kept guard around it; kingly trees, crowned with golden blossoms. They extended their graceful leafy fingers over the hermitage, as who would say:

"This dwelling is under our special patronage."

They guarded it carefully from the winds of heaven, and from their spreading hands fell—shade.

Also, it was the most charming spot in the world. Nay, the Siddhas and Chāranas preferred it even

THE HOSPITALITY OF VASISHTHA.

to heaven, and loved to linger within its hallowed precincts. The holy anchorites flocked to it from far and near to profit by the words of the sage Vasishtha, and to vaunt the unusual gifts of his fascinating cow, the immaculate Sabalā.

The hermit greeted Visvāmitra most courteously, and invited him to be seated on the sacred grass, Kusa—than which, to the pious and devout, is no more honourable throne; then he presented him with sweet roots and berries, and water to wash his feet, and neglected not to offer him the eight things of the Arghya. Having thus complied with the ordinances of etiquette, he proceeded to make polite inquiries as to the monarch's health and well-being.

Visvāmitra, in his turn, expressed his delight at thus conversing with the distinguished Brahman, and asked whether his sacred fires, his groves, and his disciples gave him entire satisfaction.

Now, after this interchange of compliments and friendly solicitude, the monarch and the saint were mutually delighted with each other.

"Stay with me a while, O Tiger of Men!" said the holy Vasishtha. "I would prepare a feast for yourself and your army that may be worthy of your reverences."

"Nay," replied the considerate monarch, "I know that these sweet roots and berries are the sole fare of the holy men of your profession, and truly they have an excellent flavour. The sight of your magnanimous countenance is also a feast for my eyes, and the sage words which fall from your lips a delight to

Chap. IV.

The hermit invites the king and his army to a feast.

CHAP. IV.

my soul! You have already entertained me munificently, O Bull among Anchorites. I am more than satisfied."

But the Brahman continued to press him to remain, so that at length, not to appear discourteous, the amiable Visvāmitra consented to accept his hospitality. At the same time, he had some misgivings as to the nature of the festival of which he had promised to partake.

"No doubt this excellent anchorite will be at infinite pains to collect many varieties of roots and berries," he thought; "in these wilds he will not be able to procure other comestibles. My soldiers and myself are not accustomed to so simple a diet; but we must put a good face on it and simulate a hearty appetite, that the worthy saint may not perceive how little we relish his fare."

Accordingly, he strictly charged his followers to show no disinclination to the repast offered them, whatever it might chance to be.

Meanwhile the most eminent of anchorites was conversing with the miraculous Cow.

Vasishtha requests his miraculously gifted cow to furnish the repast.

"My pretty Sabalā," he said, "my docile, tractable, well-beloved friend! Thou knowest how much we owe to the protection of princes; they are invaluable as friends and irresistible as enemies. Besides, it is a duty to recollect their divine right. This Visvāmitra and his army are both hungry and thirsty; shall it be said that they left this hermitage unrefreshed? O inestimable Quadruped! if thou hast any love for thy master's honour, supply forthwith a bounteous feast for these illustrious guests! And let not only the quality of it be excellent, but the quantity superabundant; for, O Light of my Eyes! the appetite of kings and of warriors is larger than that of ordinary mortals."

Then Sabalā rubbed her cold nose lovingly against her master's cheek, as a token that she would fulfil his behests. Vasishtha, proceeding to milk the magnanimous Quadruped, was speedily gratified by the sight of all manner of delicious viands; such as sugar-canes, honey, fried grains, mountains of boiled rice, succulent pastries, cakes, preserves, and sweetmeats of all sorts, &c.; and by way of beverage, Maireya liquor, extracted from the flower of Maireya, the delicious essence of āsava, and rivers of curdled milk.

At the sight of this excellent cheer the hearts of the soldiers, whom the injunctions of Visvāmitra had somewhat depressed, bounded for joy. They feasted and caroused to the full bent of their pleasure, and praised the generous Vasishtha and admired the marvellous gifts of his inestimable Cow.

But Visvāmitra grew pensive. His heart sickened with envy, and he had no appetite to enjoy food.

"How comes it," he thought, "that this anchorite has here a more splendid feast than any served at my royal table? Is not this nearly treasonable?"

Occupied by such reflections, the monarch gloomily declined Vasishtha's pressing invitations to partake of these delicacies.

"Listen, holy anchorite," he said presently; "this

CHAP. IV.

The king wants to buy Sabalā.

Sabalā is truly a Pearl amongst ruminant creatures, and kings have, as you know, a right to the jewels discovered in their realms. Nevertheless, in consideration of my friendship for your person, I will not press my claim in this instance. I will give you one hundred thousand cows in payment for this Sabalā."

"Not for one hundred million cows will I sell this magnanimous animal!" replied Vasishtha. "Sooner shall the sun put a price on his radiance, or the sage on his wisdom, than I consent to sell Sabalā."

At that Visvāmitra's brow darkened.

"Is it not somewhat strange," he asked, "that one who has adopted the life of a penitent, and who in the three worlds is renowned for his self-mortifications, should care to possess a beast thus willing to gratify his appetites? The knowledge of its unusual gifts must be a sore temptation to thee, saintly hermit; I would remove this snare from thy path!"

On Vasishtha's refusal, he makes a larger offer, and warns the Brahman not to refuse.

"It is not needful," replied the Brahman; "temptation adds fresh lustre to the virtuous, and gives their fortitude wholesome exercise."

At that the angry monarch sprang to his feet and began to pace the narrow hermitage to and fro.

"I will give thee, thou contumacious troglodyte!" he cried, "fourteen thousand elephants with ornaments of gold, eight hundred ivory chariots, each drawn by four horses with golden bells round their necks, and ten million cows speckled with different colours! I would counsel thee to accept my generous offer, hermit! It has ever been the practice of kings to take by force what they could not obtain by honourable barter."

"Alas!" replied the Brahman, somewhat terrified by the king's wrathful countenance, "this Sabalā is all my life; it is she who provides me with the oblations for the gods, the offerings to the Manes, the clarified butter which feeds the sacred fire, and the grains to be scattered on the earth as a token of charity towards all creatures. Besides, she was given into my charge by Mahādeva, the lord of cattle. I cannot sell you this Pearl amongst ruminant creatures, O Visvāmitra!"

Then, in a great passion, the king turned his back on the Brahman.

"This cantankerous priest shall regret his obstinacy!" he cried. "Let my young warriors forthwith go in search of this delectable Milch Cow! Henceforth she shall minister to our royal wants, and supply luxuries to flatter our royal appetites!"

His followers gladly obeyed him.

"No doubt," they said one to the other, "when this magnanimous Quadruped is in our possession we shall have these sumptuous repasts daily."

But when Sabalā perceived that they were leading her away from the hermitage, she began to struggle and plunge, and to lash her tail wildly from side to side.

"How have I offended this sublime Maharshi?" she exclaimed. "Have I not always taken delight in watching his divine gesticulations, and his ecstasies of spiritual fervour? Have I ever failed to supply him with those material wants which his pious exercises prevented him from providing for himself? Have I ever murmured at his authority or questioned the truth of his sage discourses? Why, then, does this resplendent saint abandon his meek servitor, his beloved and docile companion?"

Maddened by the thought, she broke from the hands of her captors; and bellowing furiously, and wildly tossing her head, rushed through the ranks of the army. On all sides the soldiers gave way before her.

"After all," they said, "it was scarcely justifiable to rob the hermit of this impetuous animal."

Panting and exhausted, Sabalā flung herself at the feet of Vasishtha, and looking up at him with her soft, liquid eyes, and lowing plaintively, asked:

"Have you abandoned me, O master?"

Then the virtuous Brahman and the affectionate Quadruped intermingled their tears.

Vasishtha tells Sabalā he dare not resist the king.

"I have not abandoned thee, Sabalā," he cried, flinging his arm round her neck as though she had been a cherished sister. "Thou hast ever been a docile and faithful companion; attentive to my lessons, and careful to furnish me with my modest requirements. I have no fault to find with thee, thou Pearl amongst domesticated creatures. But this Visvāmitra is a Kshatriya,[1] and his army appears innumerable; what wouldst thou have me do? I am alone in this forest, but for the few blameless anchorites who are all unlearned in the art of war. Farewell, then, light of my eyes! I dare not resist this Visvāmitra."

[1] *Kshatriya*—warriors' caste, next to the Brahmans in rank.

At that the devoted Cow rose from her master's feet and tossed her head proudly.

Sabalā tells him to milk her, and she will provide him with an army.

"Have I supplied your wants for so many years, holy Brahman," she asked, "that you have ceased to appreciate my miraculous gifts? Why do you not milk me, O master? I can furnish you with an army twice as numerous as that of this truculent monarch."

Accordingly, Vasishtha milked once more this inestimable Cow; and lo! there rose up before him an innumerable host of warriors, turbulent, impulsive, and loyal, as was the devoted Sabalā herself. The army of Visvāmitra was soon overthrown by these vigorous heroes, whose ranks it was impossible to thin; for if a man fell, straightway another sprang, as it were, from the ground to take his place. After the combat, however, when all the king's warriors had either perished or fled, this miraculous army disappeared as rapidly as it had sprung into existence.

Visvāmitra's army overthrown.

Now the illustrious Visvāmitra had a hundred sons, gallant youths all of them, to whom the sight of their father's discomfiture was intolerable.

"We will punish the insolence of this niggardly Hermit," they said, "and teach him and his ill-natured Cow to respect the Divine Right of Kings!"

So saying, they rushed with one accord on Vasishtha. But the holy Brahman awaited them with perfect composure, and when they were within a short distance blew at them with all his might. His sacred breath blasted them into ashes, and they crumbled into dust at his feet.

His sons blown to pieces by Vasishtha.

CHAP. IV.

Visvāmitra espouses the life of a penitent.

Siva gives him the weapons of the gods.

Then the exultant Cow tossed her head in the air and bellowed again with delight.

But Visvāmitra, having thus beheld his army destroyed and his sons blown into fragments, began to entertain doubts as to the omnipotence of kings. Like the bird whose wings are broken, or the sea that has no waves, or the sun in times of eclipse, he realized his weakness and was sad!

His indomitable resolution, however, was not shaken. Having given his empire into the hands of his only surviving son, he retired into the woods and sought, by his self-inflicted penances, to earn the favour of the deathless gods. After a time the resplendent Mahādeva appeared to him and bade him name his request.

"Give me," said Visvāmitra, "all the arms in use with the gods, the Dānavas, the Yakshas, and Rākshasas."

"So be it," replied the king of immortals, and returned to heaven.

Then, full of pride and delight, the triumphant Visvāmitra set out for the Brahman's hermitage.

"It is the duty of kings," he said to himself, "to uphold their divine prerogative; at the same time leniency is a becoming virtue. I may find it necessary to extirpate this contumacious hermit, but to Sabalā I will extend my gracious pardon, and this Pearl amongst ruminant creatures shall become my loyal servitor."

Within a short distance of Vasishtha's dwelling the exultant monarch, unable to curb his impatience, shot off one of his miraculous arrows. As it sped

through the air, hissing like some venomous reptile, the trees of the forest shuddered with dread, the birds fled through the air shrieking, and the gazelles crouched low in the thicket. All the pious hermits and anchorites rushed to their huts and caverns, crying:
"The immortals are at variance, and have chosen this forest for their battle!"

Only Vasishtha, the Bull among solitaries, displayed no uneasiness. He stood at the mouth of his cavern smiling with scornful composure.

Vasishtha awaits the coming of Visvāmitra.

When he saw him thus unmoved, Visvāmitra's wrath knew no bounds.

"I will teach thee, miserable troglodyte," he shouted, "to respect the Divine Right of Kings!"

And with that he hurled at him the Dart of Rudra, and the Dart of Varuna, and the Dart of Indra; the Human Dart, the Soporific, the Smasher, the Stupefier, the Consumer, the Dart of Groans, the terrible Javelin of Dryness, and the invincible Dart of Thunder. He threw at him also the Dart of Chastisement, the Spear tipped with a Heron's Beak, two Lances of iron, and two Clubs; and after these, the awful Arrow of Death! After that he flung at him the Noose of Brahma and the Arrow of Siva: and two precious Thunderbolts, the Horse's Head and the Trident Dripping with Blood!

The king flings his weapons one by one at the priest.

It is undeniable that here was a formidable series of arms; but, amidst the shower of these appalling missiles, Vasishtha stood calmly holding his Brahman's stick over his head, and easily warding off the fatal weapons. Throughout his countenance wore the same contemptuous smile.

Vasishtha remains unmoved.

A less irascible opponent would have lost patience. Almost beside himself with rage, Visvāmitra seized, at length, the fatal Javelin of Brahma, and hurled it at his imperturbable adversary.

Then was there silence, for the awestruck winds stood still. The gods looked down from heaven with eager interest; but all mortal creatures closed their eyes and sobbed forth: "Farewell, Vasishtha!"

But even so, the invincible Brahman was not conquered. Opening his mouth wide, he received the flaming Bolt, and at one gulp *swallowed* it!

Then was a marvellous sight! In the eyes of gods and men this iron-hearted Vasishtha devoured the Javelin of Brahma! As he fed on the wrath of the god, his eyes grew crimson as blood; flames issued forth from his mouth; and the Brahman's stick, which he still held upraised, glowed like a hot bar of fire! Then all living creatures, appalled, fell on their knees to the dreadful anchorite.

"Spare us! save us!" they cried; "do not consume us with terror! Compassionate the fear of the three worlds and digest this fire of Brahma!"

At these words the resplendent Vasishtha deigned to reassure the trembling universe by resuming his wonted placidity.

But Visvāmitra exclaimed:

"The force of the Kshatriya is a chimera; the only desirable strength is the miraculous power of the Brahman. I will not rest until I have acquired this glorious title."

So saying, he flung on one side all implements of

warfare, and on the rugged slopes of the Himālaya commenced a life of most rigorous self-mortification. After a thousand years Brahma appeared to the zealous ascetic, and said to him approvingly:

"Thou hast entered the regions of sanctity, Visvāmitra. Yes, thy victorious penitence has earned for thee the title of Rishi among kings."

With these words the august sovereign of gods returned to heaven. But the recluse hung his head in mournful disappointment.

"Rishi among kings!" he exclaimed; "that is not what I desire; nor can my aspirations rest at having entered the regions of sanctity."

And so this indomitable hero redoubled his austerities.

Now there lived at this time a worthy king named Trisanku. He loved justice and truth, and governed his dominions wisely. There was, however, one fault which marred the perfection of his character; and that was an overweening love for his Body. It is true that it was an unusually comely Body, and doubtless it appeared even more so to him than to others. The thought that death would drive him forth from it, and that it would be reduced to ashes upon the funeral pile, was very grievous to him. Often would he quit the society of his courtiers, and even of his favourite queen, to caress and weep over this doomed Body in secret.

"Alas!" he would moan, "these vigorous limbs that have carried me triumphantly through space; these skilful hands that have given me mastery over

CHAP. IV.
He macerates himself during a thousand years.

Brahma gives him the title of Rishi, but, ill-satisfied, he continues his asceticisms.

Of King Trisanku and his great love for his Body.

material forms; these eyes, which have let in on me golden light and shapely beauty, which have shown my soul the countenance of my beloved: these lips, which have kissed my beloved; this breast she scorned not to make her pillow;—to all these I must bid farewell? Alas, my friendly, serviceable Body! Have I not struggled with thee to thy present stature; and has not that drift of conscious fire men call *soul* wrought thee, with burning implements, into an adequate expression of itself? How shall my being withdraw itself from thee? Abstract storm, or heat, or motion, from the forms which they impregnate, and what of them remains? An amorphous phantom, driven forth into illimitable space, how shall my soul keep its identity? Or, if incorporated in some other frame, how shall it fail to lose the individual character which it has won by dint of labour, grief, and love, in which, O faithful Body! thou hast shared?"

Trisanku requests Vasishtha to offer a sacrifice that he may never lose his body.

At length this mournful Trisanku, haunted by these reflections, sought the eminent saint Vasishtha, and exposed to him his sorrow.

"I would, O holy Brahman," he said, "offer up, through thy agency, a solemn aswamedha to obtain from heaven permission to retain this cherished Body of mine in the future state."

But when he had heard the monarch's desire, Vasishtha shook his head.

Vasishtha refuses.

"For so senseless a petition I will offer no aswamedha," he said; "be reasonable, King Trisanku, and rather rejoice that death will rid thee of thy Fleshly Incumbrance.'

But the melancholy Trisanku was so enamoured of his comely Body that he could not bring himself to look at the matter in this light. The Brahman having refused his request, he handed his empire over to his son, and wandered forth into the forest where dwelt the hundred sons of Vasishtha. To these eminent anchorites he confided his distress, and begged them to celebrate an aswamedha in his behalf. But they asked him:

"Why do you come to us, O King Trisanku? Is not our revered father the spiritual director of your house? Why do you abandon the root and seek aid from the branches?"

Then the melancholy king answered:

"I did, indeed, first seek the holy Guru, your father; but for this intent he refused to celebrate an aswamedha."

Then the sons of Vasishtha were very wroth.

"And why, thou stiff-necked, fatuous king," they cried, "didst thou not follow the counsels of the saintly Vasishtha? We will offer no sacrifice for the preservation of that wretched Dust-Body of thine."

At that Trisanku was incensed.

"They were free to refuse my request," he thought, "but they need not have insulted my unoffending Body."

"Farewell, then," he said haughtily; "I shall seek no more counsel from you nor Vasishtha. It is clear to me that you are unable to obtain my petition, and that this insolence is but a veil for your helplessness."

And so he turned away from them.

Trisanku and the sons of Vasishtha.

Meeting only with mockery, he speaks slightingly of their power.

Trisanku is transformed into a Chandála by the curse of the sons of Vasishtha.

But the infuriated sons of Vasishtha rushed after him.

"We will give thee a proof of our power," they shouted; "may this precious Body, thou thinkest so surpassingly beautiful, assume the degraded form of a Chandála!"[1]

As they spoke, the figure of the unlucky Trisanku was twisted and bent; his eyes became copper-coloured, and his teeth yellow and green; his kingly raiment disappeared, and a miserable bear's skin alone covered his nakedness.

In this deplorable plight the unhappy monarch dared not return to his palace.

"Alas!" he thought, "my most obsequious courtiers would scoff at me, and my lovely queen turn away from me in disgust."

So, having heard of the astounding self-macerations of Visvámitra, he sought out that elephant among men. When the royal ascetic saw the condition of Trisanku, he was filled with compassion, and exclaimed, in affectionate accents:

"Alas! my kingly brother, who has dared to reduce the graceful frame which thou didst once regard with such justifiable pleasure to the pitiable form of a Chandála?"

Trisanku tells his wrongs to Visvámitra

"The hundred sons of Vasishtha," answered Trisanku: and then he told his story.

Now when Visvámitra had heard the facts of the case he was filled with indignation.

"This overbearing Vasishtha and his sons, and his

[1] *Chandála*—the lowest caste.

ill-natured Cow, are quite insufferable," he said; "it is a duty to oneself and to the world to impress them with some respect for the Divine Right of Kings! By virtue of my unrivalled asceticism, I will obtain this boon for thee, O King Trisanku."

Then Visvāmitra proclaimed a great asvamēdha, and sent messengers far and near to summon to it all the anchorites, and hermits, and devout men who devoted their lives to prayer.

But when the hundred sons of Vasishtha saw the messengers, they burst into derisive laughter.

"Oh, the famous sacrifice that this will be!" they cried; "offered by a Kshatriya, and in honour of a Chandāla!"

The anchorite Mahodaya, hearing their scornful speech, refused also to attend the asvamēdha.

The messengers of Visvāmitra came and told him this.

Then this Elephant among Kings, whom resplendent penances had rendered terrible as the storm-god Indra, launched his potent curse against the sons of Vasishtha and the anchorite Mahodaya.

"May these scornful anchorites," he said, "in whose sight living beings are objects only for derisive mirth, be banished to the tenebrous kingdom of Yama; there, as guardians of the Dead, let them learn due reverence for the Living. As for Mahodaya, in whose ears their scorn rang more pleasantly than the soft pleadings of pity, let him become a ferocious hunter, unmoved at the spectacle of suffering, and taking pleasure in destroying life!"

CHAP. IV.

The Gods disregard the sacrifice: so Visvāmitra seeks to do the miracle unaided.

Trisanku ascends till his head strikes the sky, then Indra commands him to fall in mid-air; he is restrained by the command of Visvāmitra.

Now when the other anchorites heard of the doom of Mahodaya, and of the hundred sons of Vasishtha, they lost no time in obeying Visvāmitra's summons.

"This royal ascetic is soon put out of humour," they said; "and his displeasure is truly redoubtable." However, when all was ready, and Visvāmitra had celebrated the asvamēdha, the deathless gods remained calmly in heaven, and paid not the smallest heed to his sacrifice. Then this Tiger amongst Men, burning with passionate fury, exclaimed:

"Listen, noble Trisanku. By virtue of my severe mortifications, I myself will perform this deed. Mount up into heaven with the Body thou lovest. I, Visvāmitra, in the hearing of gods and men, command it!"

Then, like a bubble of air through the water, Trisanku began to ascend, conquering the waves of space, and striding through the intangible ether, easily as an antelope bounds up the side of a mountain. But when his head struck against the celestial azure, Indra, the lord of the firmament, looking over, said: "Fall, Trisanku!" and, head downwards, reeling and tumbling hither and thither, the luckless monarch began to fall through the ocean of air, clutching desperately at empty space.

"Save me, Visvāmitra!" he shrieked.

Then this indomitable Lion among Ascetics flung upwards the words:

"I command thee to stop, Trisanku!" and, obedient to his voice, half-way between earth and heaven swung the Body of the terrified monarch.

Then, in an ungovernable rage, the invincible

Visvāmitra set to work to create new gods in the place of Indra and his colleagues.

"What is the use of these supine Immortals?" he said. "One offers them sacrifices, of which they are too languid to partake; one prays and goes into ecstasies, and sings, and shouts, but they are too drowsy to hear. Only when, having vainly implored their aid, one makes up one's mind to do without it, they take their heavy heads off their cloud-pillows and undo all one's work, to teach one to be less presumptuous, forsooth! For my part, I am tired of these mischievous laggards! Let us either have gods who will heartily lend us their aid and labour with us, or who will sleep altogether and let us do our work undisturbed."

When the Immortals heard this resolute man speak thus, they were seriously uneasy; and Indra himself forsook the skies to seek to appease his wrath.

The anger of Visvā- mitra causes Indra to expostulate with him.

"Wherefore are you thus incensed, Visvāmitra?" inquired the persuasive Indra. "Up in heaven we have a specially warm regard for you, and hope some day to count you in our brotherhood. It was with great reluctance that I did you this displeasure just now; but you know, holy man, that to defend the laws is a duty for those who know them; and it is really out of the question for this king, whom a priest's curse has defiled, to enter the celestial abode with his Body."

The royal penitent was naturally gratified to learn that he was regarded with special favour by the Immortals; also, he at once renounced all intention of

CHAP. IV.

deposing such judicious rulers. He answered Indra affectionately:

"I understand your difficulty, most radiant of Immortals, and yet how can I fail in my promise to this Trisanku? May he not remain, as now, half-way between earth and heaven? You perceive he is supported easily by this galaxy of stars."

"It shall be as you desire," answered the Immortal; and with that returned to heaven.

At the request of the Penitent, Trisanku remains in mid-air.

So Trisanku remained in the celestial vault; and the ignorant, or uninformed, imagine him to be merely an astral constellation.

But Visvámitra, the merit of whose past austerities had been exhausted by this miracle, withdrew into the forest Pushkara, and during another thousand years persisted in his opiniative macerations. Brahma at length visited the royal penitent.

"Why do you continue these cruel austerities?" asked the august sovereign of worlds; "have I not accorded you the rank of Rishi among Kings?"

But the zealous Hermit answered:

"The title of Rishi does not satisfy me, O Brahma."

Now the lower gods were alarmed at the perseverance of this Lion among Ascetics.

"He will conquer the empire of the universe," they said; "no one seems capable of mastering his resolution."

Mēnakā declares she can conquer the Hermit's resolution.

Then the Apsara, Mēnakā, laughed, and said: "I am."

A Dream, that love had wrought into the form of a Woman, such seemed this lovely Mēnakā. Tenderness softened her eyes and deepened the shade of their lashes; laughter played with her mouth, and kissed her cheek into dimples; fancy unbound her hair, and twisted it into wavelets; grace moulded her form, and passion touched it with languor.

Visvāmitra is enslaved by the beautiful Apsara.

Down among the rushes and sedges, by the shores of the lake Pushkara, the Nymph laid her in the still eventide. Her sombrous hair floated down to the water, and swam on the glistening ripples. The timid reeds just touched her with their shadows, and the golden flags leant towards her, and grew pale. Listening to the babbling waters, singing low with the babbling waters, Mēnakā lay, gazing upwards through the sedges, watching the soft tints of even.

Thus Visvāmitra found her.

"Who art thou?" exclaimed the startled anchorite. "How camest thou hither, ineffable Star of Beauty? Hast thou fallen from heaven, or crept from the heart of the lustrous waters? Hast thou no pity on these trembling reeds, and these flags that have grown so pale?"

"I love thee!" she answered.

Then Visvāmitra crushed through the reeds and the sedges, and snatching the Nymph to his heart, bore her with him to the hermitage.

For the next five years, the anchorite, casting his penitence behind him, lived, as it were, one long dream of passion.

He lays by his life of penitence for five years.

Then he awoke.

Awoke to find the fruits of his austere life scattered to the winds, his power of self-control gone, his resolution broken, his science dimmed.

CHAP. IV.
He flies from the Nymph and resumes his self macerations.

"Oh, these women!" he exclaimed; "surely the gods created them to prevent man from rivalling their greatness!"

Prudently avoiding to bid her farewell, the Hermit fled from the enchanting Apsara, and sought the desolate solitude of the mountains. There, exposed to the inclemency of the weather, and the torments of hunger and thirst, for ten long centuries did the resolute anchorite afflict his wretched body. At the close of this period the terrified Immortals appealed to Brahma, saying:

"Oh, illustrious ancestor of worlds, we are filled with anxiety by this opiniative penitent! Give him the title of Maharshi; grant him what boon he desires, lest, by his invincible zeal, he gain a power equal to our own."

Then once again the august Brahma appeared to this Bull among Penitents, and thus addressed him:

"Cease, O resplendent Visvámitra, to afflict yourself thus cruelly; I give you the title of Maharshi, prince among Rishis."

But Visvámitra, clasping his hands devoutly above his head, replied:

"The title I would obtain, O King of Immortals, is that of Brahmarshi, saint among Brahmans."

Brahma tells him he cannot obtain the desired title till he has completely subdued his passions.

"Nay," returned the god, "that cannot be thine, O Visvámitra, until thou hast wholly daunted thy passions. Is the fever of anger unknown to thee, or the fiery ardour of love? Tread these passions under thy feet, daunt thy senses, and establish serenity in thy mind, then mightest thou attain to this supreme dignity."

After that, Visvāmitra imposed on himself a still more terrible discipline. His arms held over his head, standing on one foot, with no aliment save bitter roots, in summer surrounded by five fires, and in winter exposed to the drenching rains, for one hundred years he sought to obtain a perfect mastery over his passions. Watching him, the immortals became sore afraid.

"This time he will surely obtain what boon he wills," they said.

Then Indra, the most wily of gods, called to him Rambhā, the Apsara, whose eyes were like the petals of the lotus, and whose smile was like a flash of sunlight.

Indra urges Rambhā to conquer the resolution of the Hermit.

"O Nymph of the radiant smile!" he whispered, "you can conquer this hermit's resolve; you alone in the three worlds. Appear to him, then, charming Rambhā, and dazzle him by the sight of your beauty!"

But the trembling Apsara raised her hands prayerfully over her head.

"Nay," she said, "gracious Indra, lest this irascible anchorite detect the scheme and wither me by his potent curse!"

"Fear nothing, enchanting Rambhā," answered the god, "I will accompany you. Under the form of a kokila I will keep very near you."

So the Nymph of the radiant smile came like a gleam of sunlight flashing across the path of the Hermit, and seeking to conquer his coldness.

CHAP. IV.

Suspecting her design, he transforms Rambhā into a rock. But having thus yielded to anger, his past merits are lost.

But Visvāmitra at once divined the treachery. In a sudden fit of anger he exclaimed:

"Since thou hast striven to deceive me, O Rambhā, and to rob me of the merits of my penitence, may thy traitorous charms all perish; and may thy ardent loveliness be transformed into a cold rock, uncheered by the light of heaven."

As he spoke a kokila, who was fluttering near, shook the air with its musical laughter. Then Visvāmitra understood the double motive of Indra. He remembered that Brahma had charged him to conquer the fever of anger as well as the restless ardour of love, and he was very sorrowful.

Mournfully he withdrew to the wilds of Vajrasthāna, and for one thousand years remained there silent and motionless as a rock. Then all the gods sought the presence of Brahma, saying:

"We have sought vainly to awaken anger or concupiscence in the breast of this Maharshi. If you will not have the empire of heaven claimed by this indefatigable Saint, grant him his request, and let his penitence cease."

Then the magnanimous Immortal appeared to the exhausted ascetic, and said:

After another thousand years of penance, Brahma grants him his petition.

"I am content, O Visvāmitra. The Brahmarshi is yours; cease, then, now and for ever, to afflict yourself thus cruelly!"

Then, raising his hands reverently above his head, this Elephant amongst Saints replied:

"O Brahma, if by the force of my penitence I have acquired the rank of a Brahman, let there enter into me knowledge of the holy writings, and of the Vĕdas, and of Truth, and Perfection, and Constancy, and Intelligence, and Science, and Quietude, and Patience, and Chastity, and Mercy, and Tolerance, and Gratitude, and a Mind inaccessible to Error, and Emancipation from Thought, and Emancipation from Desire!"

It must be admitted that the illustrious and resplendent Saint was not sparing in his requests, but it is noteworthy that he made no mention of the immaculate Sabalā. Had he grown sufficiently indifferent to all worldly advantages to despise this Pearl amongst Ruminant Creatures? or during these five thousand and odd years had the inestimable Quadruped expired?

Chap. IV. His request.

CHAPTER V.

DASARATHA'S FAULT.

Chap. V.

*Nature, the universal mother, has sympathy with all her children. All smiles and blushes in the early dawn, she awakens the young and joyous, and with them wonders and hopes. On the bold and ardent she flashes hotly at noon; she dreams with the languid at twilight hour; at night she steps up to the mourner and puts her sweet face down quite near to his.

She speaks to him no word of comfort; there is one comforter for sorrow—*Time;* but she lays her shadowy hands upon his aching eyes, and gives to them the consolation of tears; she touches his overstrained heart, and lo! its bonds are snapped and its anguish overflows: she wraps him tenderly in her dark arms and bids him tell his grief; and, silently bending over him, she listens.

The grief of Dasaratha.

So was it that the king Dasaratha, grieving sore for the banishment of Rāma, remained for six long days petrified by his great sorrow. His venerable head bowed, and his eyes grown vague and dim, he listened to the reproaches of the forlorn Kausĺyā without one word of justification or complaint, until, at sight of this unspeakable anguish, the woman's heart within her relented, and she turned from weeping her son in exile to seek to comfort this stricken old man her husband. Nay, with the magnanimous self-devotion of pity, she undertook the defence of the very action by which she was bereaved.

The consolations of his Queen.

"Cease to reproach thyself, O righteous monarch!" she said; "thou hast shown, by this deed, thy spotless integrity and thy unflinching fidelity to truth. It was befitting thy grandeur to promise a boon to thy Queen Kaikēyī, for by her care she had restored thee to life and health when thou camest back wounded from the battle. How couldst thou foresee that her maternal tenderness for her own son Bharatá would render her jealous of the unrivalled virtue and beauty of Rāma, and of the love these brilliant qualities had won for him, and induce her to demand his banishment? And if thy great attachment to Rāma had made thee shrink from the fulfilment of the promise to which thou hadst unwittingly pledged thyself, thinkest thou Rāma had stooped to profit by a weakness which cast a slur upon his father's honour? Nay, sire, thou art guiltless; and in this world, whose government is in the hand of Brahm, where is no crime, is no just cause for sorrow."

Still Dasaratha answered not. Her words had no significance for him; his stupendous Grief stood between him and the outer world, and shut him out from all communion with it.

But at length, when this sixth day was dead, and the earth and sky were clad in mourning, the silent

CHAP. V.

The King laments Ráma's absence, but admits his punishment is deserved.

sympathy of night overcame him; and opening his arms wide to this darkness that sorrowed with him, the broken-hearted old man awoke from his despairing trance—and wept.

As he put his hands forth blindly into the night, they were clasped fondly between two soft warm palms, and to each sob of his there was an echo.

"Kausalyā . . ." he faltered dubiously.

At that, that other Watcher came forward and put her caressing arms about his neck; and so these two mourned together.

"O Brahm!" exclaimed the stricken monarch presently, "thy justice is inexorable! With Thee sin involves sorrow, as the seed the fruit; no atonement, no remorse can preclude the law.

"From his own weakness man draws the power to pity and forgive; but Thou, who art sinless, canst not pardon sin.

"I am very old; scarcely does my heart beat. I know it is because the icy hand of Yama is laid on it, —and my son is not here. My eyes are very dim. There is, as it were, a mist before them; I know the shadow of the death-god is on me,—and Rāma is not here! My limbs are feeble, my blood is growing chill. I draw breath hardly—more hardly every moment; alas! and Rāma is not here. My heart—this failing heart—is gasping for him! My eyes—these fading eyes—are athirst to see him once again. My broken voice calls on him in vain. Alas! my son! my son!

"Thou art just, O Brahm!

"I heard an old man once on his death-bed—as I am now on mine—cry, with his feeble arms extended yearningly: 'Come to me, my son!' and there was no answer; and the fault was *mine*.

"Listen, Kausalyā. It was long ago; I was young then—it must have been *very* long ago—I had not learnt the fellowship of all living things; suffering had not taught me mercy, nor sorrow, love. The vigour and fire of youth thrilled my veins so hotly that there were moments when I was actually drunk with life. Then I was wont to seize my bow and arrows and start for the chase.

"I found here a wild excitement and an exultant sense of power which satisfied me. As the winged arrows sped through the air, carrying death where my caprice willed, I seemed to myself a second god; nay, more, a controller of eternal Brahm himself! For where the great God said, 'Live; delight in the sunshine, and in the joys of love, and in the beauty of this fair earth,' I, Dasaratha, answered, 'Nay, but I will not have it so; die, rather!' And this defiant 'nay' hurled in the Creator's face triumphed!

"O dim-sighted one! And thy hand which grasped the bow, and this other which adjusted the arrow, from whence had they their skill? And this law, by which thy dart remained so long and no longer in mid-air, and fell just here rather than there, from whence proceeded it? O fool! who, in thy arrogance sawest not that God, who uses all men for the perfecting of His work, found thee worthy of the basest office only—the executioner's!

He tells how once he took delight in the chase.

CHAP. V. *Of how he went at eventide to the shores of the Sarayū.*	"One day, in the pleasant season of rains, my bow swung across my shoulders, I strolled down to the Sarayū, the sleepy river. The delicious dew spangled the emerald grass, and glistened tremulously on every fragile blade. Through the air floated slowly the azure butterflies breathing in perfumes; and the golden bees, with murmurs of delight, buried themselves amid the petals of the roses, and revelled there. On the river's breast the swans, with their large spreading wings, let the languid current bear them as it would; and along the banks the cranes, perched on one leg, watched dreamily the slowly flowing waters, seemingly struck with wonder that their own reflections and the shadows of the reeds and sedges did not float away also adown the drifting river.

"The peacefulness and calm appealed to me, and bade me forbear to mar this harmony. But in those days I was insensible to such pleadings.

"I was proud of my skill in taking successful aim, guided only by the indications of sound, the object of my pursuit being hidden from me. Accordingly, I laid myself down behind a palāsa bush, and, keeping all in readiness, waited.

He hears a sound he takes for the gurgling of an elephant in the water.	"When evening has breathed coolly on the limpid waters, the gazelles and antelopes in herds, and the elephants and buffaloes one by one, come down to the still Sarayū to slake their thirst, or to bathe in the delicious river. I felt no surprise, then, when presently the grass was crushed down and the fringe of reeds torn through, and I heard in the stream the gurgling sound the elephant makes

when drinking, and which nearly resembles the bubbling a pitcher makes when let down into the water suddenly.

"Stealthily preparing my bow from behind my ambush, I shot off an arrow in the direction of the sound. I heard the hissing dart tear through the air. There was a second's pause;—and then, O horror! the calm beauty of the even was rendered hideous by a *human* shriek!

"'Alas! I am stricken!—I am dead!' cried the voice;—and, aghast, my soul re-echoed the cry. In the heavens above, the pure clouds turned to Red; over the whole earth a mist that was Red, Red, gathered. It swam at my feet; my hands were dyed by It; my heart was steeped in It; my life, for ever and for ever, was stained with It;—Blood!

"But a moment since, and I had been guiltless, and the world beautiful; now this frightful Stain was on me; and in all the earth and sky was nothing left save Horror!—Horror!

"'Alas!' I heard the broken voice falter as I crouched behind the bush, which shrank away from me, shuddering, 'what cruel hand has murdered me? Why? I am a blameless anchorite—I never harmed a living thing! Who is it that has had the heart?'

"I could not bear this. Trembling with anguish and remorse, I sprang forth from my hiding-place, and found a poor Youth stretched on the river's brink. His face was livid, and from his side issued a little stream of blood.

G

The dying Youth's reproaches.

"Beside him, I flung me on my knees, and wrung my hands, and cursed the hour of my birth.

"'Tell me, stranger,' faltered the dying Boy, 'what cause of hatred have I given you? I, who love all living creatures; I, from whom the wild animals do not flee, when I pass them, in the forest. Willingly I have done wrong to none. I live here with my aged father; he is blind, and I wait on him. I came here with my pitcher to seek water for him. Alas! who will fetch water for him now, or lead him out into the pleasant shade, or warn him if there be any danger near? When I am dead, who will care for the old blind man? Oh, cruel stranger! this arrow will traverse my breast, and pierce his too! Why have you been thus pitiless?'

"Blinded with tears, I sought to sustain him in my arms; I pressed my agonized face against his, that was growing chill; I strove to warm him with my breath.

Dasaratha implores forgiveness.

"'Oh live!' I cried; 'live! live! Only that! I am a miserable wretch,—and yet I do not merit you should die! Alas! alas! I am a skilled archer; there are some who praise me for it, as though it were a grand thing to destroy life! And to say such praises were pleasant to me! I came here, to the river Sarayū, because I know the wild animals quench their thirst at even; and I was hidden behind yonder bush—it quite shuts out the river. Oh, believe me, one sees nothing from behind it! I heard your pitcher, and I took it for an elephant who gurgled in the water; you hear me—you understand? The sound misled me—I thought it was an elephant! I have sinned, I have been cruel and hard of heart, but I have not merited this hideous guilt! O gentle youth, for very pity do not die!'

"He answered me, with ineffable mildness:

"'I believe you,' he said — and there came a superhuman light into his large, patient eyes—'I am sure that you are in grievous sorrow, and I pity you. But thus has the Universal Father willed to show you the necessary guilt the destruction of life involves. To the heedless, each different creature seems a being with distinct hopes, and fears, and aims, confined to that slight shell he calls himself. Were this so, a life blotted out were no great matter; for who ceases to be, does not regret existence. But, as in the sensible world is no essential gap between the different forms of matter, so is there no void to rush between life and life, and make soul differ from soul, otherwise than accidentally.[1] As, also, the changed position of a single object alters the relative position of all other things, so does one death disturb the whole order of life; but here is not merely the shifting of unconscious relationships, but the rupture of hallowed attachments, the laceration of supreme affections!'

"He had raised himself into a sitting posture whilst

---

[1] "Accidentally," *i.e.* by its *modes* or accidents. Substantially the creed of the Brahmans is identical with the philosophy of Spinoza. There are only verbal differences, and these of so transparent a nature that they can conceal from no thoughtful observer the similarity of the two systems.

CHAP. V.

Ere dying the Youth bids Dasaratha seek to disarm his father's wrath.

speaking; but, at the last words, he sank back, and, but for my sustaining arm, had fallen on the ground. The light faded from his countenance, and over his lips crept that fatal blueness which reveals the kiss of Yama.

"'For me,' he said faintly, 'I must die—already the chill is stealing over me! O stranger, I would not that my father, in his grief, should curse thee for this crime thou didst unwittingly. Seek him, then, at once; kneel to him, and say: "*He* forgave me!" Perchance, then he will forbear to curse thee. But, ere leaving me, draw forth this dart from my cruel wound—I am sick with pain!'

"I bent over him, and very tenderly withdrew the murderous weapon. Then he gave one sigh of great relief; and, with a last pitying look at my despairing face, expired!

"For a while I sat there beside him, like one stunned. I could not *think;* I *knew* that the youth was dead, and that *I* had murdered him! I knew, too, that there was Blood beside me; that It had soaked into the ground; that It had bespattered the blossoms of some little flowers.

"They bent beneath it.

"I knew that overhead the clouds, that were dyed crimson, hung motionless; and that the wind was powerless to stir them, or even to carry them away! I knew the reflection of them stained the river's placid breast; and that the waters strove vainly to disperse them, or to lave them white. I knew that the shuddering reeds had heard his first despairing shriek;

and that they whispered to the waters, 'Alas, I am stricken! I am dead!' and that the stream caught up the Whisper, and said it out aloud; and, carrying it with it, went repeating it loudly, and always more loudly, along its course.

"I was vaguely conscious of all this, as I sat looking stupidly before me, wondering at the flies, who danced upon the river's face as though the horrid Colour were not there, and buzzed as joyously as though there were no dreadful Whisper in the air!

"Suddenly, I bethought me, that it was a terrible thing to be thus alone, with—with *It!*

"Then I sprang up from beside the Corpse, and fled.

"Dimly remembering that he had bidden me seek out his father, and had waved his hand towards a thicket that was near, I took that direction; more because some blind impulse impelled me thither, than because I realized his dying charge. Near the entrance of the wood I came upon a modest hut, thatched with dead branches and withered leaves.

"*Then* the recognition of the whole cruel truth came to me, in a flash: I knew that I stood outside the dead Boy's Home!

"A second time I had turned and fled, but it was too late; from within the hut a voice called to me.

"'Art thou there at length?' it said; 'oh, I am thankful! The time seemed long without thee, Yajnadatta; why didst thou stay so long, my son?'

"Then, as I stood there, silent, the voice resumed:

"'Why dost thou not speak to me? Art angry that I said the time seemed long? Nay, be not angry

Dasaratha hears the blind man call his son.

with thy old father! I meant not to reproach thee, Yajnadatta! But when thou art near me, I forget my blindness and all my infirmities; I feel them only in thine absence, and that is why I said the time seemed long. I meant not to chide thee, boy! Thou didst well to linger a while, and to sport in the cool waters; thou didst very well . . . O Yajnadatta, speak to me.'

"Then I came forward, and spoke rapidly in my grief:

"'I am not your son; my name is Dasaratha; my father is King of Ayōdhyā. I am the most miserable of men! I sought to-day the excitement of the chase; I came to the shores of the lonely Sarayū, and hid myself behind a bush. I had never heard that there were human beings in these desolate wilds; I thought only the wild beasts of the forest came down at even, to the cool river, to drink; that was why I hid myself behind the bush. I heard a gurgling sound, and thought it was an elephant who drank; it was your son who let the pitcher down into the stream; and my arrow struck him—and—he died! I tell you, it was unawares; I prayed him, bitterly, to live; I had gladly given my life to purchase his! He knew that it was unawares; he forgave me;—but, alas, he died!'

"He stood before me, his poor, sightless eyes distended, his face frozen into vacant stillness; he gasped once or twice, then he said, feebly:

"'Of whom are you speaking? I am an old man; I am blind; I have an only son——'

THE FATHER'S GRIEF.

"Then with sudden vehemence: 'Where is my only son?'

"From the ground, at his feet, I answered him:

"'Dead!'

"Then the wretched father threw his hands up above his head.

"'Dead!' he shrieked; 'dead, before me! My boy dead? No, no! I did not hear you right—I am old; you did not say my boy was dead? A short while since he went forth to fetch water; I heard him singing as he went; it seemed to me no kokila, in early spring, could have so sweet a voice! A foolish thought, you will say? Aye, aye,—perhaps, perhaps,—but I am an old, blind man, and have no joy in life, save my son —save my son. That was why I said, just now, it was not possible; I believe in God, for my part—I know it is not possible! I mistook your words; or perchance you did but jest with me? That was wrong—I am too old! But I pardon you, I pardon you! He will be back soon—it is not a great way to the river; I told you! He has gone thither to fetch me water—he—he will be here anon——'

"I answered him only by my sobs.

"'Monster!' cried the old man, grasping my arm in a sudden passion of despair, 'why do you not answer me? If this be indeed true, and my son, my only son, has perished by your hand, how dare you face my wrathful agony? What care I whether your crime were voluntary or no, since it has left me desolate? Do you despise a Brahman's curse, that you are here?'

The old man refuses to believe this possible.

In an agony of grief and rage he prepares to curse the murderer.

CHAP. V.
Dasaratha tells the Youth's dying words.

"From the dust, at his feet, I answered him:

"'He bade me come; lying in my arms, very feeble, he said, "Kneel to my father and say: '*He* forgave me; perchance then he will forbear to curse thee.'" They were the last words ere he died.'

"Then he burst out a weeping:

"'Lead me,' he cried, 'lead me to my son! He is not quite dead, perhaps; he has fainted; my voice may awaken him from his deep trance! Or if he have indeed passed into the silent World, Yama will pity me; his father[1] has kept his radiance back from me so many years, that Yama will surely pity me, and give me back my son! Kshatriya, show me where he lies.'

"And so I wound my arm about the old man's waist, and brought him to the river's bank, where lay the innocent Youth, quite stiff and dead, near to the shuddering reeds. The poor father laid him down beside the corpse, and sought to chafe the rigid limbs with his weak tremulous hands.

"'Yajnadatta! Light of my soul!' he wept, 'speak one word to thy old blind father, only one! Oh return, return; but for a little hour return to me, and we will depart together! I had died long since, Yajnadatta, but for thee; I waited,—waited,—I was tired and very weak, but I could not die and leave my boy! And now it is thou, O son! who hast forsaken the old, blind man!'

"So, pressing his withered face against the still placid countenance of the Dead, the veteran spent himself in wild entreaties and piteous complaints.

[1] The sun-god Surya is father of Yama the Death-god.

"At length exhaustion, and his great feebleness, hushed the rebellious tempest of his grief; and he wept tranquilly, as do the clouds after the lightning has spent its fire, and the thunder hurled forth its rage. Then, to the memory of Yajnadatta, we performed the ceremony of Lustrous Waters, and having piled high the boughs of scented wood, we tenderly laid the young anchorite on his last earthly couch.

"As the sacred Fire enveloped, in a shroud of gold, the Body Yama thought to dishonour by his defiling touch, floating upwards to the supernal azure, the spirit of Yajnadatta lingered a while, like an ethereal cloud, in mid-air. And as the kindly dews fall softly from the bosom of the morning, consoling words floated downwards, to cheer the aged mourner.

"'Thy loneliness is not for long, Father, not for long! The all Merciful Ruler will soon stop thee, with His hand, and say: "Life is too heavy for these stooping shoulders; I will remove the Burthen! Rest, thou poor old man!" And then shall even the memory of thy sorrow be no more.

"'But for Dasaratha is more cause for pity. A man's *deeds* are more memorable than his *sufferings;* he ceases so very soon to feel,—and then his joys and griefs are as though they had not been; but his actions, which are the reason of his life, remain. I sorrow less for thee, Father, than for Dasaratha!'

"He spoke truly, Kausalyā! In a few days, tended lovingly by me, the old man died, and his anguish was no more. And I, after these long years, am bending now beneath the guerdon of my sin!"

CHAPTER VI.

THE INTERVIEW BETWEEN SĪTĀ AND ANASŪYĀ.

Chap. VI.

*In the grey of morning, Rāma stood at the door of his hermitage. His head was very heavy; his heart, too, was not light. Leaning against the trunk of the perfumed peepul tree, he gazed with wistful eyes in the direction of Ayōdhyā. It had seemed to him that some light in earth or heaven would reveal where the fair city lay, but there was no such token; in the wide distance was no gleam of light; Ayōdhyā was so far away!

So far away;—his father, the old King Dasaratha, whom grief had slain, and who had passed into the Restful World; his mother, the loving Kausalyā; his younger brother, Bharata, who had followed him into these wilds, to seek to conquer his resolve, and win him back to his throne and country, all so far away!

It is an error to suppose that the brave are necessarily strong; to be a Giant is one thing, to be a Hero is quite another.

Rāma is very mournful.

In the eyes of Rāma swam a mist of unshed tears; suffering could not master him : yet he suffered!

Presently a ruddy glow crimsoned the heavens, and Surya, the sun-god, leapt forth from his misty chamber.

"Good morrow!" shouted he to the slumbrous earth; and thereupon she shook off her dim languor and smiled back on him, brightly, "Good morrow!" The flowers, who had been weeping, raised their gentle faces, still wet with dewy tears, and laughed in their delight. The waving grass tossed the long shadows to and fro, and played with them and said, "We fear you no longer; begone! It is day!"

"It is day," muttered the evil beasts, and crouched low in their dark lairs.

"It is day!" carolled the birds, and began to soar and sing.

Only in Rāma's heart the night still lingered.

"The holy anchorites, who dwelt on this mountain, have all fled," he said to his brother and to the gentle Sītā; "they tell me that Rākshasas and evil spirits, who hate all living things, prowl about here by night. Think you, we do well to linger here?"

He proposes to quit their hermitage.

Then Lakshmana, the impetuous young warrior, broke into a fearless laugh.

"I am not a holy anchorite," he said, toying with his mighty bow, "to dread the sight of these Rākshasas; I have no treasures of penitence to lose, if I yield to a fit of anger; there is nothing would please me more than to encounter these enemies of gods and men!"

But Sītā took Rāma's hand, and put it tenderly to her lips.

"Nay," she said softly, "let us leave this mount Chitrakūta; *I* fear these cruel Rākshasas; I am very timid, Lakshmana!"

For she read her husband's heart, and knew that

CHAP. VI.

A day's journey brings them to the hermitage of the Saint Atri.

the evil spirits he dreaded were the idle regrets which this spot, where he had bidden farewell to Bharata, fostered in his mind.

Her love for him told her that.

So they left the fertile mount Chitrakūta, and the pleasant hermitage, beneath the spreading peepul tree, to wander once more in the pathless forest.

Towards the close of the first day, they reached the humble dwelling which the magnanimous Brahman, Atri, had sanctified by his life of penitence. When the holy man recognized Rāma, the Dasarathide, he was filled with delight; and turning to the venerable saint, his consort, exclaimed:

"See, Anasūyā, here comes this youthful prince who prefers dignity to honour, and self-respect to the glories of renown. To the vulgar he appears the victim of fatality; but the enlightened see in him one who has dared to face his destiny, and say: 'Thou art strong, but I am noble; do thy worst, and I shall still pass through it, head erect!'"

So saying, the saintly hermit hastened forth to meet his guests.

At sight of the old recluse the two young heroes performed a pradakshina round him with great respect, whilst the bashful Sītā stood with downcast eyes before the holy man. When the venerable Atri had cordially greeted Rāma and Lakshmana, he turned to the gentle daughter of Janaka, and sought to reassure her by his kindly words.

"'Thou art welcome, O Flower of Beauty!" he said. "My rude hut is all unused to harbour so lovely a guest. Anasūyā, my faithful consort, had come forth herself to greet thee, but she is an aged woman, Sītā, and very feeble; but if thou wilt deign to enter, and to approach her, she will open her arms to thee tenderly, as does the waning night to the radiant star of morning."

Then turning to Rāma he added, with justifiable pride:

"Doubtless you have heard, O Prince, of this Anasūyā, this Miracle amongst saintly women? When there was a dearth in the land, she afflicted herself with terrible penances, for ten thousand years, that fertility might return to the earth. On another occasion, travelling on the affairs of the Immortals, by virtue of her astounding macerations, she made one night equal to ten. In fact this Pearl amongst women has heaped up treasures by her unequalled penitence, and can demand what boon she wills at the hands of the Immortals. She has spoken to me, with favour, of your blooming Vaidehī,[1] and will certainly receive her with a mother's tenderness."

Then Rāma turned to Sītā, and said:

"Thou art fortunate, Bride of my heart, to have won the favourable esteem of this illustrious Penitent. Enter then the hermitage, and bear, I pray thee, my greetings to the holy Anasūyā."

So, whilst the two princes accompanied the Brahman to the stream, where he bathed at even, as the sacred rites command, Sītā entered the hermit's dwelling.

She found the ancient woman seated on a couch

[1] *Vaidehī*—Sītā was Princess of Vaidēha and Mithilā.

CHAP. VI.

Anasūyā commends her as a dutiful wife.

of the sacred grass, kusa; her figure was bent and withered, her countenance wrinkled, her eyes dim, and she trembled always, as the aspen does when the rough north wind is abroad.

She had no need to macerate herself any more; nature had laid on her the supreme penance of age; which earns, too, the supreme compensation—rest.

Clasping her hands and raising them to her forehead, as the laws of politeness require, the Princess of Mithilā bowed herself before the illustrious Saint, and inquired, courteously, how she did.

Then the venerable Anasūyā looked long and fixedly at the gentle Vaidehī.

"Thou art beautiful, child," she said at length, and her voice was harsh as the mountain winds among the creaking firs; "and that is not ill: thou art young and in good health, and that is better; thou art a dutiful and obedient wife, and that is best of all! I have heard of thee; how thou hast abandoned the luxuries of the court to follow thy husband's fortunes in the pathless woods. There are many would tell thee thou hadst performed a heroic action; but I am too old to use flatteries. I say merely thou hast done thy duty. A dutiful wife is the reflection of her husband; her mind is the mirror which repeats his thoughts; her actions shape them after the model of his; and she herself follows him, meekly and self-forgettingly, as the shadow which trails behind him in the dust!"

Then Sītā answered the stern old woman, simply:

"I cannot tell whether I be a dutiful wife or no; I only know that I love Rāma. When I stood by the sacred Fire, and the Flame glowed up into my Hero's face, as he vowed to love and cherish me, his eyes met mine, and they held me, and I could not look away.

Sītā answers that she loves Rāma.

"Then my soul went out to him.

"I cannot tell if it was God did that or the flame, which lit up both our faces, or whether his dark, wistful eyes drew the heart out from me! I only know that when my gaze fell there was a Heaviness in my breast, and a Pain, and yet a strange Delight. And where there had been selfish pride before, was written Rāma; and where there had been hope, or joy, or beauty, was written Rāma; and where there had been dreams of unknown bliss, was written Rāma; and where there had been God and heaven, was written Rāma!—I know not if my mind reflects his own, but every dumb, vague thought of mine he reveals clearly to me, and tells it me in living words; I cannot say whether I shape my actions after his pattern, but all I strive to do he consummates and perfects; whether I follow him like his shadow, meekly and self-forgettingly, I know not, but where he goes, I too go all unwittingly, for I seem to nestle in his heart."

Then Anasūyā, the aged matron, stroked Sītā's cheek, and said:

"Thy words have the fire of youth, my daughter, and love sings in thy voice as through the notes of the kokila. The past comes back to me, as I hear thee name thy Beloved. The music of thy voice brings the dead past back to me."

At that the Vaidehī, half ashamed of her loving confession, hid her glowing face in the old woman's bosom, and lay there trembling.

"Listen, my gentle singing Bird," said the venerable Anasūyā. "By virtue of my austere life, I have obtained many gifts from the generous Immortals; one of them I have reserved for thee. Henceforth thou shalt walk adorned with celestial radiance, which shall add fresh lustre to thy surpassing beauty. The soft tints of thy raiment shall not fade nor be ever soiled; and these flowers I twine in thy glossy hair shall never die nor lose their sweetness."

The Recluse proceeded to deck the youthful princess in garments of tender colours, and to hang glistening gems round her neck, and her small wrists, and her round graceful ankles. Then the amorous bride of Rāma flung her arms round the aged Saint.

"I shall be more beautiful in *his* sight!" she whispered. "O Pearl among Ancient Women, you have filled my heart with gladness!"

Then Anasūyā bade the Vaidehī sit down beside her on the sacred grass; and passing her arm round her, drew her graceful head down upon her shoulder.

"Now talk to me, child," she said; "your voice is very sweet to my ears. Tell me the story of your birth, for I have heard you were born of no mortal woman."

And so, reclining in Anasūyā's embrace, Sītā told her story.

"There is a king of Mithilā," she said, "who loves his people as his own children. His life is very full of care; for, on all occasions, he feels with them, and strives to think for them, as a righteous king should do.

"It is a heavy charge to be on one man's shoulders.

"The name of this righteous monarch is Janaka; he is my revered father.

"Some time back, as he was tracing with a plough the circle which encloses the ground where sacrifices are offered, a sudden ecstasy seized him. His heart, which had been mournful and depressed, glowed with new warmth, and into his mind, which anxiety had filled with clouds, came a rush of light.

"From the loose sod thrown up round him, all threaded through with fibrous roots, he looked to the rich fields and pastures, and to the flowering shrubs and giant trees; and his heart warmed to the generous Goddess who holds the seeds of all things in her bosom!

"'O gentle Spirit of the Earth!' he cried, 'thou alone givest me comfort for Humanity. The sky draws back her azure robes, and with her myriad radiant eyes looks down, in still surprise, on this dark, restless speck called Man. The wailing World of Waters makes monotonous lament—swinging forward, ebbing backward, in dull sorrow, that knows nor rest nor hope. Standing near, the Heart, too, loses hope,

Sītā tells of her father's many cares.

Of how he praised the kindly Goddess of the soil.

CHAP. VI.

and there seems no cure for grief, nor any Purpose in the Life of Man.

"'But thou, Prithivī, noble Goddess of the Soil! who art more than generous, who art *just;* who dost not merely give, but who acceptest; who, honouring Man, sayest not, "Here, poor Creature, is thy daily food;" but, "Comrade, put thy hand in mine, and let us work together; feed me, and I will give thee food; tend me, and I will guard and shelter thee; love me, and I will cast my beauty at thy feet; observe and study me, and I will teach thee to be strong, and pure, and brave,"—thou, beloved Goddess! art my comforter and guide; and, had it pleased Heaven to give me lineage, I had brought my heir to thee, and said, "Oh, rear this child up in thy fecund heart, that I, who love thee, may possess an image of thyself!"'

Of the Earth Spirit's answer to his loving words.

"As he spoke, a dreamy haze stole over the sweet Earth's face, like to the misty tenderness which veils a maiden's eyes when told she is beloved. Little by little, the amorous Cloud merged into ethereal semblance of a Woman's form. It floated into the embrace of his extended arms, and rested on his impassioned breast most lovingly, a moment; then died back into the formless air; and left him, thrilled by that ineffable caress, enraptured, but very tremulous!

"'I have had a Vision,' he said presently, and sighed. —'*Only* a Vision!' he repeated, and half wept.

"But, as he put his hand to the plough once more, lo before him, in the gaping furrow, he saw the loose soil move; and at length, slowly and with difficulty pushing through the heavy earth, emerged before him, as he stood wonderstruck, a pretty Babe, with large bewildered eyes, who rested its tiny dimpled hand upon the broken turf, and struggled hard, and asked, by plaintive cries, to be released.

"I have heard my father say, that when he saw me thus,—my small limbs covered quite with dust, and my poor innocent face turned up to his,—that his heart cried out loudly:

"'This is my child!'

"And a whisper from the deep bosom of the Earth answered:

"'And mine!'

"So Janaka ran forward, and snatched me to his breast; then I wept no longer, but smiled happily, and nestled there.

"And where he took me from sprang up a bed of flowers, and they did not fade with summer, but grew more fragrant as the years went on. And when I grew older, and could walk and run alone, I used to steal there often, and lie down amongst them; and they would cluster round me, and whisper, 'Welcome, little sister!'

"But Janaka taught me ever to reverence the generous Earth, my Mother; and to strive to be as pure and true and brave as she. And he called me 'Sītā,'[1] because I sprang from out of a furrow of the ground.

"This, Holy Woman, is the story of my birth."

[1] *Sītā* means *furrow*.

CHAP. VI.

Then Anasūyā folded the Vaidehī in her arms:
"Thou hast indeed the courage of the brave Earth-Mother," she said, "for thou hast not feared to face the scorching heat, and the biting winds, and the angry storm! And thou art as noble too, O Sītā! For thou hast lavished thy beauty on the sorrowful; and hast sought to make even the path of exile sweet to thy Beloved! That is why I have given thee unfading charms; which, like the flowers that cradled thee, shall outlive thy summer.

"But look; through the doorway I see the anchorites, their valkalas[1] glistening with silver water, returning from the sacred river. The night must be near; the jealous night who puts a veil over all else, and says, 'Behold *me;* I am decked with stars!' Ere the darkness descend, stand forth, beside me, Vaidehī, that I may see thee in thy new apparel."

So the gentle Princess of Mithilā stood up; and Anasūyā admired her greatly, and said:

"These gems, and this radiance I have caused to dwell upon thee, Sītā, have greatly enhanced thy loveliness."

And so thought Rāma and Lakshmana, when they entered the hermitage; and when they heard that the Vaidehī was to retain her beauty through the succeeding years, they were the more delighted, and said:

"That is a favour seldom granted to mortal woman."

[1] *Valkala*—mantles worn by anchorites.

CHAPTER VII.

SŪRPANAKHĀ.

About this time lived an illustrious hermit, named Agastya. He was justly renowned in the three worlds, both for the persistency of his self-macerations, and the amazing power he had acquired thereby; neither of which had been equalled by any saint before him, nor, it is probable, will be by any that may come after. I will not attempt to enter here on the history of his astounding miracles: but when I shall have told you that, on one occasion, he devoured the Rākshasa Vātāpi, under the form of a ram; and that, on another, to please the Immortals, he swallowed the sea, with its alligators and aquatic monsters, I think you will admit I have not overrated his merits.

But these things were mere trifles to the resplendent Agastya.

It was near to the abode of this unrivalled saint that Rāma wished to establish his new hermitage.

Now, Agastya lived in the midst of the terrible forest, Dandaka, where eternal darkness reigned. The huge trees there towered up till they reached the light, branchless; then they spread forth their massive

CHAP. VII.
The evil wood of Dandaka.

boughs, and crushed them down, the one on the other, to ward off the sunshine; if any emaciated beam forced its way through the outer foliage, it was strangled, straightway, by the creeping plants that twisted them round the naked trunks, and swung their fibrous arms from tree to tree. There were few sounds, and less movement; yet one was conscious that the Forest teemed with life; the intense stillness itself revealed this. It was not the calm of solitude but the suspended breath, which betrays a Hiding Place! The large-bladed grass grew to a monstrous height; it was of a bright metallic green, that showed the dank mephitic slime which nourished it; fungi, of all sizes and shapes and colours, sprang up amidst it; but there were no flowers—none, save the spotted orchids, the impure daughters of mortality, who thrive upon the fetid air, and draw their poisonous brilliancy from corruption.

It was the home of those who loathe the day.

For all the dimness, and the evil that it sheltered, and the silent menace of the faint, musk-scented air, it was not without a dangerous fascination, and a sinister beauty of its own.

Reader, let us not deceive ourselves: the *ugliness* of Sin is an illusory supposition merely. Were it a fact, the influence of Evil would be indeed unaccountable, —*to be attracted by the repulsive*, the preachers of innate depravity will find it hard to fasten this anomaly on poor Human Nature! No; the Beautiful, the Ideal, for they are One, includes all the opposite principles of Life; here, too, all that is, involves the existence of its contrary: the Angel of Light infers the Prince of Darkness; the Music of the Spheres, the sombrous Harmony of Gehenna; the Radiance of the Empyrean, the magnificent Gloom of the Abyss!

The glamour of the dangerous Forest had fallen on Rāma. The obscurity weighed on him heavily, yet it had a voluptuous charm for him. He was, at once, disquieted and entranced. An apprehension of unknown Danger warned him not to linger here; at the same time, he was loth to go; his own misgivings had such an absorbing interest for him!

All this he did not acknowledge, even to himself.

"I would fain establish myself in your neighbourhood, O Elephant among Saints!" he said to Agastya, "were it not for my gentle Sītā. . . . It is true that I am here to protect her and the gallant Lakshmana, my brother; what think you, holy man? My timid Princess might perchance be exposed to alarms, for this wood of Dandaka is full of terror."

"It is truly a sombrous dwelling for thy youthful bride," answered the Hermit; "and since she has abandoned her home to follow thy fortunes, it becomes thee to soften for her the hardships of exile. But, at two yodjanas' distance, thou wilt find in the heart of this gloomy forest a charming spot, abounding in fruit-trees and limpid waters, like Nandana, the garden of Indra. It is called Panchavatī, and near to it flows the Godāvarī, the crystal River. There build thy hermitage, O Hero! The beauty of this blooming valley cannot but enchant thy dreamy Sītā, and thou wilt be

Agastya counsels Rāma to go to the vale of Panchavatī.

CHAP. VII.

Jatāyu the Vulture asks to share their fortunes.

within an easy distance of my humble cabin; so that the delight of seeing thee, illustrious offspring of Raghu, may yet be mine."

Accordingly, having described a pradakshina round the inestimable Agastya, the two heroes, with the lovely Princess of Mithilā between them, set off in the direction of Panchavatī. On the road they were met by the kingly Vulture, Jatāyu. This distinguished Fowl greeted them courteously, and, turning to Rāma, said:

"My son, I was once the friend of your lamented father, that late Bull among Kings, Dasaratha."

When they heard that, the two young princes saluted the king of Vultures most affectionately, and Sītā inquired softly how he did. Now, when he had responded to their politeness, Jatāyu asked what they did in the baleful wood of Dandaka; and when he heard that they intended to take up their abode in the vale of Panchavatī, he begged to be allowed to accompany them.

"For," said the magnanimous Bird, "this is a neighbourhood of bad repute; the Rākshasas and all manner of evil creatures dwell here: I will be your faithful companion, and will help you to protect this blooming Princess, whose eyes are like two dazzling stars!"

"So be it," answered the Dasarathides, and Sītā stroked the plumage of the amiable Bird, and said:

"Thanks, O Pearl among Feathered Creatures."

So Jatāyu went with them to Panchavatī; and on the way thither, he entertained them by recounting his genealogy. It was of the most distinguished order, for the grandfather of his grandmother was the illustrious Prajāpati, Daksha; and he himself was the son of Garuda, who, you know, was the Monarch of all Fowls. The names of his intermediate ancestors have so formidable and unpronounceable an appearance, that I dare not venture on them; but you will find them in the twentieth chapter of the volume Aranyakānda, together with many curious details concerning their owners, which, for several reasons, I forbear to transcribe.

The ancestors of Jatāyu.

Agastya had not praised too highly the delicious valley of Panchavatī. Issuing from the sombrous forest, the change of scene was something dazzling! Instead of the massive teak trees, with their lowering foliage, the sweet lime and feathery acacia waved their fragile boughs, and dipped them into the sunlight, as into a stream of harmless fire; the baubul shook its golden fruit, and seemed to laugh in the warm radiance; the citron and orange trees unfolded their cloudy blossoms, and gave their rich perfumes to the breeze; and, like spirits in the air, the filmy down of the lovely cotton tree hovered, or rested on the edge of flowers, like snowy shadows who paused there to dream. The birds sang here, and the azure butterflies floated languidly to and fro, like winged morsels of the blue sky itself. On the breast of the Godāvarī, the crystal river, brooded the dreamy lotos; to whom the waters sang, and for whom the reeds along the shore sighed constantly; and from the reeds across the river flashed the brilliant dragon-fly, and danced in sudden whirls,

The beauty of the valley of Panchavatī.

CHAP. VII.

Lakshmana builds a hermitage.

or darted in rapid flights, like one possessed! In the sunlight, along the bank, basked the harmless lizards; and the stupid storks and cranes, turning their backs on them, stood on one leg, and pondered how it was no creatures came crawling up to them to be devoured?

The scowling Dandaka encircled this enchanting spot on all sides. It was as though the sinister wood had paused from its malevolent delight in evil, to sigh, and for one moment to regret the light it sought to stifle, and the Heaven it willed to hide;—the name of this momentary aspiration heavenward was Panchavatī!

In the heart of this smiling valley Lakshmana, who was the most skilful builder, constructed a graceful little cabin. It was built of branches, and thatched with leaves; and over it a neem tree extended its kindly arms, and whispered something amid its rustling foliage, which was surely a blessing.

When she saw their new dwelling, Sītā clapped her hands together for joy.

"It is like a leafy nest!" she cried. "Do you not think so, most eminent of Vultures?"

To which Jatāyu answered with some hesitation:

"Doubtless you are right, Princess with the liquid eyes. But I am a large Bird, and heavy: also my experience of nests is confined to the creeks and crannies of rocks."

The Dasarathides, the Princess of Mithilā, and the amiable Vulture, dwelt in the pretty hermitage for three pleasant months. During that time they saw nothing of the sinister inhabitants of the wood of Dandaka, and, as was natural, began to lose all apprehension. When the winter commenced, the delicious season, in which Surya woos the beloved Prithivī with gentleness, rather than ardour, the inestimable Fowl, Jatāyu, presented himself to Rāma, and said:

"I must leave you for a while, O Tiger of Men! I wish to visit my relations and friends, who dwell among the mountains. Be very watchful during my absence; I regret leaving the peerless Vaidehī in the heart of this evil Forest!"

The Vulture asks leave to visit his family.

Rāma answered:

"Be without uneasiness, O magnanimous Bird! This little Sītā has our two great hearts to shield her! But when thou hast greeted thy friends and relations, do not fail to return to us; we shall miss thee greatly, Jatāyu."

And the gentle Princess, with tears in her large eyes, repeated:

"We shall miss you sadly, Jatāyu!"

Now, it happened on the evening of the same day on which the Monarch of Vultures departed, that an evil Rākshasī, named Sūrpanakhā, passed by the hermitage. The door stood wide open. Sūrpanakhā, whose monstrous form towered above the little cabin, crouched down on all-fours, and dragging herself along the ground into the shadow of the wall, stretched forward her hideous head, and looked round into the hut.

Sūrpanakhā peeps into the hermitage.

The soft light of evening stole in there silently, and kissed the faces of its occupants, giving to them the vague radiance one sees in dreams. Sītā was mournful because the faithful Bird had left them; she nestled close to her husband, and rested her head upon his shoulder. Lakshmana, who was seated opposite them, with his back to the door, sought to divert her by his talk; but Rāma, whose arm encircled the gentle Princess, said nothing; he only looked down fondly on her sweet, pensive face and smiled.

He *smiled;* it was the first time Sūrpanakhā had seen that!

Laughter is common enough among the Rākshasas; they are amused by the sight of suffering; and as there is plenty of that in the world, they have many occasions for mirth. They can, too, grin maliciously, and curl the lip with a scornful sneer; but to smile is not given to these demons. The Smile is the transfiguration of the countenance which beholds the Ideal; the Rākshasas have no such vision. It is the radiant Flash which follows the meeting of three sentiments—Love, Pity, Desire; these feelings are not much in vogue among the Rākshasas. Finally, in the Smile is always hidden a memory of past tears; the Rākshasas have no such memories,—for they cannot weep.

The Rākshasī becomes enamoured of Rāma.

And so the malevolent Sūrpanakhā crouched there, riveted by the sight! It was painful to her as though a poisoned arrow had pierced her heart! Who was this Woman of hateful beauty, whose head rested on this young Hero's breast, and over whom he leant with that serenely tender smile? His arm around her, too,—to draw her nearer to him! Who was *she?* For him, she did not stay to question who he was; she knew *what* he was to her! She beheld him faultless in face and figure, and she loved him,—as such depraved creatures love.

She is jealous of Sītā's beauty.

After the first moment it was on Sītā, rather than on Rāma, that her odious gaze rested. There was not a dimple of the lovely face, not a curve of the rounded figure, which she did not note with her eager, cruel eyes. Grovelling there, she dug her long nails into the earth, and ground her teeth together, and muttered:

"Let me learn the likeness of this Creature who has won his love! Let me learn her off by heart!"

After a while, she dragged herself back into the shade, and slunk back stealthily into the wood. Arrived there, she flung her arms up above her head, and gave one ferocious howl, which made the echoes ring; then she flung her down upon the grass, and sat there—her long sinewy arms clutched round her knees, and her chin resting upon them meditatively. Sūrpanakhā was of monstrous and repulsive ugliness; but at pleasure she could assume another form, and disguise herself in what beautiful shape she chose. Only this adopted loveliness gave her little satisfaction; she felt the homage paid to it was not won by *her*. She, the hideous, distorted Sūrpanakhā, would have had the beautiful young Hero, who had awakened this burning passion in her breast, love her as she was, and become enamoured of her very ugliness.

At the same time, she knew this was impossible, and that was why there was a bitter rage upon her, which she had fled here to hide.

CHAP. VII.

"No doubt," she croaked as she sat there, "this arrogant youth with the god-like form thinks himself the equal of Vishnu himself; and he, too, can deign to stoop to nothing, save some faultless Lakshmī! Lakshmī, forsooth! And who knows, after all, what the beauty of this vaunted goddess may be? Who sing her praises? The gods! And I? Am not I also lauded by *my* kindred, the Rākshasas?— Beauty? The word makes me mad! Am not I, Sūrpanakhā, more beautiful than this feeble Thing he loves, and wastes his melting looks upon? Well, I know his taste; I, too, can be a timid, shrinking maiden, soft and loving and gentle, and of more dazzling charm than this vapid Bride of his. Let us see if she will stand between my Beloved and me!"

The Rākshasī assumes the form of a young maiden.

So saying, the Rākshasī sprang to her feet; and in a moment her form was changed, and she became a maiden of surpassing beauty. Her height, and the shape of her features, were like Sītā's; but her eyes had not the softness, nor her gait the purity, of the gentle Vaidehī. Nevertheless there was a fire in her glance, and a voluptuous grace in her movements which were full of enticement.

Now, in the hermitage they had heard Sūrpanakhā shriek; and Rāma and Lakshmana, springing to their feet, had rushed to the mouth of the hermitage to see from whence it proceeded. They were about to return into the hut, to reassure the anxious Sītā, when, to their amazement, they saw issuing from the wood of Dandaka, a young maiden decked in dazzling raiment.

She approached them, and fixing on Rāma her large wild eyes, said to him in gentle tones :

"O Stranger, whose eyes are like the sun-god's beams! why are you here in this terrible forest? Know you not that the Rākshasas dwell here, the enemies of Gods and of Heroes? Alas! they devour the young warriors they meet in this wood! They have no pity! Why have you come hither?"

Then the noble Raghuide smiled down on her gravely.

"I do not fear the Rākshasas, gentle Star of Beauty!" he said; "the Immortals strengthen the just warriors, and fight with them against their foes. But what doest thou, O fragile maiden, here in these regions of terror—thou who hast the grace of my lovely Sītā, and whose youth and loveliness appeal for protection? Enter our hermitage, O Damsel with the liquid eyes! Lakshmana and I will honour thee as a sister, and my loving Princess will cherish and comfort thee? Lay aside all fear; henceforth we will be thy loyal guardians, thou desolate little Maiden!"

But at the kindly tones of his voice, and the pitiful softness of his gaze, the evil heart of the Rākshasī glowed with a fiery heat. She drew close to Rāma, and took his hand, and pressed it against her breast, and then to her burning lips.

"It is not *fear* that has brought me to thee," she said. "I love thee, O Hero with the radiant eyes! I am Sūrpanakhā, the terror of all living things! I roam at my ease through the wood of Dandaka; it is my home; I am happy, I am a Queen there! But now

Rāma offers her shelter and protection.

She confesses her passion to him.

Chap. VII.

the trouble of passion absorbs me; thy view, O Youthful Warrior! has thrilled me with the torments of desire; love me, O my Hero! Am I not beautiful? I am strong, and fearless, and wild. I snatch the serpents up in my arms, and twine them around my neck, and they shudder with dread; I buffet the tiger, and shake the lion by the mane, and they slink back into the thicket appalled; I outshriek the winds, and roar with the deep-mouthed thunder; the storm is my joyous playmate! Come with me, O Beloved! Wildly, wildly we will take delight and exult in the sombrous forest. My savage humours shall be thy sport; and thou shalt conquer my turbulent will by thy impassioned caresses! I am a Bride who befits thee more than this vapid Sītā; in a moment I will devour her and this paltry fellow, Lakshmana, and then we will bound forth into these wilds together, as the crooked rays break from the breast of the storm-cloud!"

Her eyes glowed like two living coals, and her hand clutched the arm of Rāma with an iron clasp. He thought: "If I anger her she will assuredly spring at me, and I were loth to use violence with one who has the form of a woman, and of a marvellously beautiful one too;" so he assumed a conciliatory tone, and said:

Rāma seeks to persuade her, he is unworthy her notice even.

"The radiance of thine own beauty has dazzled thine eyes, O transplendent Queen of the Rākshasas! I am not worthy of thy favours. I am a man whom Destiny has robbed of the delights of youth! Weeping has disfigured my countenance, frequent penances and the hardships of exile have broken my strength, and I am weak and emaciated; my spirit is broken also. How couldst thou stoop to so ignoble a consort? Besides, O Lady with the peerless form! thou hast a right to demand an entire devotion, and I am already bound by the marriage-tie. This Sītā has gathered the flowers of my heart; she came to me in my spring-tide and gathered all the flowers! What wouldst thou with me, O blooming Sūrpanakhā? The fervour of my youth is spent, O Star of Beauty! The Princess of Mithilā claimed it of me, and I poured it out at her feet! Nay, unrivalled Queen, look around thee; there are many heroes from whom the delights of love have been hidden until this hour; it is on such as these thou shouldst turn thine eyes. See my young brother, Lakshmana; he is of comely countenance, and of god-like stature; were not such an one more befitting thee, than a worn, enfeebled man, as I am?"

Rāma bids the Rākshasī give her favour to Lakshmana.

For Rāma thought it well to divert her mind from that project of devouring Lakshmana. As for Sītā, she was well hidden in the cabin, and the son of Sumitrā kept guard before the entrance.

Then Sūrpanakhā wheeled round suddenly and looked at Lakshmana. He stood out of earshot, on the other side of the mouth of the hermitage, leaning on his mighty bow.

The sunny insolence of his glance met hers.

"He is not ill," thought the Rākshasī, "and—he is Rāma's brother!"

So she ran up to him, and seizing his hand, looked up into his eyes:

CHAP. VII.

"I am Sūrpanakhā, Queen of the Rākshasas," she said. "This wood of Dandaka is mine; love me, O Warrior with the laughing eyes! and let us roam together in the delicious wilds of the forest!"

Now, Lakshmana thought:

"My brother has handed this ardent Rākshasī over to me in jest;" so he tossed back his flowing locks for joy, and said, with mischievous delight:

Lakshmana in jest assures Sūrpanakhā that she has Rāma's love.

"Sublime Sūrpanakhā, this Elephant among Men called Rāma has sought to prove thee. From here I have watched how thy charms have troubled him with the fever of passion! How could it be otherwise, Pearl amongst Rākshasīs? I myself am bewildered beyond measure by thy surpassing loveliness. But I am merely the servant of Rāma, and it is no way becoming that thou shouldst stoop to behold me even. This magnanimous son of Kausalyā is worthy to take so bright a Star to his breast; and doubtless it is the supreme nature of his bliss which has troubled him. It is true that he has a wife already, but what of that? Thou, incomparable Sūrpanakhā, canst afford to disdain this ugly, distorted Sītā, with her projecting teeth and tawny hair! She can never be a rival worth thy consideration."

But the Rākshasī, whom intense vanity led to believe his flatteries, turned from him with a savage howl.

The Rākshasī threatens to devour Sītā.

"There shall be no rival between me and Rāma!" she screeched. "I will forthwith devour this odious Sītā, whose repulsive ugliness offends me!"

So saying, she darted into the hermitage. In her fury she cast by her disguise: her distorted figure, and monstrous face, and claw-like hands returned, and bellowing hoarsely, she rushed towards the affrighted Sītā. But Lakshmana, horrified at the result of his pleasantry, sprang after her, and catching the Monster by her streaming hair, cut off her nose and ears with his naked sword.

Chap. VII. Lakshmana cuts off the Rākshasī's nose and ears.

Then the Rākshasī rushed from the hermitage, making the echoes ring with her hideous shrieks, and, staining the path with her blood, leapt howling through the forest Dandaka, uprooting great trees in the agony of her fury and pain.

After a few moments' silence, Rāma laid his hand on his brother's shoulder, and said :

"A mortal woman, whom the hand of an enemy had disfigured, would move heaven and earth for vengeance ; how much more, then, a Rākshasī ? This Sūrpanakhā, too, is of redoubtable lineage : she has for brothers the famous Khara and Dūshana; the just Vibhīshana, who condemns the deeds of the Rākshasas ; Kumbhakarna, the sleepy giant, who, when he awakes, is of more terrible strength than Indra ; and Rāvana, the lord of all Rākshasas, who has defeated the whole hosts of Heaven in battle ! Henceforth, O Brother, we have these formidable enemies to deal with !"

Rāma foresees the enmity of Rāvana.

"So be it !" answered Lakshmana, and tossed his head and laughed.

But Rāma flung his arm around his beloved Sītā, and drew her very close to him.

CHAPTER VIII.

RĀVANA'S CRIME.

Chap. VIII.
Of the splendour of Rávana.

RĀVANA, the King of all the Rākshasas, the enemy of gods and men, was, we are told in the Ramāyana, of magnificent stature and presence. Ten heads were his, and his twenty eyes were like flashes of beamy sunshine; laughter was in them, and defiant scorn, and dogged resolution, and much amorous fire; but no reverence, nor fidelity, nor pity. His colossal frame showed traces of his desperate conflict against the hosts of heaven; the thunderbolts had scorched him; Airāvata, the monstrous elephant of Indra, had torn him with his tusks; and on his broad chest was a large dint that the sharp disk of Vishnu had left there. He wore necklaces and bracelets of gold, and flashing gems; and round his head was a crown that seemed a twisted band of fire; but these glorious wounds were the ornaments he exulted in the most.

Another constant source of triumph was the tribute of horrified terror paid him by all creation. Around him the very winds crept with bated breath, or fled with howling terror to find a refuge in the shuddering sea! Meeting the scornful derision of his glance, the sad Heaven hid away its innocent blue with clouds; and the sun, passing over the isle of Lankā, where he reigned, paled, and held back his winged messengers of light and heat.

Although he felt such satisfaction at beholding all living things thus panic-struck at sight of him, he was himself quite ignorant of fear. In the early days of the world he had had but one head; but he stood on it for the space of ten thousand years, and in compensation for this eccentric penance received nine other heads, with the promise that neither Rishi, nor Yaksha, nor Dānava, nor Pisācha, nor Gandharva, nor Rākshasa, nor God even, should be able to imperil his life.

He omitted to include man in the list; it appeared to him needless to claim immunity from so contemptible a creature.

One day this splendid Rāvana, the Scourge of the three Worlds,[1] was reclining luxuriously on his sumptuous couch, surrounded by the most distinguished chiefs among the Rākshasas. The light was softened for him, and many flowers had sighed forth their odorous souls to make the air delicious. On either side of the languid demon, two young maidens, whose misty garments enhanced their charms rather than veiled the graceful outlines of their forms, waved to and fro punkas, whose handles were of dazzling gold. Gems sparkled in their hair, and veiled fire in their wild, liquid eyes; and as they swayed them near and back, with a dreamy rhythmical measure, it seemed an

[1] "The three Worlds," *i.e.* Earth, Air, and Fire,—water and air were regarded as modifications of one and the same element.

unspoken song of amorous languor, to which the undulating punkas whispered an accompaniment.

For some time Rávana had reclined thus, his numerous eyes half closed, in an ecstasy of voluptuous enjoyment, when he was disturbed by a stir and confusion among his obsequious courtiers. Looking up in angry astonishment, he perceived his sister, the vindictive Súrpanakhá, her garments torn and soiled, her tawny hair streaming, wild and dishevelled, and her face bespattered with blood. She forced her way through the startled Rákshasas, and rushing forward to the monarch's feet smote her breast, and sought to speak; but, choked by her violent emotion, fell on her face, and lay there, mouthing and struggling in vain for breath.

Then the dreadful Lord of the Rákshasas leapt to his feet, and snatching Súrpanakhá up from off the ground, shouted, his eyes flushing crimson with rage:

"Speak! Who has dared molest the sister of Rávana, the victor of the deathless gods? Dost hear me? I command thee, speak!"

Then Súrpanakhá broke into a hoarse, derisive laugh.

"Who has dared?" she said; and stood before him, clutching her heart with both her hands, as though she feared for very fury it might burst, ere she had spoken. "It is a pretty question, truly! In this pleasant town of Lanká, wrapped round by the blue sea, for all the world like a bright star in the centre of the azure sky, tales of daring no doubt are rare! Outrage, and Battle, and Slaughter,—the words are coarse, too coarse! You have musicians to play to you, rather, eh, Brother? And girls to fan you. On my word, they might be divine Apsaras, they are of so dainty a mould, and their raiment is so scanty; and perfumes in the air too! Bah! they are sickly to my nostrils; but then *I* come from the reeking battle-field! And the light,—oh the fierce, blazing sun scorches the skin; it is too fiery by half; it must be toned down, mellowed tenderly, to suit languid eyes. ... By the stupendous gates of Hell, I think I shall go mad! Brother, whilst you stretch your limbs on softly cushioned ottomans, like some mawkish saint tasting celestial beatitude, the name of Rākshasa is made the laughing-stock of the three worlds! In the country of Janasthāna, the crows feast on the corpses of our warriors! The Anchorites and pious Hermits wander, at their ease, through the wood of Dandaka, and laugh at the memory of its terrors. Khara is dead; and Dūshana, and Trisiras, the Hero with the three heads: in the whole universe, perchance, you are the only living creature who has not heard of their death! They sought to avenge my wrongs, and to destroy the audacious Warrior who dared to mutilate me thus; and they perished in this just cause; they, and fourteen thousand warriors. And now, perchance, you will ask once more, *who* has dared do this? Oh, not the armies of the death-less gods, not the Gandharvas, nor the Rishis, nor the Dānavas, but a *man!* One Rāma, an exiled youth, now dwelling with his brother and his bride, in the vale of Panchavatī! By the Eternal Heavens,

CHAP. VIII. the very worms are rising from the mud, to spit upon the name of Rākshasa!——"

Here Rāvana put out a hand, commanding silence. Even Sūrpanakhā was awed, as she looked at him. His shaggy brows were drawn down over his eyes; and his large, white teeth gnawed the nether lip. Pondering grimly, he still kept one hand extended, only the fingers of it clenched themselves unconsciously, so that he seemed to menace the universe with his fist.

Presently he dashed his monstrous hand down upon the couch; and the golden frame was shivered, and jewels sprang from it, like glistening tears of pain!

Rāvana asks the rank and power of his adversary.
"Who is this Rāma?" he asked, with intense slowness of utterance, and his low, deep voice was like the mutterings which precede the tempest. "How great is his strength? What weapons has he? To what race does he belong? And why does he dwell in the vale of Panchavatī?"

Then Sūrpanakhā answered:

"He is the son of Dasaratha, King of Ayōdhyā; his arms are long, and his chest is large as the mighty Indra's; in his eyes is a tranquil radiance, which makes one shrink. His garment is of the fibre of bark, and he has a black antelope skin thrown across his shoulders. He has a large bow, chased with gold; one does not see him bend it, nor adjust his arrows; but his shafts rush through the air like winged flames, and beat down his enemies, as the hail destroys the harvest. He has with him a young brother, named

SHE TELLS HIM OF THE BEAUTIFUL SĪTĀ.

Lakshmana; the insolence of this youth is unparalleled; he laughs in the thick of the fight, and deals out gibes with death. Like Rāma, he has one thought, one care, one vulnerable spot, where those who loathe him may deal him a more painful blow than death! His honour, and his brother's love, are bound up in the woman who dwells with them—Sītā, the youthful wife of Rāma.

"The loveliness of this Sītā . . . Heavens! the execrable loveliness of this Sītā! When I think of it—of the little pouting mouth, and smooth dimpled cheeks, and soft appealing eyes—by the Thirteen Gods! my fingers tremble to claw and tear this hateful beauty, and make it more hideous even than my gashed, distorted face :—But I know a better revenge than that—a more sweetly excruciating revenge than that! Brother, these Heroes have a charmed life, otherwise they had not stood before Khara and Doushāna; and even were it possible to slay them, death were too poor a compensation for these injuries. Death? it is over too soon by half! A man may be content to kill his enemy; a Rākshasa prefers to torture him!

"Were it not a fine thing, Demon with the dreadful scowl, to have the Heart of this grand Rāma here—thus, between your finger and thumb to toy with It, and make It the contemptible Plaything of your careless hours; while he went, desolate, through the three worlds, wearing his soul away in a vain search; famished with longing; shamed by unutterable doubts; tortured by the impotence of his wrath? You under-

CHAP. VIII.

Sūrpanakhā suggests a scheme for vengeance.

stand me? *Carry off this Sītā!* Would you wipe off the stain from our race; would you avenge your brothers massacred, your sister mutilated, your warriors given to feed the crows; would you drag your foes through the undying torments of Tartarus; would you break Rāma's spirit, and strangle the laughter of Lakshmana? Carry off this Sītā! Nay, if pride, and revenge, and hate are nought, would you win a youthful bride, more radiant than Srī[1] herself, and whose graceful charms as far surpass those of these half-naked damsels here, as the gazelle's the lynx's? Then, for your very lust's sake, carry off this beautiful, accursed Sītā!"

Once more the Rākshasī flung herself at her brother's feet; but this time he laid his immense hand caressingly on her tangled head, and said:

" It sufficeth, Sūrpanakhā;" and then he laughed.

That was very terrible. Even the Rākshasas exchanged appalled glances; the wind caught up the sound, and rushed through the wastes of space wailing:

" Rāvana, the Scourge of the three Worlds, has *laughed!* There will be cause of weeping for all living creatures soon!"

Then the remorseless Demon ordered his chariot. It was of the most refined gold, and it had many advantages besides; for it floated as easily through the air as it rolled on firm ground, and it required no coursers to draw it. Just for the sake of appearance, two Pisāchas, creatures with the bodies of asses and heads of vampires, were harnessed to it;

---

[1] *Srī* or *Lakshmi*—Goddess of Beauty.

they were useful, too, in case of any warlike encounter. Standing upright in this car, the Monarch of all the Rākshasas shook the reins he held, and shouted tauntingly to the air:

"Vainly dost thou hide thyself from sight; I feel thee trembling round me! Thou, who bursteth out a-weeping if a chill touch thee, and sobbest like a child if thou beest stirred—thou Coward Air—I command thee put thy amorphous wings beneath my chariot, and bear me upwards, close to the Home of Stars."

Reluctantly, and with many stifled sighs, the frightened Air crept beneath his chariot, and, uplifting the evil Rākshasa to the gates of the blue world, held him there suspended.

Then leaning over, his elbow resting on the side of the car, and his ten chins upon his hand, the Fiend looked down. He saw the white fluttering clouds, where the Immortals lure their best Beloved Ones that they may talk to them of love; he saw the filmy vapours in which the bright Apsaras wrap them, when they float earthward to bewilder some foolish human heart; and far beneath he saw the Sea, with its wrinkled, careworn face, hiding away with miserly care its pearls and glistening treasure, and lamenting its great poverty in a whining, monotonous voice; he saw the old grim Mountains, with the rivers flowing down their rugged cheeks, as though they were weeping at having grown so far beyond the reach of the flowers' perfumed sighs; he saw,—more marvels than I have time to tell, or you,

Rāvana soars aloft in his magic car.

CHAP. VIII.

Reader, the patience to care to hear. But, among other things, his eyes rested on a monstrous nyagrodha tree, which the exploit of Garuda had rendered famous. For one day that this Monarch of all Birds, having a tortoise and an elephant in his beak, on whom he was minded to make his dinner, had perched on this tree, behold, a gigantic branch gave way beneath him, and fell smashing down to earth! This was a disastrous event; for the branch was a hundred yojanas, that is rather more than a hundred of our miles, in length; and so a great many hermitages were broken down by it. However, the amiable Fowl hastened to repair as much as possible the mischief he had done; he picked up the branch forthwith, and with it, and the elephant and tortoise still in his beak, flew off to the country of the Nishadas. Here he chose a solid mountain for resting-place, and finished the repast that had been so inopportunely disturbed. Afterwards he made use of the large branch to ravage the country of Nishada. Its inhabitants were a bad set of people, who had allied themselves with the Rākshasas.

The Rākshasa sees the hermitage of Mārītcha, and descends thither.

Well, near to this monster nyagrodha tree, Rāvana beheld the hermitage of the Rākshasa Mārītcha—a Demon of much vigour and daring, but who had lately assumed the garb of a penitent, and embraced an ascetic life, that his strength might be redoubled. Swooping downward, as a kite who perceives its prey, the Lord of Rākshasas sprang from his chariot to the ground, close to the abode of Mārītcha. The recluse hastened forth to greet him, and invited him to enter, and prayed him courteously to name his errand.

"How can I serve you, O Bull amongst Malevolent Beings?" he said "You are my sovereign; demand of me what you will!"

Then Rāvana thanked him, and answered:

"There has come into the vale of Panchavatī a pestilent fellow, Rāma by name, who has been sent into exile by his father. As in his own country, so in the forest of Dandaka he has rendered himself obnoxious by his bloodthirsty atrocities. He has cut off the nose and ears of my sister Sūrpanakhā; he has murdered my brothers Khara and Dūshana; and Trisiras, the Hero with the three heads; in fact, there is no end to the story of his crimes! This accursed Rāma has a youthful bride, Sītā, the Princess of Mithilā. They say that Srī herself is of less radiant beauty. It is not befitting so scurrilous a fellow should possess this Pearl amongst women. The account of her unusual loveliness has filled me with a fierce unrest; there is a fever on me, and a heaviness of heart nought can remove till I behold this Sītā! My glory and strength, and the tribute of terror paid me by all living, are nought if I cannot possess this Sītā. Even my thirst for revenge, and my hatred of this upstart, who dares to beard the Rākshasas, are nought compared to my unruly passion; yet they, too, urge me to this deed. Mārītcha, help me to rob Rāma of this incomparable Star of Beauty!"

But when he heard this request, the judicious Demon shook his head.

Chap. VIII.

He tells the object of his visit, and claims the aid of the recluse.

CHAP. VIII.

Marītcha warns Rāvana of the virtue and valour of Rāma.

"You have been deceived, O Victor of the deathless gods!" he said. "This Rāma is no rebellious son; his banishment is a tribute of respect paid to the memory of Dasaratha, who unwittingly gave his word that for fourteen years this young prince should inhabit the woods. I have heard it said that his exile in these forests was ordered by the Supreme Ruler of Life, that the world might be cleansed of such beings as you and I, O Rākshasa! If this be so, let not Destiny compel us blindly to measure our strength with his. You know me of old, O Master! I was not a Demon of a timorous disposition, when it was my pleasure to roam through the forest Dandaka, feeding on human flesh, and wresting from the lions and tigers their prey. It was my delight to afflict the blameless anchorites; to frighten the more timid, and to excite the fiery to hurl after me profane blasphemies, which might rob them of the fruits of their penitence. Especially I loved to torment the saint Visvāmitra, for I knew that in his youth he was of an irascible temper, and I hoped to provoke him to some outburst of unholy wrath. But the Brahman, unwilling to give me the chance of ruffling his equanimity, appealed to Dasaratha, and claimed the protection of Rāma, then a youth who had not counted sixteen summers. At the head of a troop of unruly Demons I came to the Saint's Hermitage at the hour of sacrifice; we burst into scornful laughter at sight of the boy warrior, and began to sing the cradle song with which mothers rock their babes to sleep. But paying no heed to our derision, the youthful Rāma drew his bow, and like lightning flashes a stream of fatal shafts brought death among us! I alone of all the company escaped with life; but I was sore wounded, and bounding high into the air in agony, a gust of wind took me and threw me on the shores of Lankā, more dead than living. No sooner did I recover from my cruel wound than I espoused this solitary life, hoping by my self-macerations to escape from this invincible Hero. Since I have heard that Rāma dwells in these forests my days are full of terror. Each bush and thicket seems to shelter him; and behind every tree my fancy shows me a youth clad in the fibre of bark, with a black antelope skin thrown across his shoulders. I *know*, Rāvana, that when I look on Rāma again my hour will have come, and death will beat me down! O Monarch of the Rākshasas! I fear me, Destiny has involved you in this doom."

Then the Demon with the ten heads laughed aloud.

"Most excellent Mārītcha," he said soothingly, "I perceive thy sojourn in these wilds has somewhat damped thy spirit. It is but natural. Truly, night in these dark forests must have an utter gloom. It is a scene for sad forebodings, when the trees throw their long shadows down, and one sees them writhe and twist about, like tortured spirits, chained to the knotted roots! It is an hour for dread presentiments to breed a nameless Terror, when flying foxes, like abortive offsprings of a monstrous Night, flap their blurred, distorted wings; and when, across each open

CHAP. VIII.

Rāvana laughs at the Hermit's fears.

Chap. VIII.

Marītcha seeks to convince Rāvana of his danger.

path, the noiseless reptiles twist their crooked way, leaving a slimy track behind; whilst worms and meanest insects wrap them in pale, unearthly fire, that flickers and expires fitfully. Alone, amid such scenes, the Thoughts no fellow-being shares, grow too stupendous for the Brain that conceived them. Either they burst the casket of the Soul, so that it has no longer any concentrated power, but merely the general consciousness of being shared by all nature; or if, as in thy case, noble Demon, the mind be of too strong a tone to be driven mad, they obscure the intellect, they cannot obliterate, and lead it to give consistency to shadows, and being to empty words, such as 'Destiny' and 'Doom' and many of the same worth. Thy solitary existence has made thee too poetical, most excellent Marītcha!"

Then, very gravely, the Recluse led Rāvana to the mouth of the cavern, and pointed upwards with his hand, to where the moon, putting aside the filmy mist, came forth to make Night beautiful.

"Think you," he said, "that yonder planet is conscious of her full mission; of how she rules the tides of ocean and of air, of the check she puts on evil, and the encouragement she gives to innocence? Not the less is it, that she may perform this work, that she shines there and is beautiful. Nay, raise not your eyes so high. Behold this flower at your feet; is it there chiefly for itself, think you? Doubtless, if it could speak, it would answer, 'Yes,' and if questioned further on its complex organization, would reply, 'This care was taken that *my* life might be sustained and nourished!' Yet we know the flower is there, rather that its juices may nourish more life, and that its very breath may render the air more pure and healthful. And you, Rāvana, think you that you are an isolated being, independent of this great Law of Life? Monarch of all the Rākshasas! it may be that the purpose for which the Master of Gods and men allowed Demons to plague, and tempt, and sadden His creatures, is at an end. It may be that there is no longer any place for such as you and I in this God's World! In the early stage of the life of man, it was needful to show him the loathsome form of Sin; now, perchance, is it rather the Divine Will to keep ever in his sight the ineffable loveliness of Virtue; fixing his eyes no longer on the yawning Gulf, whence issue flames, it may be that he should rather, henceforth, raise his eyes to the still Heavens, where smile the stars! Comrade, our day is waning. This Rāma, who is to encourage man to lead a noble life for honour's sake, and not for fear's, is doubtless sent here as our Destroyer. O Demon with the flaming eyes, do not despise my counsels! If die we must, let not our own act hasten on our doom."

Again Rāvana laughed; but this time in grievous wrath.

"I was rash just now," he said, "when I thought thy sanity had resisted the attacks of loneliness. I came not here to ask thy counsels, but to claim thy service. Now here is a question I would have thee solve: whether it were better for thee to do what I require, and to perish, possibly, by Rāma's hand,

CHAP. VIII.

The Recluse seeks to dissuade Rāvana from injuring Rāma.

Rāvana threatens to slay Māritcha if he refuses to help him.

CHAP. VIII.

With many misgivings Māritcha consents.

or to refuse the aid I demand, and be slain by me, here, and in this moment? Thou knowest, Rākshasa, I use no empty threats! Come, what is thy decision?"

"I will follow you," answered the Recluse, sadly; "you are my sovereign, let me die with you, rather than by your hand!"

And so, mournfully enough, Māritcha rose, and flinging round him his valkala, prepared to follow the infatuated Demon. Having reduced the other to obedience, Rāvana's good-humour returned.

"Come," he exclaimed joyously, "thou faithful Māritcha! Let us lose no time. That silvery moon, of whom thou didst, just now, so sagely describe the mission, beckons us with her long shimmering fingers: 'I will guide you,' she says, 'to the home of this my best loved Star!'"

"May it please the deathless Gods," muttered the other, "that she lead us not rather to where lie the uncleansed ashes of Khara, Dūshana, and Trisiras."

"What sayest thou?" inquired Rāvana; "the fate of these heroes renders thee uneasy? Nay, most noble Māritcha, thou hast too low an opinion of thine own power. I should know somewhat of the acquirements of Khara and Dūshana, for they were my brethren. I tell thee they were feeble children compared to thee! And as for Trisiras; what though he had three heads? In all of them, was there the half of the prudence, craft, and resolution stored in thy brains? Come, Bull amongst Rākshasas, the way to escape their fate is to avoid their errors. This is no occasion for blind rage, nor senseless daring; skill will serve us more than strength, and coolness than courage; we who possess cunning as well as daring can scarce fail in such an enterprise. The great object to be gained is the separation of Rāma and Lakshmana; that must be thy work. Thou must devise some means to lure one of these warriors from the hermitage, and during his absence I will carry off the Vaidehī. Thy fleetness of foot will secure thy escape; for me,—my mind is too firmly set on this adventure not to ensure me triumph!"

As he spoke, the two Demons passed into the blackness of the deeper forest; and as they trod the sombrous aisles, carpeted with the spoils of many a dead summer, the sinister Worshippers of night came forth to glare on them. When the two swarthy Shades had passed, they looked the one on the other, asking: "On what ill errand is the Lord of Rākshasas abroad?"

On the morrow, when the young Dawn was kissing through the filmy mists, wooing them to linger,—whispering, "I, too, am fond of dreams!"—the fanciful Bride of Rāma stood at the door of the hermitage. Perchance she was *too* fanciful! It seemed to her that the young Morning rose ever, decked in tender hues, that were too dreamy to be bright, and glistening over with sweet dew, that trembled between smiles and tears; and that she was so hopeful, and so able to forget the night she sprang from, and so brave to run on to meet the night that awaited her, because *she was beloved!* And then the gentle little Sitā won-

Sītā stands in the early morning at the entrance of the hermitage.

CHAP. VIII.

*The beauti-
ful Gazelle.*

*Sītā asks
Rāma to
capture it
for her.*

dered who it was loved the Morning?—whether the pretty clouds, who flushed beneath her glance; or the birds, who sang to her; or the plants, who flung back their petals at her touch; or the blue heavens, that cradled her; or the fair earth, in whose arms she seemed to play?

Thus, very full of wonder, the gentle Vaidehī watched the gradual awakening of day.

Now whilst she stood in the doorway, glancing forth from the wood of Dandaka, and traversing the open glade, passed several times, forward and back, a marvellous Gazelle, the like of which was never seen by mortal eyes. Its coat seemed of burnished gold; and round its neck was a wreath of lilies, shimmering with brightest water; round its small horns strings of large pearls were twined; and in its forehead was a flashing jewel that seemed a living coal of fire! Pausing a second before the cabin, it looked at Sītā, and its large, startled eyes seemed to show that it had half a mind to seek a shelter near her. Then it bounded into the thicket; but only to return once more,—and once more to fix its wistful gaze on the young Princess.

"See, Rāma!" cried the delighted Sītā, clapping her hands for joy. "Oh the beautiful Gazelle, with the lotus wreath and the golden fur! Well have we chosen this forest Dandaka for our home, since there dwell in it such marvellous creatures! Rāma, Light of my soul! had I the bright skin of this radiant beast to cover my couch of leaves, were I not like a Queen, though dwelling in these savage woods?

Thy Queen, my Rāma! I would recline on it, and dream of thee; and thou, too, wouldst stretch thee beside me on my divan of golden fur. I fear me the desire is evil; but if it be not *very* evil, O thou Dear One, capture for me this Gazelle!"

At that, Rāma took down his large bow from the wall.

"Thy desire is not very evil, Little One!" he said, smiling, "and thou shalt have this golden covering for thy rude couch of leaves!"

"Nay, but, Rāma," faltered the gentle Princess, whose heart already relented, "if the pretty beast flee not too rapidly, capture it rather living, that it may be our playmate. It shall be the wonder of Ayōdhyā, when we return, that we possess a Gazelle with a coat of burnished gold!"

Now Lakshmana had been in the inner part of the hermitage; but, hearing these words, he came forward.

"A Gazelle with a coat of burnished gold!" he exclaimed; "from my boyhood it has been my delight to roam in the forest, but never saw I such a creature as that! Rāma, this is some device the Rākshasas have imagined to mislead our simple little Princess here."

"I am not so very simple, Lakshmana," pouted Sītā, prettily.

"Nay," said Rāma, passing his arm tenderly round her neck. "I, too, saw this wonderful Gazelle; and if it be indeed some evil spirit in disguise, I shall be doing a good deed in destroying it. In any case

CHAP. VIII this is the first boon my little Bride has craved, and it shall not be refused her. Lakshmana, do not thou leave the hermitage during my absence; I trust my Treasure to thee, for I know thy loyalty and courage."

Rāma starts in pursuit of the Gazelle, and leaves Sītā in his brother's care.

So saying, the Hero bounded forth in pursuit of the radiant Gazelle. Oh the chase it led him!—luring him on by its slackened pace for a few steps, then leaping onwards into the tangled thicket, and hiding there; and as he sought for it, springing up close beside him, and shooting by in a new direction, like a sudden rush of wind! He was already far in the dangerous Forest, when, perplexed by its caprices, and provoked at being led so far, he renounced his first intention of capturing the Gazelle living, that it might be the playmate of his youthful bride.

"No innocent creature," he thought, "were capable of these innumerable wiles."

Rāma wounds the Gazelle, and it is transformed into Mārītcha, who screams for help in a voice like Rāma's.

So he drew his bow—the miraculous weapon given him long since by the saint Visvāmitra—and the unerring dart sped from it, and struck the radiant beast between the horns. But lo! as it staggered and fell head foremost, its form was changed, and the Rākshasa Mārītcha, bleeding from a mortal wound, lay stretched upon the grass!

Dying, the Demon raised him on one arm, and shrieking in a voice that copied the tones of Rāma, "Help, Lakshmana! Help! help!" he fell back, and expired.

Now, the Rākshasa's treacherous shriek went ringing through the wood of Dandaka, and reached the hermitage, where Lakshmana and Sītā were awaiting the return of Rāma. The startled Princess sprang to her feet at once.

"Dost thou not hear, Lakshmana? He calls thee. Alas! he is in peril! Oh fly to him; do not lose an instant!"

Sītā hearing the scream, bids Lakshmana run to his brother's aid.

But Lakshmana answered her with a smile:

"Fear nothing, Sister of my heart! This is not Rāma's voice; some evil creature has stolen his accents to lure me from thy side. It is not Rāma's wont to call on me for aid!"

But Sītā beat her small hands together in her distress and anger.

"Do I not know the voice of my Beloved?" she asked. "Is there a Being in the three worlds who could deceive *me*—his Love? Lakshmana, art thou mad,—or cowardly,—or what,—that thou sittest there unmoved when thy brother calls to thee? O Heavens! that I should have to urge thee thus! For pity's sake,—for very shame's sake,—begone! How dar'st thou linger when he calls? How dar'st thou, I say? Here is thy bow,—Oh he stirs not! Eternal Brahm, this man will not stir! What can I, can I, do? Alas! my Love will die for want of help!—Thou dear Lakshmana,—pity me!"

Here she flung her on her knees, and, her face all bathed in tears, seized Lakshmana's hand, and sobbed:

"Brother, dear faithful Brother, go to him! Forgive me, dear Lakshmana, if aught I said seemed harsh; forgive me—and save my Rāma!"

CHAP. VIII.

Lakshmana replies that this is not Rāma's voice, and that he will not leave Sītā alone.

Then Lakshmana clasped her two little hands lovingly. "Thy Rāma has no need that *I* should save him, Sweet One!" he said. "There is no hero with a strength like his; and he has on his side the sinless Gods, who will not let him perish ere his large destiny be accomplished. But thou, my Pretty One, mayst not be left in this solitary spot with no protector. The Gods, who made woman feeble, gave her beauty that man might love to shelter her with his strength; but there is so much evil in the world, that what should serve to compensate for her weakness, is but a fresh danger; because thou art so very lovely, Sītā, thou hast more need of guardianship than other women. And therefore came I into these woods. Rāma needs not my protection; shall I abandon thee, when for thy sake I am here?"

Then Sītā drew herself up to her full height, and looked at him with flashing eyes.

Sītā accuses him of treachery to Rāma.

"For *my* sake thou art here?" she said with bitter scorn; "not for Rāma's, but for mine? Oh I thank thee! It is a pity thy devotion should be wasted on another's wife! Thy brother's too; so much nobler a man than thou,—so much more precious to me than thou couldst ever be, that if he die to-night I would rather cling to his cold corpse than touch thee with my hand; I would rather dwell with him in the dim world of Yama than sit by thee on the most gorgeous throne in the pleasant town of Ayōdhyā! Oh thou wilt gain little by this treachery! Thou thinkest, doubtless, 'If my brother die, this Sītā shall

LAKSHMANA YIELDS TO SĪTĀ'S PRAYER.

be mine?' Nay, thou shalt have nought of Sītā, save her lifeless frame; her soul shall fly from thy loathed presence, and find a shelter still near her true Lord!"

Then, stung by her reproaches, the Warrior leapt to his feet, and stood before her also scornful and stern.

"It is woman's nature to be unjust," he said coldly. "I will not plead with you, that I have ever honoured you as my brother's wife; and that it as such, as dear in the sight of him whom I revere and love, that I have willed to be your watchful guardian. Think what you will of me,—your suspicions are a shame to you; they cannot reach me even! But since my care is loathsome, I will leave you; as Rāma's wife I owe obedience to you; I will go hence in search of him. Meanwhile, if any mischief befall you, thank your own wilfulness, ungrateful woman!"

So he turned away from her in wrath.

But ere he reached the door, the impulsive Warrior's heart relented, and he came back to her, and said, very tenderly:

"Be not uneasy, little Sister! Thy Rāma will soon be here; I am going now to seek him. Oh I beseech thee keep close within the hermitage during my absence! I am not angry with thee, Sītā! I know it was thy love made thee unjust to me in words—*only* in words; thou knowest my thought of thee is reverent. Farewell, my Princess! If in this atrocious forest there be any good Divinities, oh may they guard thee, Sītā! My heart misgives me at leaving thee alone...."

To which she answered:

Stung by her reproaches, Lakshmana consents to seek for Rāma.

CHAP. VIII.

"If Rāma come not back, I will not live; I will hang myself on the large neem-tree, or drown myself in the deep river, or throw myself down some hideous precipice, or leap into some devouring fire. I will not live without my Lord!"

And so, to satisfy her, Lakshmana wandered forth in search of Rāma. At first he walked slowly, hoping that, finding herself alone for the first time in this solitary hut, the timid Vaidehī might call him to return; but no such summons came, so he quickened his pace, thinking, "I shall not be absent long."

Left to herself, Sītā began, little by little, to reflect on her alarms, and to assure herself they were unfounded.

"Lakshmana was right," she thought, with fond pride. "What living creature could conquer Rāma? It could not have been he who cried for help."

And then she began to smile as she thought of how she had treated Lakshmana.

"Poor fellow," she thought, "he is so generous he will never reproach me. But I will be, oh so loving to him when he returns!"

Sītā goes to the mouth of the hermitage to see if they are coming.

And so she dried her eyes, and prepared herself to meet the two young warriors with her most sunny smiles. But, ah me!—they did not come. The time seemed very long,—and everything was so still; the old neem-tree even did not murmur among his boughs; he seemed to be waiting too,—and not to have the heart to talk at all. She went to the entrance of the hermitage, and stood there, shading her eyes with her hand; it was very strange they should be so long!

As she stood gazing wistfully towards the wood, and feeling, oh so terribly alone, issued from the forest an old Man clad in the garments of a Hermit, with a pitcher in one hand, and in the other a stick, on which he leant. He seemed very feeble and weary,—this poor old Man. He approached the Princess of Mithilā, and bowing to her very courteously, said:

"O Lady, whose dazzling raiment and whose peerless beauty seem that of the divine Lakshmī herself, if thy heart be as kind as thy countenance is lovely, let me rest a while in this pretty hermitage; I am footsore and weary."

An old Pilgrim issues from the wood, who claims hospitality.

Now Sītā thought, "This is doubtless some holy Pilgrim who comes from the abode of the Saint Agastya;" so she said courteously:

"Enter and repose yourself, Holy Man," and brought him water to wash his feet, and hastened to set before him what viands she had, and bade him freely satisfy his hunger.

"My husband and his brother will be here anon," she said; "they will be delighted to find you here, worthy Pilgrim, for they love to discourse with the pious anchorites who journey through this wood."

Sītā invites the Pilgrim to rest and satisfy his hunger.

"Thou art marvellously beautiful!" exclaimed the Pilgrim, who had partaken of nothing, and who had not since his entrance removed his gaze from the countenance of the youthful Princess. Sītā was somewhat startled.

CHAP. VIII.

Sītā is perplexed by his strange words and mien.

"How strangely bright and piercing his eyes are for a Penitent's!" she thought:—and then she reproached herself. "It is not the fault of this Holy Man if there be an evil light in his eyes," she said to herself; "a man may, too, be quite a Saint, and yet have a bad habit of staring."

Nevertheless, she was not quite at her ease; and though she chatted away to her visitor, that he might not imagine he was unwelcome there, she kept as far away from him as possible.

"Who art thou, Maiden with the faultless form?" asked the Stranger presently, in the midst of her little courteous speeches. "Never have I beheld so wondrous a vision of beauty! Assuredly thou art no mortal woman? Yet hast thou the voluptuous charms of a child of earth, combined with the ethereal grace of a daughter of the air! Whence art thou, Lady whose eyes kindle the fierce flames of desire? How cam'st thou hither? Know'st thou not that this wood of Dandaka is the home of savage beasts of prey? So bright a loveliness as thine should rather grace some monarch's court!"

More and more troubled by his ardent gaze, the Princess of Mithilā answered simply :

In answer to his questions she tells her name, and asks who he may be.

"I am the wife of Rāma, the Dasarathide; they call me Sītā. Obedient to his father's word, my Lord dwells here in exile; I am happy here, though I know this is an evil wood, for I love my Lord, and know no fear when he is by.—And you, O Hermit with the bold, keen eyes,—who are you? And oh—wherefore are you come?"

Then the Stranger sprang to his feet.

"I am the son of Visravas!" he shouted; "Rāvana, he that is called the Scourge of the three Worlds!—I am here because I love thee, Sītā!"

And then he seized the shrinking Vaidehī by the two hands.

"Is it a small thing to have the love of such an One?" he cried. "Oh think of it!—I,—the King of all the Rākshasas, the Terror of the Universe, before whose face fled Indra, King of Heaven, and the armies of the Deathless Gods,—am here, in this poor garb, because thou, O little fragile Child, hast thrown trouble into my soul! Sītā, there is an ecstasy in a love like mine, which Brahma himself could not give to thee! Behold, I stand erect beneath an Eternal Curse,—Remorse and Pity touch me not,—Hope cannot reach me,—all Fear is centred in myself! My soul dwells lonely in an atmosphere of high gloom, and there is no emotion left it,—save the stormy delights of passion: accept, thou frail and gentle Flower, the ardour of this flame, which defies all Law and limit: rule, with thy low voice and thy small weak hand, this Rebel, who laughs the Will of Highest Heaven to scorn! Be the one cherished Darling—amid a hated Universe; the worshipped Bride—of the Enemy of all else that lives! Step up beside me, Child with the appealing eyes! Make thou the Chaos of this Heart thy home—and let me show thee how the Damned can love!"

He glowed on her with all his eyes as he spoke, and his voice had the sadness of intense desire.

Chap. VIII.

Rāvana flings by his disguise and tells his love for her.

CHAP. VIII.

He seeks to conquer her terror by promising her a life of pleasure.

He depreciates Rāma and says he is an exile for lack of courage.

But Sītā, half dead with terror, shrank away from him to the ground, and lay there, like a flower of the prairie whom the hot wind has seared. Then Rāvana changed his tone; he stooped down to her, and whispered softly:

"Why tremblest thou so, Pretty One? I mean thee good, not harm. This forest is too dreary, and too rough a home for thee; there is a pleasant island, —the fairest isle in all the rippled sea,—it is called Lankā; I have a gorgeous palace there, which shall be thine; thou shalt have raiment, and jewels, and young maidens to wait on thee, and all that makes the heart of woman glad! As for this Rāma,—oh thou shalt be spared all self-reproach! I will carry thee hence by force; by such a loving, careful force that it shall not harm thee, little One, although it let thee struggle to be virtuous. And then amidst the joys I will surround thee with, thou shalt soon forget this Rāma. Why should his memory cling to thee? What has he given thee in exchange for thy young love? A poor hovel in this wilderness; a couch of leaves; the fare of a Penitent; a life of solitude; and this to *thee*, whose beauty alone makes her a Queen! And how despicable a man is he! Women of high rank have ever held cowardice to be the most repulsive vice; in what esteem canst thou hold this Rāma, who without a struggle, or a word even, has let a woman rob him of his birthright; has obeyed, with the abject submission of a beaten cur, the voice that sent him into exile, and let another usurp his crown, without so much as uttering a menace or remonstrance? Sītā, I am not made of such a servile stuff; the blood is red and hot that thrills my veins. If I know not mercy, at least I know not fear; power is mine, and wealth, and learning;—am not I a nobler consort than this Rāma?"

Then Sītā, her great love conquering her fear, stood up before him without trembling.

"Is the viper, that crawls upon his belly through the dust, more noble than the kingly eagle, who soars up close to the golden sun, because he has a fatal venom in his tongue? Is the savage beast, who tears and destroys his prey, more powerful than Vishnu, the kindly God in whose sight life is very precious? *Then* art thou more noble and more fearless than my Rāma! As for the courage of my Rāma, it is not of the same stuff as thine; to obey is more courageous than to resist, if virtue issue the command. But thou, vile Rākshasa, shall have dire proof whether my Lord be strong or no! Hide thee, in thy pleasant Isle of Lankā, if thou lovest life; touch not the bride of Rāma, whom the Gods have armed and strengthened, or thy fate is sealed!"

At that Rāvana laughed scornfully, and said:

"Scarcely, O large-eyed Lady! The Gods were put to shame by me; the Gandharvas, and Dānavas, and Nāgas, and Pisachas helped them, and yet I triumphed! Shall a man conquer me?"

Once more all hope died out of Sītā's heart.

"Alas!" she wept, "if thou beest indeed so powerful, how canst thou stoop to this dishonour?"

"Because I love thee," he answered.—And then he

Sītā tells the Demon how Rāma's courage differs from his own.

CHAP. VIII.

Rāvana snatches up Sītā, and rushes off with her in his chariot.

assumed his own gigantic stature, and snatching up the trembling Sītā, shouted for his Chariot, Pushpaka. And lo, it came, flaming through the air, like a cloud ablaze with lightning; and he leapt into it, and laughed in joyous triumph!

Then the daylight faded; despair seized the hearts of all creatures.

"Shall evil triumph?" they wept,—and looked up to the dimmed heavens.

Then, struggling in the Demon's arms, and turning her tear-stained face away from him, towards the hermitage, Sītā cried out wofully:

Sītā's farewell.

"Farewell, my cherished Home, that was like a leafy nest! Farewell, old neem-tree, with the spreading boughs! Sob, sob among thy spreading boughs! Oh wail the story of my wrongs into my Rāma's ears!

"Farewell, O pleasant vale of Panchavatī, where flows the languid Godāvarī, amid its reeds and sedges! Wake up, O languid Godāvarī! Weep, weep among thy reeds and sedges; moan plaintively the story of my grief into my Rāma's ears!

"Farewell, O country of the Janasthāna! Farewell, O sombre Forest, amid whose leaves and blossoms the little Birds twitter, and nestle side by side! O little Birds who nestle side by side, flutter very near to Rāma, and sing, oh sing to him my message of undying love!"

And thus, her voice much broken by its load of tears, she bade to all farewell. And through the valley swept a sudden sigh that seemed to answer her, "Alas!—Farewell!"

CHAPTER IX.

THE DEATH OF JATĀYU.

THE heavy leaves of the giant teak-trees were whitening in the growing dimness; the shadows were lengthening, and the tears of even were saturating the trailing ferns, when Rāma turned away from the slaughtered Rākshasa, and sought to retrace his steps. The excitement and heat of the chase were over: —there was a chill at his heart, too.

"The shade hangs heavy in this wood of Dandaka," he said, and shivered.

As he pushed his way through the long damp grass, rose up behind him a wild, unearthly Shriek, that made the echoes scream back for fear! He knew it was the jackal, screeching its hideous greeting to the twilight; yet it intensified his forebodings, and sent him rushing onwards, wrung with fresh terror.

Presently he saw Lakshmana bounding towards him through the wood. At that his heart failed him utterly.

"What means this?" he cried to the young Warrior from far. "Did I not leave my gentle Sītā in thy charge? What dost thou here, Lakshmana?"

Rāma's forebodings.

"Thy Sitā sent me," answered the other, breathlessly; "she thought she heard thee cry for succour, and would not let me stay; she called me 'Coward' and 'Traitor,' when I sought to reason with her! And so, perforce, I came. Could I bear to be called false to thee, O Brother?"

Then Rāma, his voice full of tears, cried out aloud:

"This is some scheme of vengeance, and we are undone! It was a Rākshasa who decoyed me from my home, and he cried to thee in a voice like mine:—Alas! an evil Destiny has brought me to this Wood! Brother, if Sītā greet me not on my return, my life is over!"

Side by side, and in anxious silence, the brothers hurried on through the darkening forest. As they came forth into the open vale, Rāma, darting by Lakshmana, rushed on to the little hermitage; where the torn earth before the entrance, and the confusion of all within, bore witness to a recent struggle.

The Dasarathide stood upright a moment in his desolate home:

"Lost!" he cried out at length. "First,—my Home, my Throne, my Father! Now,—my Love! This is too much; let me die!"

He flung himself, face downwards, to the earth, and lay there motionless.

Kneeling down beside him, the large tears brimming in his eyes, Lakshmana called to him eagerly:

"Rāma! Rāma! this thing cannot be! Thy Love has not suffered ill! What crime hast thou committed? Was not Sītā innocent? The Gods are not dead in heaven; I tell thee it is not possible! Perchance thy Beloved has wandered forth into the wood,—or perchance she does but hide from us in jest. Call to her! call to her!"

Then Rāma, his face distraught with grief, sprang to his feet, and rushed to the door of the hermitage.

"Sītā!" he cried, "my large-eyed, gentle Sītā! if thou hast willed to prove my love,—if thou art hiding from us,—let the agony of my fear suffice. Come to me, my Love,—come to me!"

He stood there, both his arms held wide, as though half hoping she might run forward to his embrace. The country of the Janasthāna lay very still around him; only, above his head, the old neem-tree shivered in every leafy spray, and seemed to wring its hands for pity.

Slowly that gleam of hope quite faded, and his arms fell down nerveless by his sides.

"Nay, Brother," implored Lakshmana, "yield not to despair; she is not gone; our Sītā has not left us! Perchance in our absence she has gone to sport with the little fawns, that know her voice, and come round her when she calls; or she has strolled down to the river's brink to wreathe herself a crown of lotus flowers; or to dream by the slowly-drifting waters."

Rāma shook his head despondently; yet he let his brother lead him where he would. Into the grove, where the asokas fluttered their delicate blossoms, and seemed to try to speak; then, forth into the open glade once more, under the ebony and the

CHAP. IX.

Rāma's momentary weakness.

sandal trees, whose dark foliage cast mournful shadows; then down by the shores of the Godāvarī, where the flags drooped, and the rushes folded up their flowers; and where the flowing water asked the breeze wherefore it was so sad, and drifted on, saddened also by the answer;—here, and through every nook and glen in the Vale of Panchavatī, they hunted for any trace of Sītā; they called to her,—and received no answer; but each time they breathed her name the shadows deepened, and the light grew more pale, and all nature seemed to weep!

At length Rāma paused, and flung his bow down upon the grass—and clenched his fist—in wrath!

"Do the Gods mock me?" he said. "Is the pain of man a pleasant jest to the Eternal Powers who look down from Heaven? or, as thou sayest, are the Gods dead,—and has a blind Destiny, ignorant of justice, become the ruler of our fates? Was not I virtuous? Was not my Sītā innocent? What means this evil fortune which pursues me, and culminates with this crowning misery? Why am I, who have made Truth and Purity and Kindliness my rule of life, thus hated by the Gods? It were best to change my conduct, since this is the meed Heaven keeps to pay the righteous!"

"Ay," returned the impetuous Lakshmana, with flashing eyes, "let the Gods look to it! Let them restore our Sītā, or every living thing in earth and heaven shall feel our rage! We will throw moderation and pity to the winds, and exact vengeance where justice is refused us!"

For a while Rāma stood there in moody silence. The black clouds of anger and despair strove hard in the inner Heaven of his soul; but the Sun that tabernacled there, the luminous Conscience which no guilt had dimmed, burst through them at length, and triumphed.

"I was wrong!" he said, and dashed a spray of softened tears from his eyes; "Virtue is a service man owes *himself*, and though there were no Heaven, nor any God to rule the world, it were not less the binding law of life. It is man's privilege to know the Right and follow it. Betray and persecute me, Brother Men! Pour out your rage on me, O malignant Devils! Smile, or watch my agony with cold disdain, ye blissful Gods! Earth, Hell, and Heaven, combine your might to crush me,—I will still hold fast by this Inheritance! My strength is nothing—time can shake and cripple it; my youth is transient—already grief has withered up my days; my heart,—alas! it seems well-nigh broken now! Anguish may crush it utterly, and life may fail; but even so, my Soul, that has not tripped, shall triumph, and dying, give the lie to soul-less Destiny, that dares to boast itself Man's Master!"

"It may be, Brother," said Lakshmana thoughtfully, "that it is for the ruin of the Rākshasas, and to give to man a pattern of high endurance, that this grief has befallen thee. Meanwhile, O Brother! let us be up and doing. There is no refuge in the three worlds for the wretch who has carried off thy Bride! The trees and mountains, and the clouds and stars, and

The Hero subdues his wrathful passion.

Lakshmana seeks to encourage him.

every living thing that Vishnu thrills, shall turn traitor to him, and show us his retreat! Sītā sprang from the heart of the kindly Mother-Earth; and thou, Rāma, in whom reigns the love of universal nature, hast conquered the devotion both of simple animals and half-conscious plants, and even of the wild elements, whom patience and justice alone can tame. The Universe is with us, Rāma! Shall Brahm, who gave the Universe its laws, fight against us? Let us take courage, and shake off this torpid grief!"

Then Rāma seized his brother's hand.

Rāma puts himself under his brother's guidance.

"What shall we do, O Tiger of Men?" he cried. "I will be guided by thee! Say, how shall my Sītā, who is like a Daughter of the Gods, be given back to me?"

Lakshmana answered:

"Let us recommence our search. To the east of this country of the Janasthāna is a mountain that has caverns and grottoes, whither resort the Gandharvas and Kinnaras, the dwellers in the ethereal Blue. One hears sweet music there by night, as though the mountain were singing softly to itself. It is hard to discover the entrance to these caverns, for the celestial Visitants love mystery. Perchance the Robber who has stolen thy Bride has fled to one of these for shelter."

Then, seizing his great and terrible bow, Rāma followed Lakshmana to the eastern side of the valley.

"O Mountain!" he cried out in his bitter grief, "is thy heart quite made of stone? There are innocent flowers fluttering on thy breast, and grasses, and thou givest shelter to harmless little beetles; surely thy heart is not all of stone? Thou seemest very sad thyself when the grey clouds cling round thee, and thy rivers are swollen with too many tears. Pity me, old Mountain! If my Love lies hidden in any of thy grots or caverns, fling back the creeping plants, or roll away the heavy stones that block the entrance, and keep her from my arms! Give her back to me, old Mountain!—by memory of the passion which tore thee from the bosom of the earth,—give my Love back to me!"

As he spoke, the large Mountain, as though in answer to his prayer, showed to him on its fertile slope the impress of a huge Foot, that could not have been that of mortal man. Near to it was a garland of flowers, that Rāma quickly stooped and gathered up, and pressed with fond emotion to his lips;—he had seen Sītā twine them thus, and wreathe them in her hair!

The Footprint that was not of mortal man.

But now Lakshmana, who had advanced a little, shouted to him to come. Rushing forward, Rāma beheld a broken chariot of war, and two Pisāchas, harnessed to it, lying there dead. Down by the chariot—his feathers ruffled, his large wings drooping, his once-piercing eyes bloodshot and dim, lay the King of Vultures, Jatāyu!

Then Rāma cried out in fury:

"This malignant Fowl, who called himself the friend of the splendid King Dasaratha, is probably a Rākshasa in disguise! He it is who has devoured

They find the bird Jatāyu.

my Sītā! Behold him in a hideous sleep, having gorged my large-eyed Princess!"

Then Jatāyu turned his mild gaze reproachfully on Rāma.

"I am not sleeping," he answered; "I shall soon die—Rāvana, the Lord of Rākshasas, has slain me because I sought to rescue thy Love from his clutch!"

At that, the Dasarathide flung himself on his knees beside the magnanimous Vulture.

"O Jatāyu! O my Friend!" he cried, "forgive me. Sorrow has well-nigh maddened me, or I had not conceived the thought! And it was in the service of my Sītā thou didst receive these cruel hurts? Rāvana has robbed me of her, thou sayest? O Best of Feathered Creatures! pity my despair, and tell me all thou knowest!"

Then, supported in the Hero's arms, the King of Vultures strove hard with the feebleness of approaching death, and answered in a faint yet clear voice:

"I was slumbering on the highest peak of the Mount Vindhya, when the wind came trembling to me bearing a piteous cry, 'Save me, save me, Rāma!' I knew the voice of the Princess with the starlike eyes,—and I sprang up—and flapped my wings to assure myself I did not dream,—and threw myself forth upon the air. As I hung there, pondering on what course to pursue, lo, I beheld Pushpaka, the war-chariot of Rāvana, the Enemy of Gods and Men, —and behold the dreadful Fiend clasped in his arms the youthful Vaidehī, the Flower amongst beautiful

Women. She held her little hands out to me, and screamed, 'Thou good Jatāyu, rescue me!' Then I rushed after the chariot, and flung myself before it, and shouted to the Demon, who reigns at Lankā, 'Halt!—if thou hast any love for life,—release this woman!' But the Rākshasa answered me in scorn: 'I have much love for life, thou aged Bird!—and yet shall I not, at thy puissant word, release this Sītā!' I said, 'It is true I am an aged Bird, but I am still vigorous and brave; if thou do not restore his Bride to Rāma, I will slay thee here, for the Gods will lend me strength!' Then Rāvana, his ten faces aflame with passion, shouted, 'Out of my path, Meddler!' and hurled at me a shower of javelins. But I sprang upwards, and then swooped down upon him with all my force, and as I am a very heavy Bird, my weight broke down the car Pushpaka, and, like two fearful thunderbolts flaming against each other, we tumbled through the air, and this great mountain shivered when we smote the earth! Then Rāvana, bounding to his feet, at once snatched up the Vaidehī, and, borne up by two dusky wings, rushed off towards Lankā. 'Farewell, venerable Fowl!' he shouted mockingly. 'Thou hast proved thy friendship to this fellow Rāma. Now forbear to tire thyself, for I must use a speed scarce suited for such ancient wings as thine!' But I darted after him, and, pouncing on the Demon's back, dug my sharp claws into his naked shoulders, and tore his flowing hair, and pecked and bit him till his twenty eyes were blinded with his blood! Then, howling hideously with rage and pain, the Rākshasa

Chap. IX.

How he battled with Rāvana.

How the Demon gave Jatāyu his death-wound.

swooped down to earth again; and,—swiftly laying down the fainting Sītā,—drew forth his mighty sword, the same that conquered Indra in other days. As in my impetuous fury I rushed on him, he dealt me a blow with it that staggered me; and then he battered me about with it until sense failed, and flames of blood seemed flashing before my eyes.—Yet, even so, I heard the plaintive voice of Sītā, and through the death mist, that made all vague, I knew that, as the Demon bore her off, she stretched her pitying little hands towards me, and wept, 'Alas, Jatāyu!—my poor loving friend, Jatāyu!'"

The dying Vulture gasped here for breath, and over his eyes the film thickened; he essayed to flap his poor wings once more, but he could not; they hung powerless by his side.

"It is well," he said in broken accents, "that I should die now—when the day is fading—for I have loved the sunlight: its splendour never made me blink;—it was pleasant when the fiery beams thrilled through my ruffled plumage: it was pleasant, too, to float on the bosom of the air, and to skim across the open country, and to hover above the forests and listen how the trees sighed—because they could not fly. My wings are broken now; I feel they could not stretch them in the air,—there would not be any joy in life. I am glad to die—with the waning light!"

The Heroes grieve for the good Vulture.

Then Rāma stroked fondly the plumage of the noble Bird. Lakshmana said:

"Thou shalt not die, O Bull amongst Feathered

Creatures! I will tend thee, and bear thee always in my arms, or across my shoulders! Thou shalt yet see the Princess with the starlike eyes restored to the love of Rāma!"

"I know she will be restored to Rāma," returned Jatāyu feebly, "and I die content. I could not live with broken wings. Turn me, I pray you, Heroes, towards the west. Is there still a streak of sunlight in the sky?"

"There is yet one last, faint gleam," answered Rāma.

"One last faint gleam," he faltered. "Gold—that flushes to crimson; crimson—that deepens to purple, and fades,—fades,—fades to sombre grey . . ."

He sank back into Lakshmana's arms, and passed away—with the sunlight!

Then Rāma, gazing down with reverent tenderness on the large Vulture, said:

"*Of a certainty, Son of Sumitra! there are amongst the animals many good and generous beings, and even many heroes. For my part I do not doubt that this compassionate Bird, who gave his life for my sake, will be admitted into Paradise!*"[1]

And so they erected a funeral pile in honour of the King of Vultures; and when the fire had reduced his corpse to ashes, they cleansed them by the ceremony of lustrous waters. Then Rāma recited over the remains of the magnanimous Bird the same prayers that holy Brahmans use at the obsequies of honourable men.

[1] Translated literally.

CHAPTER X.

RĀMA ALLIES HIMSELF WITH THE ORANG-OUTANG, SUGRĪVA.

Chap. X.

THERE was a River that sang all day long, and even through the night. In every one of its ripples a water nymph seemed weeping: there were never heard such mournful songs as those it chanted to itself. It was called the River Pampā, and close to it was the wood of Rishyamūka; so close that the banks were quite lined with flowers, who had crept out from under the shade of the trees, and stolen near to listen; for the music of these waters was as sweet as it was sorrowful.

The melancholy Ape.

Now there dwelt, in exile, in the wood of Rishyamūka, a Prince of the Simian tribe, the august Orang-outang, Sugrīva. He had ever been an Ape of a sentimental and mournful disposition; but, since his banishment, melancholy had become a passion with him. He did not like to see the trees in blossom; the sunlight vexed him greatly,—so did the song of birds; he looked on flowers as most frivolous beings: but he loved to wander by the shores of the River Pampā; because, though the sunbeams kissed it, and the lotus flowers lay upon its breast, and the kokila fluttered near, and sought to teach it a less mournful strain, it refused to be comforted—and wept always—day and night!

The Monkey takes fright at sight of two Warriors.

One day that the lachrymose Sugrīva was seated on a grassy knoll that overlooked the River,—his chin resting on his knees, and his eyes half-closed, as is the way with thoughtful Apes,—he saw approaching on the opposite bank two young Men of kingly stature, clad in the garb of anchorites, yet carrying bows, and with well-filled quivers hanging from their girdles. Filled with apprehension, Sugrīva sprang to his feet, and summoned by a shrill cry the four loyal followers who shared his exile—Nala, Nīla, Tārā, and Hanuman, Son of the Wind, the noblest among quadrumanous creatures. Gathering round their Lord, these four heroic Apes watched gravely his anxious countenance; waiting, in respectful silence, till he should inform them of his pleasure.

"As a rule, Men are cruel and malicious," he said at length. "They are, too, especially jealous of the superiority of the Simian tribe: it were wise to put ourselves out of the reach of these young Warriors' arrows!"

His followers flee with him a safe distance.

And with that, he sprang from the hillock into cover of the wood; and his followers, their sensitive natures at once infected by the terror of their chief, leapt after him; shrilly screaming, breaking down trees, and bounding over thickets, and making the wood of Rishyamūka tremble by the impetuosity of their flight. They paused only on the northern slope of the Mount Malaya. Staying there to take breath, they sat round in a circle, and rested their chins upon their knees,—and reflected on what was to be done next.

"It seems to me, Indra amongst Monkeys!" said the Son of the Wind to Sugrīva, "that we have been wrong in fleeing from these warriors. Exiles, we have nothing to tempt the covetous, nor to awaken the jealousy of the envious; on the other hand, we stand grievously in need of friendship. These two Heroes might prove valuable allies, were we to treat them with courtesy, and offer them hospitality during their sojourn in this wood."

But life, which had not dealt kindly with Sugrīva, had taught him to see people, as well as circumstances, in their blackest colours.

"Thou art too rash, Hanuman," he rejoined, distrustfully. "I tell thee, men are a malicious race! They have all manner of ingenious devices for slaying from a distance those with whom they dare not risk a struggle. If we let these warriors approach us, we put our lives in their power; and who shall assure us that they are not sent hither by our enemy, the rancorous Bālin, Monarch of all the Simian tribes?"

"That will I!" answered Hanuman. "Give me permission, O Ape with the powerful countenance, and I will straightway accost these strangers, and discover what motives bring them to the wood of Rishyamūka."

"If thou choosest thus to imperil thy life, do so," returned Sugrīva; "but remember it is thy own impetuous rashness, and no command of mine, which takes thee into this danger."

Upon that, the fearless Son of the Wind wrapped himself in a sombre valkala,[1] that had been given him by a holy recluse, to whom he once rendered a service, and, assuming the staid gait and stooping carriage of a mendicant friar, approached the two Warriors, who had just climbed the river's bank, and whose mighty limbs were gleaming with the bright waters of the River.

"Who are you, Heroes, whose limbs are like young fir-trees?" asked the Monkey in a courteous tone. "Are you of the Sons of Men, or of the Company of Celestial Warriors, who do battle for the Storm God, Indra? What cause has brought you to this wood? If your errand be as worthy as your gallant bearing would seem to testify, I will be your guide, lest this wood of Rishyamūka entangle you in its network of winding paths."

Then one of the young Warriors smiled, to see the Orang-outang in the garb of a religious mendicant; but the other, the taller of the two, whom the majesty of an ineffable sorrow seemed to raise above sight of the ludicrous, said gravely:

"It is courteously offered; I pray thee, answer for me, Lakshmana, for my voice is choked, and speech is cruel to me."

Then Lakshmana, in whose eyes, spite of all his anxiety and distress, a gleam of laughter still lingered, answered:

"We are much beholden to thee, magnanimous

[1] A garment made of bark.

Chap. X.

Lakshmana says that they seek Sugrīva.

Saint! We are the sons of Dasaratha, King of Ayōdhyā; this Hero is Rāma, who is known in the three worlds as the Friend of living creatures. We are here because an evil Rākshasa has carried off the cherished Bride of this King of Men, my Brother; and Danu, the son of Lakshmī, counselled us to come to Rishyamūka; 'For,' said he, 'there dwells there an eminent Orang-outang, by name Sugrīva, who will give you tidings of your lovely Sītā.'"

Then Hanuman threw on one side his disguise, and laughed for joy.

"This same Sugrīva is my Lord and Sovereign," he said, "and he will assuredly give you all the assistance in his power, for he also is an exile, who has lost the wife he loved. Mount on my back, O Kings among Men! and I will straightway bring you into the presence of him you seek."

Hanuman brings them to his master.

So Rāma and Lakshmana climbed on to the back of the generous Monkey, and he brought them to the Mount Malaya; where Sugrīva and the other Apes sat in a circle,—their chins upon their knees.

When Hanuman had introduced the Strangers, and told their errand, the Prince among Simians shook them warmly by the hand; and, moved by the sorrowful countenance of Rāma, he went farther, and embraced him lovingly. And, in his turn, Rāma, the noblest of the Sons of Men, embraced the exiled Ape!—When the Son of the Wind saw that, he made a Fire, according to the Brahmanical rites, by rubbing together two pieces of wood; and then these two Princes—Rāma, the Dasarathide, and

Sugrīva, the melancholy Orang-outang—performed the ceremony of a Pradakshina round the Fire, to celebrate their newly-formed friendship.

"Tell me, O magnanimous Sugrīva!" pleaded the Dasarathide, when he had thus complied with the exigencies of etiquette. "I was sent to thee by one Danu; he told me thou couldst give me tidings of my Beloved? Thou hast heard how she was stolen from me? My Friend, I know not what has befallen my Love with the dark, soft eyes! I know not whither they have carried her; and I wander, groping through the world,—blinded by a great darkness; knowing not where to seek for the Star my heart has lost! If thou canst give me news of her, or of my enemy's hiding-place, tell me, O tender-hearted Monkey! I starve for tidings of her!"

Then, shedding copious tears, the mournful Ape answered:

"Alas! my Rāma, I have no comforting news to give thee;—though I have beyond a doubt seen thy Beloved. But three days since, I was wandering by the shores of the River Pampā; it was early morning, and the mists hung heavy on the stream; presently, as though a great cloud had obscured the heavens, darkness fell on the River and on me; I looked up, and beheld Rāvana, the King of Rākshasas, sailing overhead; and struggling in his swarthy arms, a lovely Daughter of Man, whose garments seemed woven out of sunbeams. She screamed to me, but the distance kept back her words; only, as the Demon sped on with her, fell at my feet a little golden Anklet, and

Marginalia:
CHAP. X.
Rāma begs Sugrīva to tell him all he knows.
Sugrīva tells how he saw Rāvana carrying off a daughter of man.

CHAP. X.

Rāma recognizes the Scarf and Anklet of Sītā.

a Scarf of pale, soft azure. Then I, at sight of these mournful tokens, wept long and sore over the hard fate of the beautiful Child of Man,—and the River Pampā wept with me! I have treasured up this Scarf, and this little Anklet of gold, and from time to time I look at them, and bedew them with my tears. They are stored in my cavern, near at hand; I will fetch them, that thou mayest judge if they belong to thy Love with the dark, soft eyes."

Then Sugriva ran and fetched the Scarf and the golden Anklet, and at sight of them Rāma cried out, "Alas, my Queen!"—and held out both his hands for them,—and kissed them, as though they had been living things.

"Ah!" he cried, "little Scarf! that art so soft, that art so blue,—that hast been wound across my Sītā's throat, and round her waist, and that hast felt her heart beat, and her bosom swell,—is there nothing in all thy folds and fringes to speak one thought of comfort to me? Thy brightness is not dimmed, although my life has lost its radiance! It is strange —harshly, bitterly strange! Love, Happiness, Faith,— a poor piece of stuff outlives them all! Man's heart grows sere, the large emotions of his soul wither and die, ere ever the garb he wears have lost its colour!"

And then he gazed upon the golden Anklet, that was so small it had but just clasped round his wrist! And he burst out a weeping, and cried:

"Poor little Sītā! my childlike, fragile Sītā! whom I took away from the loving care of the old man,

Janaka, and brought into these savage woods to meet so hard a fate! So timorous, my Sītā! So gentle, and so very, very timid, that when the wind howled, even, thou didst nestle close to me, and with thy large eyes ask, 'Protect me, Rāma!' And yet so brave, my Sītā! so patient and so generous, that though I saw the terror in thine eyes, and felt thy little heart flutter against mine, thou didst never tell thy fears, nor utter a complaint, nor one regret, lest I might fancy thou wert suffering through following my lot. And so beautiful, and so loving, Sītā! Alas! my Sītā,—and so beloved! It had been better otherwise, my Queen! It had been better far for thee, poor Child, if I had loved thee less; for I am a man accursed by Destiny, and my love has been thy ruin!"

As he lay upon the earth, quite beaten down with grief, Sugrīva came near, and said, amid many sobs:

"I, too, am one accursed by Destiny. Let us mourn our several griefs together!"

The ghost of a smile flitted across the noble countenance of Rāma. He dashed the tears from his eyes, and tossed back his head, as though he were defying despair to overpower him. Then he said kindly to the dismal Monkey:

"Nay, let us rather strive to help each other to overcome misfortune. What are thy sorrows, worthy Simian? Tell them me, that I may make their remedy my care."

Then Sugrīva plucked a branch from a shorea, that was all in flower, and bade Rāma sit down on

Sugrīva tells Rāma he too is in grief, and the hero bids him tell the cause.

CHAP. X.

it beside him; and when Hanuman saw that, he gathered a branch from a sandal-tree, and beckoned Lakshmana to sit by him; and when they were all comfortably established, the Prince among Simians commenced his story.

"Doubtless, O Elephants among Men!" he said, "you both know the name of Bālin, the invincible Orang-outang who governs all the Simian tribes? He is my elder brother,—and my most bitter and relentless enemy. You shall hear how, and why he became so. After the death of the eminent Ape our father, Bālin inherited with his crown the affectionate loyalty I had ever paid my rightful superior. Also, there had never been a dispute between us; when the Asura, Māyāvin, jealous of Bālin's great renown, declared war against him. One night, when the Lord of Monkeys was calmly reposing in his cavern, Kishkindhyā, the malevolent Asura, came and stood without, and shouted a thousand outrageous insults, and dared Bālin to come forth and wrestle with him. Then my intrepid Brother leapt from his couch, and rushed forth to avenge the insult. I followed him, wishing to share his danger. But when Māyāvin saw us both, his courage failed him, and turning back into the forest, he fled with the speed of the wind. We pursued him for many miles, but his swiftness of foot was extreme, and the morning dawned ere we had come up with him. Then, just as we were close upon his heels, the wily Demon stepped on one side, and rushed into a cavern, whose entrance was concealed by shrubs and creeping plants. But Bālin had

Sugrīva tells how Bālin pursued the Asura Māyāvin.

How the Asura fled into a cavern.

seen his place of refuge, and turning to me with a smile, said:

"'Await me here, Sugrīva; to wrestle with this Māyāvin one suffices,—but to prevent him running away from this combat he so desired a while back, is a more difficult matter. If he seek to pass thee, drive him back into the cavern, but do not thou enter it; I choose to overcome this blustering Asura unaided.'

How Bālin charged him to guard the cavern's mouth.

"So, obedient to my brother's word, I took up my stand at the mouth of the cavern. All that day I waited. The night drew on, and the moon came out to wonder; every little star bewildered itself to know why I stood there! The morning woke up, and laughed—'What, *you* there still?' The noonday sun streamed down its hottest beams: 'I will make this infatuated Ape move from here!' he said;—but I did not stir. Only as the night came on again, I gave up hope. I am naturally of a lugubrious disposition; there appeared to me no longer any doubt that my Brother had perished by Māyāvin's hand; and as I stood there, my tears streamed down like rain, for sorrow at his supposed death. At length came oozing out from the fatal cavern a little stream of thick, dark crimson; when it wetted my feet, I started back appalled, for I never doubted that it was the murdered Bālin's blood.

How he thought Bālin had perished.

"'At all events, the assassin shall not escape!' I muttered. 'I should be powerless to slay him, for Bālin's vigour was twice as great as mine, ere I had been enfeebled thus by grief and fasting; but he shall not escape.'

CHAP. X.

And having blocked up the cavern, mourned sore for his brother.

"And so I blocked up the entrance of the cave by a huge stone. Then I returned to the cave of Kishkindhyā, to tell the doleful news to the whole Simian tribe, that they might mourn for Bālin as never Ape was mourned before! And so they did; for three days there was no sound heard in all the forest but the discordant wailings of all sorts of Monkeys; —and among them all, was none who grieved more wildly, nor wailed more shrilly than myself!

"At the close of that time, Hanuman, the noble Son of the Wind, came to me, as a messenger from the whole Simian tribe.

How Hanuman persuaded him to assume the crown.

"'Magnanimous Sugrīva!' he said, 'deign to repress thy grief, for the sake of those who now look to thee for support and guidance. Thou art our sovereign, Prince of Monkeys! and to mourn for any length of time disturbs our loyalty, and is repugnant to our characters as Apes: the assembled tribes long to do homage to the new Monarch of Simians; put on thy robes of state, Sugrīva, and come forth, to delight their eyes!'

"Rāma, I swear it, I had preferred to spend my life in perpetual tears for the unhappy Bālin! But they would not listen to my protestations. Much against my will, they invested me with the royal mantle, and proclaimed me king in my brother's stead.

"However, one day that I was seated amidst my ministers, deliberating on some affairs of state, strode in no less a personage than the Bālin I had mourned as dead! Overcome with joy, I sprang from my throne, and was about to fling myself on his neck, when his wrathful and forbidding scowl checked my joyous emotion.

"'Brother!' I faltered, 'is it indeed thou? My Lord, —my King,—my Brother? I wept for thee as dead! Thanks be to Vishnu, the kindly God, in whose sight life is precious, and praise be to thy strong heart that has brought thee triumphant through this conflict! Oh, with what joy I give thee back thy crown! It was a bitter grief to me to set it on my head! Bālin,—look not on me thus coldly; say thou dost not doubt me, Brother!'

"He put me on one side without a word. Striding past me, he mounted the steps of his high throne; and stood there, his colossal frame worn and spent with hunger and fatigue, and his two eyes gleaming like living coals! Then the whole Simian tribe, carried away with pride and delight in his lordly bearing, shouted till the leaves fell down, and the forest trees trembled to their roots! But Bālin put forth a hand — to silence them. Where I stood, stricken and abashed, his eye found me out; and his scornful finger showed me to them; so that each one there looked from him to me,—and back from me to him,—and held his breath.

"'Men of the Woods!' he cried, and stabbed me with his accusing finger, though his gaze despised to rest on me, 'ye are called "wild" by those who dwell in cities,—it may be; for my part, I would not change my title of King among the Wild Men of the Woods, to have the government of every smooth, tame slave, who lets himself be bound by laws and formulas, im-

CHAP. X.

posed on him by others. I do not *give* you laws; they *exist*—for me as well as you; it is not *I* who have made it a base thing to plot, betray, and murder; it is not *I* who have said that to design to slay, and then to rob one of such near kinship as a brother is a worse outrage, a more flagrant blasphemy against Nature! But it *is* I,—your King, your Lover, to whom your honour as a race is dear,—who ask you now, if you will harbour in your midst a Traitor who has violated the obligations Brahm has laid on him, and shamed the One Creator's name, by being the despicable thing he is?'

"As a large wave, sweeping onwards to shore, rose in the crowd a murmur, that grew and swelled,—and then died, hushed into a deep-drawn breath, as he turned on me all the passion of his rage.

"'Simians, you behold this Sugrīva; oh, look on him,—take in every line of feature and of form,—whilst I am telling you what manner of creature this is who dares to wear our shape! You know that, some while back, an open enemy, Māyāvin, the Asura, dared me to a combat, and then fled, and sheltered himself in a cavern? I, not witting I addressed a more treacherous and ruthless foe, bade this Sugrīva here await me at the cavern's mouth, and if the Demon sought to flee, drive him back to the conflict he had courted. What did this estimable Brother,—my own Mother's son? Lusting for my death, yet not daring even to unite his strength to the Asura's to master me, *he blocked the cavern's mouth*, and returned to steal my crown. But the Immortals willed that, as my life had not been inglorious, so death should not be dealt me by a miscreant's hand! I flung myself against the rock,—what could a dead block of a stone against a soul drunk with its own rage? The barrier yielded; bleeding and lacerated, I rolled with it down the slope, and lay there, liberated, yet fain to die, so shaken was my life by this supreme achievement!—But yet I died not! It was not meet, my People, I should let a Dastard rule my brave Men of the Woods! I am here,—less to reclaim my rights than to denounce that Traitor!'

"As a large wave, sweeping onwards to shore, the murmur rose again and swelled;—but this time it died not;—it grew louder, and ever louder, in my ears; a sea of threatening faces, grinning with rage and hatred, swam before my eyes; and, my heart quite failing me, I turned and fled! Then, shrieking hideously, the whole band of Apes, led on by Bālin, rushed after me; and I, only to keep life, sought refuge in this wood of Rishyamūka; for I knew the ferocious Bālin dared not pursue me hither. Long years back he slew the giant Dundubhi, whose mighty skeleton you see whitening there; and in his arrogant delight, he flung the Demon's body here, and the blood defiled the hermitage of the Saint Matanga; in his wrath the holy man cursed my reckless Brother, and charged him, under pain of death, never to enter this forest. So I have dwelt here in sanctuary; and Hanuman, and these three noble Apes, who know my innocence, have shared with me all the woes and hardships of my exile.—This, Rāma, is the story of my wrongs and sorrows; and alas! noble Dasarathide, I see no remedy nor hope; this Bālin will never temper with mercy any judgment he has passed; and though I am innocent, he is powerful; and there is none able to subdue his will!"

Sugrīva says none can conquer Bālin.

At that Lakshmana laughed in scorn.

"Thou art enamoured of melancholy, Ape!" he said. "Look to the right of thee; thinkest thou Bālin could hold his own against Rāma, King of Men?"

Sugrīva looked at Rāma; then bowed his mournful head upon his breast.

"I am not of a hopeful disposition," he said meekly. "It seems to me that none could conquer this Orang-outang, who tears the forest trees up by the roots, and who in sport tossed here that monstrous carcase of Dundubhi, as one would throw a pebble."

Without stirring, Rāma placed his foot beneath the huge skeleton, and raised it high in air; then kicked it from him into shattered fragments! But even then Sugrīva shook his head.

"It was weighted with flesh and blood," he said, "when Bālin cast it hither. I would not have this young hero, whose beauty seems more than mortal, fall a victim to this indomitable Warrior. Once Rāvana, the dreadful Lord of Rākshasas, having heard his fame, desired to wrestle with him. The Demon came to Bālin at sunset, when he was busy at his prayers.

He tells how Rāvana was subdued by him.

"'Leave these mummeries, Ape!' said the Rākshasa; 'they tell me thou hast some strength; I would try a combat with thee!'

"Bālin answered: 'When I have finished my devotions to the Gods I will wrestle with thee, Rākshasa.'

"'The Gods?' laughed Rāvana in scorn; 'I am beyond them in strength and power. Attend to me first, pious Ape, and then address thy prayers heavenward!'

"At that, without more ado, my vigorous brother clutched the insolent Rākshasa by the throat, and held him as in a vice, till his ten faces flushed a dusky purple. Meanwhile Bālin rinsed his mouth, as the rites command, and looking towards the east, recited tranquilly his prayer. Then, carrying the Demon with him, he marched off by way of the air to the western coast, and from thence to the southern ocean, and finally towards the northern district, where reigns the kingly Himālaya. Having thus addressed his adorations towards the four points of Heaven, the intrepid Monkey released the Rākshasa, and said to him:

"'I am ready now to wrestle with thee, resplendent Demon! if such be thy pleasure.'

"But Rāvana shook his head:

"'Nay,' he said smiling, 'my breath is not yet in a condition to struggle with thee, gallant Bālin. Also, I require no further proof of thy unusual vigour. Accept my felicitations, invincible Orang-outang! Thou hast earned my respect, and I will not battle with thee!'

"'So be it,' answered Bālin, who saluted the Rākshasa courteously, and went his way.

CHAP. X.

"If the Scourge of the three worlds failed to conquer this doughty Ape, who shall master him?"

Then Lakshmana sprang to his feet.

"What proof dost thou require, thou obstinately despondent Ape!" he asked impatiently, "to assure thee that the strength of this Simian is as a feather to the might of Rāma?"

"Once," returned Sugrīva, "Bālin traversed with one arrow the hearts of three palm-trees; let Rāma show me a like deed, and I will believe my brother has found an equal."

Rāma convinces Sugrīva of his power to subdue Bālin.

Without a word the noble Dasarathide took his bow, and shot from it an arrow that sped shivering through the hearts of seven palm-trees, and finally pierced the mountain's side beyond, and stuck quivering in the hard rock.

A gleam of hope sprang into Sugrīva's eyes.

"O Elephant amongst Men!" he exclaimed excitedly, "thou art indeed Bālin's master! Under thy puissant aid I shall not fear to abandon the shelter of this wood of Rishyamūka. Say, O Hero with the radiant eyes! wilt thou indeed help to restore me to my home and family, of whom Bālin has robbed me?"

Rāma answered him:

"Return, Sugrīva, to thy native woods; assert thy innocence, and claim thy rights. If Bālin menace thy life I will slay him; for an innocent life is of more worth than a guilty one!"

And so, for the first time since his banishment, Sugrīva ventured forth from the wood of Rishyamūka. Hanuman and the other Apes followed him at a distance with Lakshmana. As for Rāma, he walked side by side with the Prince of Orangoutangs, until they were within a short distance of the cavern Kishkindhyā; then he paused, keeping his bow in readiness, in case Sugrīva's life should be in peril.

Sugrīva defies Bālin.

The outlawed Ape, standing before the cavern's mouth, shouted to Bālin to come forth to him.

"After long years of exile," he cried, "I come, determined to resist this unjust oppression! Brother, I am innocent of the crime you accuse me of. Retract your cruel judgment, and restore to me family and friends, or battle with me here, that or you or I may quit this world, where life, and peace, and honour are impossible for us both!"

Maddened by the sound of a voice he hated, the ferocious Orang-outang rushed forth from the cavern, and fell on the luckless Sugrīva. The two tussled and flung each other, and tore each other with their nails; they reeled here and there, clutched in each other's arms, and stumbled, and fought upon their knees; and, still fighting, rolled upon the ground in a delirious frenzy of rage, which their near kindred rendered more intense;—for hatred is love gone mad: one feels no rage against the stone which falls on one, and maims one; and if one's heart were cold to one's fellows, their wrongs and insults would never awaken the passion of revenge.

But Rāma, standing at a short distance, could not distinguish the Brothers from each other, so like were

CHAP. X.

Sugrīva overthrown.

they in size and colour; and he dared not seek to free Sugrīva from that fatal embrace, lest his arrow might strike the innocent Monkey in mistake for Bālin. At length the exiled Ape, covered with blood, broke from the desperate grasp of Bālin, and screaming shrilly for pain and grief, fled towards the wood of Rishyamūka.

Thither Rāma followed him; and the disconsolate Monkey, laying his hand on a grievous wound upon his chest, asked with tearful eyes:

"Why didst thou deceive me, Hero? I had never dared to face this Bālin hadst thou not promised to protect me; for I knew his strength to be three times that of mine!"

Rāma explained how he had not dared to shoot an arrow lest it might wound Sugrīva instead of Bālin, so nearly were they of the same size and colour. And upon that Lakshmana gathered a branch of Gaja-pushpa that grew on the mountain's slope, and tied it round the throat of the ill-used Orang-outang.

"By this sign," he said, "shall Rāma recognize thee in to-morrow's combat."

Next day he defies Bālin again.

So the following day Sugrīva, the four other Orang-outangs, and the two noble Dasarathides, sallied forth again. Before the cave of Kishkindhyā, the outlaw, once more, defied the Lord of Simians.

"Come forth," he shouted; "acknowledge thy misdeeds, or expiate them!"

Then Tārā, wife of Bālin, sought to restrain the impetuous fury of her Lord.

"Thou dear Husband!" she pleaded, "venture not

forth to-day; I beseech thee, for this one day, stay with me, in this cave of Kishkindhyā! A presentiment of evil hangs over me. Is not thy great fame established? In all the three worlds is there one who questions thy courage? This Sugrīva is not wont to be so valorous; there may be treachery afloat—treachery and danger to thy dear life! O my Lord, is there shame in avoiding the snare of a traitor?"

Tārā seeks to dissuade her husband from accepting the combat.

Bālin, laughing, embraced his favourite Queen upon the brow.

"Nay," he said, "gentle Tārā, fear nothing! It has been granted me, by the Immortals, to die at the hands of a Hero, grander by his virtues and his courage than any among living creatures! Shall this paltry Sugrīva alarm me? And if death indeed awaited me, still could I not refuse this challenge; for to tolerate an offence were harder far than to die!"

And with that he came rushing forth upon Sugrīva. But when Rāma saw that the vigorous Monkey was about to triumph, once more, over his innocent Brother, he drew his bow, and pierced the heart of Bālin by his unerring shaft!

Bālin rushing on Sugrīva is wounded by Rāma.

Relaxing his grasp of Sugrīva, the mighty Ape screamed forth, "I am slain!" and fell, with a monstrous crash, to the earth!

When they saw that, Lakshmana, and Nala, Nīla, Tārā, and Hanuman shouted for triumph!

But Rāma approached the dying Orang-outang, and said, with grave respect:

"Forgive me this deed, heroic Bālin."

CHAP. X.

Bālin reproaches Rāma.

Then he knelt down beside him,—and drew the arrow forth from out the wound.

Turning his failing eyes on the young Warrior, the dying Monkey said:

"Rāma, Rāma the Dasarathide, thou who wast known in the three worlds as the Friend of living creatures, why hast thou soiled thy soul? Had I fallen by thy hand in open warfare, I had met death, as it was promised me,—at a Hero's hand; then had I pardoned thee, and died content! But now has this needless cruelty dethroned thee from thy nobility; destroyed thy treasures of past mercy; and snapt the cord that bound to thee the hearts of living creatures! Wherefore hast thou abandoned thyself to this senseless fury? Had Sugrīva slain me, it had been in fair battle, and to avenge many wrongs; but thou, how had I injured thee? And if thou hadst no grounds to hate me, what motive prompted thee to this ill deed? We lead a harmless life, we Wild Men of the Woods; we feed on fruits and grains, and never store up wealth. Our flesh is not good for food; the Brahmans forbid its use; for we have five fingers on our hands, and our construction resembles man's; our skins, even, may not be worn as clothing. Wherefore, then, Rāma, hast thou slain me? This deed, which has nor vengeance, nor interest for motive, will load thy name with ignominy!"

Rāma, supporting him the while, that he might not suffer needless anguish in his last hour, answered: "Thou reasonest, Bālin, with the shallow judgment of an ape. Had my action indeed vengeance, or interest, as motive, it would, as thou sayest, dim my fair fame, and render worthless my past reverence for justice. Or had I, from vainglorious delight in the strength the Gods had given me, challenged thee to a combat and slain thee, to prove myself more vigorous, it were not less a shameful deed. There is but one just reason for destroying life,—and that is, its *preservation*. To save a worthier life, we may take a less noble one; under no other circumstances can we innocently destroy the meanest son of Brahm! I slew thee, Bālin, because, otherwise, thou hadst slain Sugrīva; he is innocent, whilst thou hast been suspicious, rancorous, and cruel. It was just that I should count his life of more value than thy own; but thy death is a sorrow, not a triumph to me."

Rāma justifies himself.

Then the dying Lord of the Simians turned him, painfully, towards Rāma:

"Thou art right," he said, "and I have erred. It is meet that I should die, since I have been unjust; but let my death expiate my offence. If Sugrīva be near—I cannot see whether he be near, there is a mist that hides from me who are standing round—let him note how the death agony convulses me, and let him say, 'It suffices!' Let him not visit my sins on the innocent; Tārā, my faithful consort, and Angada, my son, who stands yet in the young dawn of life, have committed no offence. They have loved me; but surely to love, even the guilty, is not a crime? For me, I regret the past; but can I change it now? I cannot do more than die!"

Bālin asks mercy for his queen and for Angada.

CHAP. X.

Rāma promises to protect them.

"Thou canst do no more," said Rāma, gently; "also thy sins die with thee. What thou hast done that was noble, and generous, and brave, passes not away; it lives, and testifies that thy spirit dwelt upon the earth, in mortal shape. Have no fear, noble Bālin, for Tārā and Angada; they shall hear of the great deeds of the Lord of the Simians; and it shall be their pride to have loved such an one. Leave thy fame, and the welfare of thy dear ones, in my hands; and thou, rest thee from pain, and die in peace!"

"I leave them in thy hands," he returned feebly,—and died in peace.

CHAPTER XI.

THE LOVE OF INDRA.[1]

"The Breath which is in the midst is Indra. He, by his might, kindled other breaths in the midst: inasmuch as he kindled them, he is *Indha* (the Kindler)."

Muir's Sanscrit Texts.

"He who *kindles;*" Indra, God of Celestial Fire! It is he who troubles the air, and fires the clouds; it is he, also, who touches the thoughts of man with flame!

Have you watched the changeful sky—crimson, and gold, and amethyst, sinking into a depth of azure?

It is the Mantle of Indra.

From its folds glance forth the beamy stars. He is called the God with the thousand eyes; for stars look out from the folds of his mantle!

He rides on the snow-white Elephant, Airāvata, whom the Storm lashed out from the foam of the Sea. In his hand is Vajra, the Thunderbolt; the forked Lightnings are his arrows.

Have you heard the shriek of the East Wind? Have you seen the trees wrenched up, and thrown,

[1] *Vide* Note.

CHAP. XI.

crushed, back to earth; the sand torn up in eddies, and the white salt dust of the Sea flung in the face of heaven?

It is the Wrath of Indra.

The sunlight is his Laughter; when the clouds give their lives forth in rain, he is in grief.

In earth or heaven, there is none like him. His Beauty has the wistful passion of a man, and the splendour and might of a God! A Flash of Supernal Fire, he has thrilled through the earth's dark places; he has learnt Sorrow, and Guilt, and Desire; and the dark, wild Heart of a Man struggles through his Divinity!

"Let us worship with reverence the mighty Indra, the exalted, the undecaying, the youthful!"[1]

In all nations, through all ages, he has been so worshipped. The Celestial Fire has not cooled, the "Breath that is in the midst" still kindles other "Breaths" to its heat. The God of Sunlight and Storm still bids the world dream or struggle, lust or aspire; and the great ocean of man's passions obeys him!

There were some young maidens standing just on the threshold of Life; for Childhood is the vestibule merely; it is hung with pretty Pictures, too, so that one does not look on to the World-chamber at the end until the glare, of a sudden, bursts on one, and one hears the uproar made by the over-numerous guests.

Just at this point paused our young maidens, half awed by the tumult, half fascinated by all the movement and the light. It chanced that at this moment

[1] Rig Vēda.

the gaze of Indra fell on them, and beholding them, so beautiful and so pure, he loved them. Flashing earthward, in a Form of Fire, he kissed them on the lips, and left them with blanched cheeks, and eyes aflame. For they knew a God had been with them, and thrilled them by his touch, and yet had winged his way back to his High Home ere they had tasted aught of passion, save its first sudden pain!

So, with a fever on them, and a vague desire in their innocent breasts, seeking Whom they knew not, what they could not say, they wandered forth; and Love, who breathes only in the upper air, led them to a Hilly Country, where the large stars seemed smiling near.

And there, still far beyond them, but looking down with deeply passionate eyes, they saw the great God, Indra; and he held out his large arms, wooing them to the fire of his embrace!

The hearts of the young maidens failed them. Fain had each been to turn her back; but her soul within of a sudden found its wings, and bore her, in a rush of superhuman ecstasy, to the arms of the enamoured God!

Thus, ignorant of the bitter cost to mortals, who press up, with quivering lips and heaving breasts, to meet the desire of the Sons of Heaven, did they receive the "sorrowful great Gift," *the Love of Indra*.

Bear me witness, Ye, who have tasted the Kiss of Fire, how closely anguish and rapture are interwoven here. Whether is greatest, I know not; the bliss and suffering alike strain all too fiercely the human brain

CHAP. XI.

and heart; yet who would cage his soul and bar it round with shade, if the Sun-god claimed it of him, saying, "Let my large pulses thrill thy being through, and draw thy Spirit forth from thee in Flame?"

But our little maidens, having no previous knowledge of all an Immortal's love involved, fretted against the Crown Indra had laid on them; because, although it wrapped them in a Light, it scorched and tore their smooth young brows, and mingled with its Beams of Gold the lifeblood of the wearers.

"We are faint," they said, "and weary! The bloom has faded from our cheeks, and all the youth of our hearts is dying! Our eyes are tired with Beauty! Tired—and Light is but a splendid Pain. Our hearts are spent with passion, this eternal Rapture will destroy us. Oh that we could rest! Rest—rest, from the fever of our lives, ere it exhaust our power, and we die!"

The Brides of Indra wander from Mount Mēru.

So, one day that this longing for rest overcame them, they strayed from the Mountain of Mēru, where the Gods quaff sparkling nectar, and hearken to the Song that dies not, but flings forth the Soul of its music half-way between Hell and Heaven; gathering voices, from Hell and from Heaven, that merge their might and their glory to swell this Ocean of Harmony!

With their hands to their ears the faithless Brides of Indra fled from the witching strains, and sought the sheltered valleys, where life is calm, and men and women pass slowly through the stages of time; marking progress merely by the succession of season, and dying, at length, because they have dwelt too long, not lived too much. And in their wanderings they came upon the country of the Uttarakurus. Oh, that was a pleasant land, and surely just the spot where our weary Fugitives might find the peace they longed for. There were no extremes of heat nor cold, no excess of light nor depth of gloom; all was equable and tempered calm—like the inhabitants themselves, whose dispositions were inaccessible to all violent emotions, which overstrain a delicate frame. There was no need for any exertion either; for in a wood, called Chaitraratha, hung from the boughs of the trees all that the heart could desire; jewels, and raiment, and luxurious couches, and delicious viands of every description; one had only to walk thither and gather them. The flowers in this country were of gold, so were the mountains; the rivulets were so choked up with gold that they slept between their banks, that were strewn with gold too, and did not attempt to sing. The Women who dwelt there were all youthful and lovely; the Men were all courteous, and learned in saying pleasant things: old age, or disease, or poverty, or suffering, or grief, were not known here; it is probable that all such things were soaked away out of the land by the black and terrible River, that swept with its sinister floods the borders of the Land of Gold, and rolled, muttering ever words of menace and despair—that were not understood by the smiling Uttarakurus.

Amid this luxurious people the pale Wanderers paused; and, struck by their strange beauty and their wanness, born of an ardour unknown to any here, the inhabitants flocked around them, saying, "Stay with us and share our lives."

Then, at first, a pang of unsatisfied longing held back the souls where Indra had set his Love. But, little by little, each sought to reason herself out of the memory of those rapturous moments spent up among the mountains.

"Help me to live it down!" cried out each weary heart; and the appealing hands went forth, seeking for some stay.

They met the smooth palms of the bland Uttarakurus.

"Let us lead you along the path of pleasure," they said to the Brides of Indra.

But the Beloved of the Sun-god found no delight in the golden country, nor in the wood of Chaitraratha, nor in the company of the smiling Uttarakurus.

"Better to have died in a god's embrace," they moaned, "than to crawl through the long days in this hateful City."

But they had made their choice; and Mahēndra, God of the Firmament, has no welcome for renegades! In the heart of the Golden Land his curse found them out.

The Curse of Indra.

"Have ye forgotten," he cried to them, "how, in the lone Hill Country, ye lay awhile on my breast, fainting almost with rapture, while the large stars were smiling near, and the night hung, still, around? Have ye forgotten how, pale and beautiful, ye stepped through the groves of Nandana; and how Light robed ye in splendour; and the Stars I had laid in your bosoms glowed there, and flamed with a glory that shamed the pale orbs of heaven? Why have ye thrown by your Crowns, whose gems flashed through the ages, witnesses to the past and the future that ye were chosen as the spouses of Indra? What though your slight heads were bowed, and your fragile strength near broken: was not my arm around you? Who would not totter and fail, to be upheld by the amorous Indra? What though your spirits' growth were too swift for your delicate frames? As guerdon for your shortened lives, my Love had made ye immortal!

"But ye have loved ease better than glory! O foolish Ones! ease can never be yours! Ye have tasted an Immortal's Love! And your glory ye have abandoned! Dwell, then, as Exiles and Strangers in this town ye have preferred to the mountains; and, since ye have dreaded the Tempest, endure the torments of the Calm."

And so, in the city of the Uttarakurus, dwell these pale Women with the lustrous eyes, who were once the Beloved of Indra; and they hold no friendly intercourse nor have sympathy with any; each morning gives fresh birth to the wild Desire, that gnaws their hearts; each night finds them in a dead despair; for the pitiless Curse of Mahēndra drives them down to their unhonoured graves!

CHAPTER XII.

THE ANCIENT VULTURE SAMPĀTI.

Chap. XII. *A LARGE company of Monkeys, that had for chiefs Hanuman and Angada, son of the deceased Bālin, paused to rest on the slopes of the Mount Vindhya.

The despondency of Sugrīva's envoys.

It was glorious weather! There was not a leaf, nor a blade of grass, but was saturated through with sunlight, and seemed half delirious with happiness! Our Monkeys, who were, for their part, in very low spirits, looked on this as an insult, heaped on to the afflictions which distressed them. It is indubitable, that there is a satisfaction in contemplating the depths of one's own misery, and in recalling the ill-treatment one has met with at the hands of fate, or of one's fellows. As they sat there, their chins upon their knees, a certain gloomy complacency overspread their countenances.

Angada was the first to speak.

"The time allowed us by Sugrīva, to scour the country for tidings of the Vaidēhī, has long elapsed," he said; "we have failed to discover any trace of her; but, entangled in the labyrinth of the recluse Svayamprabhā, and seeking in vain an exit from the enchanted cavern, we have incurred the penalty of death, with which the Monarch of Apes threatened those who failed to return within one month, to report the result of their search. My innocent Brethren, our fate is sealed! Implore, if ye will, the pardon of Sugrīva : for me, I prefer to die here of thirst and hunger, on this lonely mountain, rather than trust to the mercy of my Father's Enemy!"

"We will die with thee," returned the others; and, with melancholy resolution, they grouped them round the young Chieftain.

Now it chanced that, on a crag somewhat above them, Sampāti, the aged King of Vultures, was taking a midday doze. The firm resolution with which the band of Simians seated themselves, to set about dying forthwith, shook the Mount Vindhya, and awakened the ancient Bird, who, looking over, perceived the group of disconsolate Monkeys.

Sampāti was a very devout Fowl.

"Beyond a doubt," he exclaimed, casting up his eyes, " it is an admirable Wisdom who directs the course of events for my profit! The Immortals have brought these quadrumanous creatures here, and put the thought of self-destruction into their heads, so that, after my long fast, I might delight my appetite with a food I love!"

This pious ejaculation reached the ears of the dejected Monkeys.

Now, one may be heartily weary of life, and even have made up one's mind to be rid of it; but one does not care to have the ways and means made *too*

Chap. XII.
Angada counsels self-destruction.

Sampāti, overhearing this proposal, contemplates a satisfactory meal.

CHAP. XII.

Angada speaks of the Vulture Jatāyu.

Sampāti, hearing this, says Jatāyu was his brother.

easy to one; in such a matter, one likes to choose one's own time and path of exit. So the exclamation of Sampāti was anything but agreeable to our Monkeys.

But Angada was possessed of a shrewdness and sagacity beyond his years.

"Alas!" he exclaimed, in a loud tone of voice, "this lamentable exile of Rāma, how many misfortunes has it not occasioned? Already Dasaratha has perished, and Bālin,—and that inestimable Vulture, Jatāyu! Ah, that was the most grievous of all! Dasaratha was a worthy King, but he was already enfeebled by age; and Bālin had been guilty of injustice; we, too, if perish we must, have failed to accomplish our sovereign's commands; but Jatāyu? that elephant among Vultures was resplendent in honour, and beauty, and virtue, when he sacrificed his life in this cause!"

When he heard that, Sampāti dragged himself to the edge of the shelving rock.

"Do you speak of Jatāyu, the son of Garuda?" he asked; "he who dwelt in the country of the Janasthāna?"

Then Angada turned, and looked up with simulated astonishment, as who should say,—"Is there a Bird, above me, on this mountain?"

"I beseech your Highness," implored the aged Vulture, meekly, "to relieve the anxiety of a brother's heart. I am a bird of a noble race; but, alas! the sun has scorched my wings; and for many years I have been confined to this Mount Vindhya, and have had no tidings of my family. If this illustrious Vulture of whom you speak be indeed my brother, the magnanimous Jatāyu, who dwelt in the Janasthāna, I would beseech one of your company, noble Simians, to climb up hither, and bring me down among you, that I may hear the sad details of his death."

The Vulture begs them to tell how Jatāyu died.

Then some of the Apes demurred, saying:
"Shall we bring this monster down among us, that he may devour us the more easily?"

But Hanuman, Son of the Wind, said:
"He is a Vulture of good family, and treachery is not compatible with high breeding;" and so he climbed up to Sampāti, and brought the large Bird down in his arms.

Then the ancient Vulture turned his dim eyes on Angada. "Tell me, noble Orang-outang!" he asked, "who is this Rāma, for whose sake my brother gave his life; and for whom ye, too, seemed minded, a while since, to die? How has he thus earned the devotion of living creatures?"

Angada answered: "Rāma is a King's son, who loved honour better than his father's crown; that is why he is an exile. As he has been true to his own soul, so has he been just to the lower creatures, whom Brahm made to be his younger brothers. He has despised none; he has not thoughtlessly inflicted pain; he has taken pleasure in winning their simple, trustful love; that is why he possesses, unimpaired, Man's sovereignty over every living race and tribe upon this earth.

Angada relates the virtues of Rāma.

CHAP. XII.

How Jatāyu was slain by Rāvana.

"Rāvana, the Scourge of the Three Worlds, has stolen his Beloved, the beautiful Princess of Vidēhā. The noble Vulture, your brother, was the first to give his life, in seeking to rescue Rāma's Bride from the Demon's clutches. Rāvana slew the gallant Bird in the country of the Janasthāna. We have been sent forth by our King, Sugrīva, to discover the hiding-place of the ravisher of Sītā, and Jatāyu's murderer. Our search has been fruitless; and rather than return to face the wrath of Sugrīva, and the grief of Rāma, we had determined to die, here, on this mountain side!"

Then Sampāti, very sorrowful for Jatāyu's death, drooped his head awhile; and lay, quite still, upon his side; and the Simians, in reverence for his grief, kept silence round him.

Sampāti mourns for his brother.

"Ah me!" he said at length, with a deep sigh, "the empire of the air is large; the earth is a great place; and I have heard it said by birds, who have plunged and dived into it, the ocean seems to have no bounds nor limit! Yet, though a nest is of such insignificant size, it fills the heart more than a whole universe! Up among the crags of the old Himālaya, I used to roost beside Jatāyu; and as we grew to be large Birds, our stony nest could scarcely hold us, and we had to press close, close together; so close, that we could hear and feel each other's hearts beat; and they kept time so nearly, it had been hard to say which was Jatāyu's, and which mine!

"It chanced, one day, that my brother and I being thrilled by the wild air, started to fly a race together, through Indra's world. But when noon came, and the fierce sun looked straight at us, Jatāyu fainted, and tumbled through the air, head foremost! Then, full of love and pity, I outspread my large wings between him and the cruel sun; but the hot beams withered them up; and, maddened with pain, I staggered earthward, and fell on the summit of this Mount Vindhya. Long I lay there unconscious, because my agony had exceeded what life can know; at length I awakened, to the loss of death, without its restful gain. I had no wings; my sight was dimmed; only the sense of pain was left! For some time I remained there, hoping all would be over soon. But death came not! Wearied out with suffering, I dragged myself down the rocky slope, to the entrance of the cavern of the Saint Nisākara. There, leaning against a tree, I waited till the Saint should pass, that I might ask him why death refused to give me rest. Towards even, when the sleepy breeze was hushing the flowers to sleep, Nisākara came walking towards the hermitage; and behind him came a troop of wild animals, lions, tigers, leopards, bears, &c., lovingly escorting the Holy Man to his abode. The Hermit looked at me, with mild pity, as he passed, but he entered the cavern without speaking to me. Then, very disconsolate, I thought to drag myself back whence I had come. But, after a time, the good Nisākara came forth to me, and said, compassionately:

"'I saw two bold, young Vultures, sons of the great Garuda, bound forth, to fly a race through Indra's

CHAP. XII. world. The shape of one of them was like to thine, O poor wingless Bird!'

"Then, mournfully, I told my story.

"'And wherefore hast thou come to me?' asked the Saint, when I paused.

"I looked up into his face with great despair.

Sampáti begs Nisá-kara that he may be released from life.

"'I would have thee ask the Lord of Creatures to let me die,' I said. 'Of what good is life to a Bird who has no wings?'

"'Of what *pleasure*, thou wouldest say,' answered Nisākara, gravely. 'Were thy life of no good, the Lord of Creatures had not left it thee! But I understand that it seems hard to thee; thou art but one of the younger sons of Brahm, and even his eldest-born, Man, frets often at the fact that his own happiness is not the object of his being. Know then, for thy comfort, thou shalt have thy wings given back to thee some day. Wait patiently till the chance be given thee,

Nisákara promises that his wings shall one day be restored to him.

of serving a more noble being than thou; afterwards, thy power to float through Indra's world shall return, and thy love of life shall be redoubled.'

"And so I have lived on patiently. Perchance this noble Rāma may be he of whom the Saint spoke; for if I do not err, I can give you tiding of his lost Queen. But first, I would ask your Highnesses to carry me to the shores of Varuna's[1] world, that I may celebrate the ceremony of lustrous waters, in honour of my deceased brother."

So the Simians led the noble Bird to the seashore; and there Sampāti offered the funeral honours,

[1] Varuna is Lord of the Ocean.

which the rites command, to the memory of the magnanimous Vulture, who perished by Rávana's hand; and he mourned there for the good Jatáyu, and the impressionable Apes mourned with him.

Chap. XII. Sampáti performs the ceremony of Lustrous Waters in Jatáyu's honour.

Afterwards, they carried Sampáti back again to the mountain, and the princes of their company surrounded the kingly Vulture; who, having purified himself in the cleansing waters, was resplendent with beauty, as though youth were returning to him.

"O magnanimous Fowl!" said Angada, kindly, to him; "our lives are, so to speak, between thy claws! If thou canst tell us anything of the Rákshasa, or Ráma's Bride, we may yet escape the cold of death."

"I will give you all the help in my power, noble Simian!" returned Sampáti. "Would that I had the vigour of my early days, and could bear you on my wings to the hiding-place of this Rávana. At least, I can tell you where to seek him. My son, Supársva, who had tended me during my long years of exile, returned a short while back to me, bringing no food, though I had fasted many days. When I am hungry, I am prone to irritation; so I chid Supársva.

The aged Vulture tells how his son returned once with no provisions.

"'Thus it is,' I said, 'that young Birds of the present day neglect their aged Parents! As they wing their way lightly through the air, it never occurs to them,—My Father, that old Bird whose wings are scorched, has had no dinner: or if the thought strike them, they say, most likely, 'Let the old Fowl starve! that way, the trouble of him will be off my shoulders." That is the way with young Birds nowadays.'

O

CHAP. XII.

How Supārsva encountered Rāvana carrying off a daughter of man.

"Then Supārsva answered my reproaches, meekly:

"'My Father,' he said, 'I scoured the country far and wide, seeking some provisions for thee; but all creatures, both eatable and other wise, seemed hiding out of the way of some great peril. Whilst I hung on the air, wondering, I saw a Monster with ten heads, and large swarthy limbs, sailing towards me; and in his arms he held a young daughter of man, clad in bright raiment; who looked like a pure bright Star in the dark bosom of a Cloud! As they neared me, I heard her scream, "Rāma! Help! dear Rāma!" And I hesitated whether to succour her or no. But he with the ten heads cried to me, courteously, to make way for him; and no bird of breeding answers a polite request with a challenge to combat,—so I let him pass. When he was out of sight, crept out of the folds of the air the Bhūtas, the ethereal spirits that float in mist. "Supārsva!" they cried to me, "thou hast been near to death! It was Rāvana, the Terror of the three worlds, who passed thee awhile back! We were all hidden, crushed together, and wrapped away in a shred of vapour: and we trembled for thee, so! But that he held a woman in his arms, the dreadful Rākshasa had not let thee live!" And so, Father, I return to thee, glad that life is mine; though, like thee, I am weary and a-hungered.'

"Now, what think ye, illustrious Apes? Who was this woman like a gleaming Star, that Rāvana held in his embrace?"

"Sītā!" cried the Simians, leaping to their feet.

"What direction did they take, magnanimous Vulture?" Sampāti strove to raise himself.

"At one hundred yojanas hence," he said, "is the sea that washes all the southern coast; there at a hundred yojanas from the shore is the Isle of Lankā, where Rāvana dwells; thither, beyond a doubt, he has carried Sītā."

As he spake, the air was troubled by a sudden tempest, the leaves were blown into a flutter on the trees, and the trunks swayed them forward and back, as though they were about to snap off from their roots. It was Supārsva, returning. He swooped down beside his father; and when he heard the errand of the noble Simians, he confirmed Sampāti's story, and gave them many valuable instructions about the road they ought to take.

CHAP. XII.

The return of Supārsva, who tells the Apes the way to Lankā.

Whilst he was conversing with Angada and Hanuman, little by little, Sampāti felt renewed vigour and lightness thrill him through; and presently, a sudden impulse kindling him, he essayed to fly; and, lo, a spreading pair of wings were his,—and with wild delight he put them forth into the air,—and felt that he had mastery over it once again.

"See! see!" he cried out, in the voice of song, "my wings are given back to me! Oh, the delight! Once more I am upborne by the cool air; the clouds hold out their misty arms to me; the blue sky beckons me to wander there! Once more I shall spring upwards—my feathers ruffled by the pleasant wind—and laugh with the stars because the earth looks small! Once more shall I sink slowly, slowly to the

Sampāti feels power in his wings.

Chap. XII. mountain top, and roost in the old nest among the Himalayan crags—and dream that Jatāyu is by my side, and that I feel his heart answer to the beatings of my own. Farewell, O Friends! Let this favour done me prove that your enterprise shall succeed!"

And with that, he flung himself upon the wind, and Supārsva followed him; whilst the admiring Simians looked after them with straining eyes, until they seemed two specks, soon swallowed up by the blue distance.

CHAPTER XIII.

THE ADVENTURES OF HANUMAN, SON OF THE WIND.

THE Simians are a very impressionable race: one cannot fail to discover that whilst perusing Valmiki's story. It is probable, too, that were one to investigate the matter, one would find that they display the same characteristics now; for evidently human nature has not changed much since the times of which he wrote; —then why should monkey nature have done so?

Their interview with Sampāti had quite driven all suicidal notions out of the heads of Sugrīva's envoys. In fact, they went on their way as merry as needs be, —speculating on what would be the gratitude of Sugrīva, and the delight of Rāma, when they brought them the news that the missing Sītā was found at last,—until they reached the sea-coast.

It was very different then!

Night wrapped the earth; but one could dimly see the huge white-crested Waves roll them up, grimly moaning; then, with a cruel hiss, sweeping back, dragging the stones and shingles with their white foam-fingers! It was not a reassuring spectacle, and

CHAP. XIII.

The army's dismay at sight of the sea.

suggested somewhat forcibly to our heroes' minds, that, whilst it is doubtless desirable to know whither one is bound, it is not precisely the same thing as being landed safe and sound at one's journey's end.

So, not choosing to express their misgivings, yet too dismayed to make any attempt at dissimulation, the band of Monkeys, in doleful silence, came to a standstill, at a little distance from the moaning waters.

"Let us encamp here for the night," said Angada, in a voice that sought to be encouraging; "in the morning we shall be better able to decide what course to pursue."

So they waited there through the night: they seemed to have come to a tacit understanding that their uneasiness was not to be discussed,—but it was not the lighter for that.

The morning did not materially alter matters; except that they could see the turbulent ocean, and judge how far the Isle of Lankā must be off, since the most keen-sighted amongst them could discover no trace of it. Yet, as with nature, so with her children, there is a renewal of life with the dawning of day; besides, there is no encouragement to hardihood like light. So our adventurous Monkeys, still looking dubiously at the heavy, angry-looking mass of waters, so unlike the blue rivers that flowed singing through their native woods, began to question how in the world it might be possible to traverse it;—that was already, you see, a step removed from the hopeless despondency of the preceding night.

Angada looked anxiously from one to the other of his followers, seeking where was displayed the most resolution.

"The eyes of all the Wild Men of the Woods are upon us, comrades!" he cried. "Who loves the honour of his race well enough to undertake this perilous adventure? Which of you, Heroes, dares to leap across this foaming sea, and explore the Isle of Lanka, in search of the Vaidehī?"

At that the gallant Apes, who were ranged in a line along the shore, leant their heads to the right, and looked at the sea;—and then leant their heads to the left, and inspected it that way;—afterwards they all looked at Angada, and none spoke a word.

"It is a dangerous enterprise, I admit," he said, in answer to their mute appeal; "but we are in desperate circumstances already. Do not forget, O Bulls among Apes, that, ere our encounter with that distinguished old Vulture, we had decided to die of inanition, rather than face the wrath of Sugrīva! In what is our position altered now? Come, who will extricate himself and his fellows from this difficulty? Let those who have spirit and energy beyond their comrades step out from the ranks, and we will compare together, that we may know who has most vigour here!"

Then Gaya, Gavāksha, Gavaya, Sarabha, Gandhamādana, Maīnda, Dvivida, Nīla, Nala, Tāra, and Jāmbavat, the most ancient Ape amongst them all, separated themselves from the company.

"I can leap ten yojanas!" said Gaya.

"And I twenty!" said Gavāksha.

CHAP. XIII.

Next morning Angada asks who will venture on this enterprise.

None presenting themselves, he bids the most mighty tell what power is theirs.

CHAP. XIII.

"I should think nothing of thirty!" said Gavaya.

"Nor I of forty!" rejoined Sarabha.

"Fifty yojanas would not alarm me!" said Gandhamādana.

"Sixty would be an easy leap for me!" observed Mainda.

"I have leapt seventy yojanas between sunrise and sunset!" said Dvivida.

"And I eighty between dawn and midday!" returned Nīla.

"Ninety yojanas is the measure of my usual leap!" said Tāra—and flung back his head, as who should say, "Will any of you exceed that?"

"Ninety-two is the average extent of mine!" retorted Nala—putting his face close to the others, with a grin that answered, "Ay, *I* will!"

All confess themselves incapable of springing across the sea.

"Well," observed the venerable Jāmbavat, "my vigour is doubtless much impaired by age; but it seems, all the same, able to surpass the capabilities of this arrogant youth. For all that, this exploit is more than I could accomplish!"

"Or I," said Angada, sadly. "I could leap a hundred yojanas, which Sampāti told us was the distance to Lankā; but of what use were it to Rāma and Sugrīva that I should reach the evil island, and perish there? To return thence would be beyond my power."

"Nay," returned the most ancient of Apes, "let who will go, thou must not abandon us, Angada! Sugrīva may efface from the minds of the frivolous young Monkeys of this court the memory of the redoutable Bālin; but the pride of the warriors and veterans is wrapped up in thee, O Angada! Whilst thou remain amongst us, we are content!"

"Content to perish by my uncle's hand?" asked the young Simian, with a mournful smile.

"If needs be—content even to that!" returned Jāmbavat.

Now, all this while that his companions had been boasting of their energy and strength, Hanuman, Son of the Wind, had observed a contemptuous silence. The venerable Jāmbavat walked up to where he stood aloof, and said:

"How is it, Indra amongst Quadrumanous Creatures! that thou hast no word to say of thy daring, nor strength,—thou who art the Pride of the Simian Race, and who, alone, art capable of this astounding prowess?"

At the praises of Jāmbavat the gigantic Orang-outang seemed to grow and swell in stature; and the eyes of the whole band, turning on him of a sudden, flashed with delighted gladness.

"Step forth, Hanuman!" they shouted; "thou Lion amongst the Wild Men of the Woods!"

Then the noble Son of the Wind laughed lightly:

"This enterprise does not alarm me," he said. "I have a heart not prone to recognize defeat. Look on me, comrades! I am not one whose beauty lies in elegance, nor smooth comeliness; there are some ugly scars about me that do not lend me grace—yet it is on *them* I would have you fix your eyes, and not on my well-proportioned limbs and stature! A large

Hanuman is silent, till called on by Jāmbavat.

The Son of the Wind declares his willingness for this expedition.

CHAP. XIII.
He tells them of his youthful daring, and asks if they can trust him.

carcase is of little value without a will to match, and strong muscles require a fearless spirit to work them. Simians, you know me! I am Hanuman of the broken Jaw! When I was yet a babe, lying in my mother's arms, the ruddy Sun laughed down into my face; and I, thinking it was some splendid blossom, flushed with excess of sap, sprang from my mother's arms five yojanas into air, in my eagerness to clutch the radiant thing. In the fall that happed me then, I broke my jaw. Comrades, I am no longer a babe, and have learned to accomplish what I undertake; but my daring and resolution have not cooled. Say— will you trust this matter to Hanuman of the broken Jaw?"

"We will!" shouted they, till the earth shook and the mountains shouted back, "We will!"

Then Angada wound a garland of scarlet flowers round the neck of the noble Orang-outang, and they led him to the Mount Mahēndra that he might take his spring from thence. When Hanuman planted his feet firmly on the ground to give impulsion to his leap, the great mountain groaned, and, from between its shattered rocks, gushed forth foaming cataracts, that rushed headlong down the precipices, to the destruction of the Nāgas and great serpents, who had their holes and caverns there.

The Simians wish him a good voyage as he springs away from them.

Having addressed one prayer to the Immortals, and bidden farewell to his fellows, the heroic Ape stretched his long arms towards Lankā, and bounded forth upon the air; and all the Simians shouted to him, "Good voyage and safe return!"

THE MOTHER OF NAGAS.

As this highly-gifted Ape sped through the home of birds, his size was developed to an enormous extent, and his tail[1] waved majestically from side to side, like the cloud-signal hoisted by the Storm-god. His shadow, that covered ten yojanas, struck terror into the hearts of all the fishes and aquatic monsters. Then the Nāgas, who made the ocean their home, clamoured to their mother, Surasā:

"Who is this Large Creature, whose shadow darkens our world? Stop his voyage, we pray thee. Devour this Quadrumanous Animal, O Mother of Nāgas!"

So Surasā assumed the form of a monstrous Rākshasī with gaping jaws, and rose up through the water.

"Stop, O colossal Ape!" she shouted to Hanuman; "the Immortals have given thee to me for a meal! Therefore enter my mouth without more delay. Of what avail is it to resist one's Destiny?"

Then, in consternation, Hanuman looked down at her mouth, that was like a yawning cavern.

"Magnificent Parent of Nāgas!" he said, "I am employed on an important errand just now; it concerns Rāma—he who is known as the Friend of Living Creatures. I beseech thee, let me continue my voyage now, and afterwards I will return to be swallowed by thee, if such be the will of the Immortals!"

But Surasā was impatient—or perhaps she thought it possible that Hanuman might prefer another route to return by.

"It is needless thou shouldst be troubled by this

[1] *Vide* Note I.

Chap. XIII.

Surasā bids Hanuman enter her mouth.

The Ape tells her his errand, and begs her to let him accomplish it.

CHAP. XIII.

Hanuman makes himself large and then small, and darts in and out again of Surasā's mouth.

errand, thou whose last hour is so near," she said. "Waste no more time in discussion, but enter my mouth forthwith!"

"Make thy mouth large enough to hold me then!" shouted the doughty Son of the Wind, making himself twenty yojanas in length. But when Surasā saw that, she stretched her mouth to thirty yojanas; whereupon Hanuman elongated himself to forty; the Rākshasī straightway expanded her jaws to fifty; and so they went on, until Surasā's mouth was a hundred yojanas wide!

"Of what avail is all this fatigue?" asked the Mother of Nāgas; "it is evident our force is equal in this matter of expansion; then wherefore give thyself and me this trouble? Yield to thy Destiny without more ado, for I swear by the deathless Gods thou shalt not continue thy voyage ere thou hast entered my mouth."

"So be it," answered the dauntless Ape; and quick as thought reduced himself to the dimensions of a man's thumb—then he slipped into the monstrous jaws of the Rākshasī, and as quickly darted out again.

"Farewell, Surasā," he laughed; "I have obeyed thy behests, and entered thy mouth. I must now continue my voyage."

"Farewell, gallant Monkey!" cried the Mother of Nāgas; "I wished only to put thy ingenuity to the proof."

And having thus cleverly made a victory of defeat, Surasā sank down to her clamorous children.

Now, whilst she felt his Shadow lie on her bosom,

MAINĀKA, THE GOLDEN-HEARTED MOUNTAIN.

the impulsive Spirit of the Sea put back her waves and looked up at Hanuman.

"Ah," she thought, "this gallant messenger of Rāma shall have my aid. For is not this noble Dasarathide the descendant of Bhagīratha, who brought the lovely young Gangā from heaven to be my delight?"

So she whispered to Maināka, the golden-hearted Mountain:

"Hanuman, Son of the Wind, is in peril, Maināka! Thou dost owe thy life to his father: rise up from the depths of my kingdom, O Pearl among Mountains, that the gallant messenger of Rāma may rest on thy summit."

So the golden-hearted Mountain rose up through the whispering waters, all clothed in fluttering verdure, that was shimmering with ocean spray.

But Hanuman thought, "Here is another obstacle to my voyage," and redoubled his speed.

Then the gentle Spirit of the Mountain stood forth on its summit, and cried to him:

"Do not mistrust me, Hanuman. Rest awhile on my Mountain. I have journeyed up through the rough billows to bring my summit near to thee. The kindly Wind, thy father, saved me once from danger;—I should be glad, O noble Hero, if thou wouldst pause upon my Mountain!"

Then the courteous Simian smiled kindly on the Mountain Spirit.

"It was generous of thee, O Maināka," he said, "to force thy way through the waters, to afford me a rest-

The Spirit of the Sea tells Maināka that Hanuman is in peril.

Maināka rises out of the sea to afford him a resting-place.

ing-place. But tell me, why was thy golden-hearted Mountain sunk away thus in the depths of the sea?"

Then the Spirit answered:

"In the early days the Mountains had wings, and could roam through Indra's world. But all creatures were in constant terror lest they should be crushed by these flying monsters; so the great Father, in whose sight life is precious, charged Indra to take their wings from the Mountains. But it is a glorious delight to fly. There is no joy in life to be compared to it. Who would not rather die than lay on one side his wings? So I fled from the God's command. But Indra pursued me, and in his wrath burned my wings by Vajra, the Thunderbolt! And he had slain me utterly, but that thy Father, the kindly Wind, who had fluttered often among my groves and prairies, snatched me up in his arms and carried me to the large-hearted Sea. 'Thou hast known sorrow,' he said to her; 'have pity then and shelter this poor Maināka.' So the generous Sea took me to her breast, and hid me away from the Storm-god. And I have dwelt many years beneath the waters; but when I heard thou wast weary, Hanuman, in spite of my dread of Mahēndra, I came forth to bring thee rest. Stay then on the summit of my Mountain, and then continue thy voyage refreshed."

Then Hanuman raised his hands to his brow and saluted the golden-hearted Maināka with an anjali.[1]

"O magnanimous Mountain Spirit," he said, "I

---

[1] "The cavity formed by putting the hands together and hollowing the palms; being in this form carried to the forehead

had gladly rested on thy pleasant slopes, but I promised my comrades to perform this exploit without taking any repose. But to show I am grateful for thy courtesy—see—I lay my hand on thy brow, in token of friendship. Farewell, Maināka, I must no longer linger; "and with that he continued his journey.

Chap. XIII.

Hanuman thanks the Mountain, and continues his voyage

Then Indra, Lord of the Firmament, smiled down on the golden-hearted Mountain.

"Rest without fear, noble Maināka," he said; "for this kindness thou hast shown to the messenger of Rāma, I forgive thy rebellious petulance about that matter of the wings."

Indra allows the Mountain to remain in the midst of the sea.

So the golden-hearted Mountain, all a-flutter with trees and verdure, remained in the midst of the sea; once more brightened by sunbeams, and sung to by birds and zephyrs.

Meanwhile, an old Rākshasī, by name Sinhikā, who was hungry, saw the gallant Monkey sailing on through the air.

"It is a grateful chance," she thought, "which brings this large creature here, just when my hunger is so keen."

Then she seized the shadow of Hanuman between her claws.

Sinhikā seizes Hanuman's shadow.

The illustrious Orang-outang, feeling himself shaken from side to side, as one who is dragged by the cloak, looked down to the surface of the water, and saw Sinhikā holding on by his shadow, with her large

it is an appropriate salutation to a superior."—*Wilson's Sanscrit Dictionary.*

mouth open wide, expecting him to drop into it; and her bleared eyes shut, because they were not used to look up to the sunlight. So, doubling himself together for a spring, Hanuman darted into the monster's throat, and with his claws tore his way out through the evil creature's back!

Hanuman kills Sinhikā.

So Sinhīka died; and that was a very good thing, for she had destroyed many harmless beings by that way of catching hold of their shadows.

That was the last adventure which befell the heroic Simian ere he reached the shores of Lankā. Swooping down on the beach, the daring Son of the Wind rested awhile to take breath, and to reflect on what it behoved him to do next.

Reaching the coast of Lankā, he meditates on what course to pursue.

"Here I am, in this Isle of the Rākshasas!" he laughed; "to traverse the sea has been a mere excursion of pleasure to me! Now, how am I to accomplish the rest of my mission, and discover the retreat of Sītā?"

So, taking his chin in his hand, the Orang-outang pondered the matter over.

"These Rākshasas are a crafty race," he said; "were I to be discovered in their city, they would doubtless suspect my errand; for they know the virtuous disposition of the Simian, and his sympathy with such of the human race as deserve encouragement. Were I to enter Lankā, clothed in this colossal shape, the curiosity of the public would infallibly awaken the apprehension of Rāvana's confidential followers; so, though it hurts my vanity, I must assume more modest proportions."

Accordingly Hanuman reduced his size to that of a cat; and when night had let down shadow on the town, he sprang on to the ramparts, and, crouching down, surveyed the position from thence. The magnificence of this city, built by Visvakarman himself,[1] and of as surpassing splendour as Amarāvatī, the residence of Indra, filled the intelligent Orang-outang with wonder. As the sky is adorned by its constellations,[2] so was Lankā embellished by its glorious palaces, high as the summit of Kailāsa, and white as the clouds in autumn. There seemed no end to the turrets that tore through the blackness, and carried their wreaths of balconies close to the home of stars.

Chap. XIII. At nightfall Hanuman commences his search.

At this hour the streets were silent; but from these gorgeous palaces issued the sound of music, and the tinkling of the nūpuras of the dancing girls came sweetly to him on the still night air. As he left his post, and crept stealthily along the deserted streets, the delicious odour of savoury dishes provoked his appetite, and revealed to him how merrily these jovial Demons whiled away the night.

Some houses he passed, though, accepted the soft dimness night gave to them, and were very still; love reigned within them; that was why they respected the sweet mystery of night.

Hanuman, profiting by his small size and great agility, examined every dwelling he passed; and, as you may think, saw some strange and memorable sights.

[1] Visvakarman, the Celestial Architect.
[2] This comparison is translated from the Ramāyana

P

CHAP. XIII.
Hanuman enters the Palace of Rāvana.

At length he neared a magnificent Palace, the colour of the sun itself; pinnacles, that seemed so many beams fretted into radiant lace, ran up far into the sky; whilst garlands of lights, like fire-blossoms of every colour, twined round and amongst its turrets. As a great forest is guarded by its lions,[1] so was this splendid Castle watched over by savage Rākshasas, clad in sombre garments, and armed with weapons of every description.

These gigantic sentinels paid no heed to the diminutive Ape; if they observed him at all, they despised to exhibit any sign that so insignificant a creature had attracted their attention. So Hanuman slipped by them easily enough, and found himself in the midst of a vast and lofty corridor.

Keeping as near the wall as possible, the adventurous Son of the Wind crept on towards a distant apartment,—whence proceeded vague music, such as the sea-nymphs make when whispering to the pink conch-shells.

He comes to the Harem of the Rākshasa.

Strange light flashed on him as he put back the heavy curtains and looked in,—it glanced from the walls, that were studded with dazzling gems, which seemed so many lustrous eyes keeping guard over those who slumbered there! Like roses that had swooned to earth,—drunk with the wealth of their own perfume,—a cluster of lovely Maidens, sunk in softest cushions, lay stretched on the floor, in calm and smiling sleep. Their soft breath tossed their filmy veils, and

---

[1] This comparison is translated.

played with the airy draperies that floated round them, like the mist around the star of morning!

Here, some beautiful, unconscious Child smiled in her sleep, letting her little pearly teeth glance from between her rosy lips:—There a more thoughtful Maiden sighed in the tender mournfulness of some dream of love:—One had flung her graceful arms around a dear companion's neck, and, even in slumber, seemed to be caressing him, with pretty childlike grace; and with her blooming upturned mouth to be pleading, "Kiss me, please!"

"Is not this Svarga, the retreat of the Gods?" asked Hanuman, amazed.

But then he remarked a certain voluptuous frailty, that fluttered over all this loveliness, and gave it a tinge of light and warmth unlike the ethereal radiance of heaven.

"No doubt this is the Harem of the Monarch of Rākshasas," he said.

And this time he was right in his surmise.

So, curbing his admiration, and doing his utmost to look sternly on the slumbering Maidens, the virtuous Ape stepped on into a further apartment, whence issued a sound like the muttering of distant thunder.

It was Rāvana snoring.

Thrown on a splendid couch, adorned by wrappings of gold and crimson, the magnificent Rākshasa lay sunk in a deep slumber. His brawny arms were thrown back upon his pillow, and his large breast, with its many scars, was bare; his ten mouths were open, and his ten noses were snoring, all at the same time;—so

Hanuman reaches Rāvana's chamber.

CHAP. XIII.

Mandôdarî, the Diamond among beautiful Women.

it was no wonder if the chamber were shaken by the noise.

Nevertheless, beside him, on a lower couch, whose wrappings were of blue and silver, lay Mandōdarī, the Diamond amongst beautiful Women, in a still and peaceful sleep.

Her smooth young cheek lay upon her little hand, —the other hand hung carelessly over the couch's edge. The long, trailing lashes lay, so still—so still, —one might almost have feared this was a vision and no living woman,—only the mouth smiled! The little dimples in the cheek smiled too, and seemed to say: "Do not be afraid! Though I have such a wide, low brow, and such sombrous waves of hair, I am not stern, nor sad; only passionate,—not at all stern!"

For a moment, dazzled by her unusual charms, Hanuman thought: "Can this be Sītā?" Then the impossibility of the Vaidehī's being thus tranquil and contented as another's bride than Rāma's occurred to him.

Hanuman's conscience misgives him, and he quits the Palace.

Also, at the same moment, his sensitive conscience misgave him.

"I have gazed on the consorts of Rāvana, in their sleep," he thought. "Is not this an abominable fault?"—so, with modestly averted eyes, the conscientious Monkey picked his way cautiously by the lovely sleepers; then slipping through the long corridor, and darting by the unwary sentinels, found himself once more alone with the night.

He soon assured himself that he had been over-scrupulous: he had not intruded himself into the

Harem for any personal gratification, but in the service of Rāma.

"And where should one look for a woman, save in the company of women?" he said.—But this was an awkward reflection; for it suggested that he had, as yet, failed to discover anything with regard to Sītā.

Walking on, absorbed in reflection, Hanuman had by this time reached the ramparts of the town. He seated himself on one of them, in a very melancholy frame of mind.

"Why have I come here?" he exclaimed, drooping his tail, and dejectedly gnawing his claws. "The Vaidehī is not at Lankā; or perhaps, unable to bend her to his pleasure, this monster, Rāvana, has devoured her! How am I to return with such mournful tidings? The noble Rāma will assuredly die of a broken heart, when he learns the fate of his large-eyed Sītā. Lakshmana will not survive his brother; and then, what chance of life will there be for Bharata, or Kausalyā, or any one of the Queen-Mothers? Sugrīva, the Monarch of Apes, will assuredly expire under the weight of these misfortunes; and Tārā, seeing thus a second husband abandon her, for the empire of Yama, will, beyond a doubt, choose to perish on the same funeral pile! Angada, who has so tender a love for his mother, will certainly refuse to live without her;—and if he die, I do not see, for my part, how the whole Simian tribe will be able to exist any longer! I will never be the herald of these misfortunes. On these shores I will erect a pyre, and forthwith take my departure for Yama's world, amid its purifying flames!

Marginal note: CHAP. XIII. *Hanuman enumerates the evils that will result from his unsuccessful search.*

CHAP. XIII.

Or I will espouse the ascetic life of an anchorite in these woods of Lankā. The joys of life are over for me!"

Thus the impulsive Offspring of Marut bemoaned himself, shedding copious tears the while. Presently crept over earth and heaven a faint grey light, promising the advent of dawn.

"It will never do for the Rākshasas to find me here," thought Hanuman. So, springing to his feet, he fled for shelter to a grove of flowering asokas that was near at hand.

Hanuman in the asoka grove.

The trees were all in blossom; and, as he passed under them, they pelted the mournful Simian with their yellow petals. The birds, too, sang with the evident desire of encouraging him; and, as he neared a little thicket of oleanders, a River, that ran through it, began to murmur in the most significant manner.

Somewhat consoled, Hanuman climbed into a sinsapā-tree, and concealing himself in its foliage, waited till day should break. When at length the sun drowned the dreamy grove in a golden shower, he climbed to the topmost branch, and scanned all the pathways of the wood.

He sees a group of hideous Rākshasīs.

The impulsive Son of the Wind could scarce contain his exultation at the sight which met his eyes! At a little distance from him stood a group of hideous Rākshasīs. Some of them had large, flapping ears, in which they might have utterly enwrapped their faces—which would have been a good thing, so ugly were they; others had no ears at all. Some of them had snouts like wild boars, with yellow projecting teeth; the noses of others grew out from the centre of their skulls. Some were quite bald; others had long shaggy hair, that hung in tangled wisps, or stood out straight round their distorted faces!

In fact, it was quite curious to see how much variety there can be in ugliness.

Like a Star, in the clutch of the monster Rahu, Sītā sat, surrounded by these virulent Hags! The Simian had no doubt about it; the moment his glance fell on her, he knew who it must be; there were not two such visions of loveliness!

Sītā is sitting among the Rākshasīs.

She was seated on the grass; her black, silky hair streamed down to the ground, and lay, heaped up in a gleaming mass, beside her; her eyes were downcast; on their long lashes gleamed two brilliant tears, that would not fall; her mouth—it was so small a mouth to be so sad!—trembled a little,—that was the only movement; her arms stretched forth,—her little hands clasped,—were flung heedlessly to the side of her, and had fallen upon the glossy coils of hair: she seemed quite to have given up hope!

She wore a silken tunic of a soft, bright, amber hue; its tint had not lost its tender brilliancy, as the Recluse, Anasūyā, had foretold; and surely it was the holy Woman's favour which made the youthful Princess still retain the blooming charms that Rāma loved; for grief is more cruel to beauty and youthfulness, as a rule.

Presently, swung through the wood the sound of music and merriment; and, drawing nearer and nearer, the silver laughter of the nūpuras of the

CHAP. XIII.
Rávana comes to visit Sítá.

Dancing Girls. It was the Lord of Rākshasas, escorted by a brilliant company, who came, thus early, to visit his captive.

Like some beautiful, wild creature brought to bay, Sītā sprang to her feet; and shaking her long hair round her, stood,—one hand holding to the trunk of a tall tree, the other held to her breast to still its tumultuous beat. As the Lord of Rākshasas advanced to her, alone,—the others falling back somewhat to let him speak unheard,—Sītā met his amorous gaze with bright defiant eyes, and Hanuman saw the mighty Rāvana pale and tremble somewhat; whilst the frail and timorous Sītā never shrank nor faltered;—and thus he learnt how much more powerful is love than fear.

Then the Rākshasa, his impassioned eyes bent on her, spoke, in softened tones:

The Rākshasa seeks to win Sítá by fair promises.

"Why dost thou gaze on me thus wildly, Sītā? Have I been so harsh to thee? Child! child! am I thine enemy because the love of thee has so taken up my soul that life has no delight nor warmth save in thy presence? The tears are heavy on thy lashes, O my Queen! And yet joy beckons thee. My wealth, and power, and all the pleasant luxuries of my court, are thine; stoop only to gather them, my fawn-eyed Sītā! Let me hang jewels in thy silken hair, and robe thy peerless form in raiment like the sun! Thou shalt choose to wait on thee the loveliest maidens in this isle of Lankā; my Lords and Warriors shall be thy slaves; and I, their Monarch, will sit me at thy feet, and read thy pleasure in thy dark large eyes! Is there a caprice or fancy in all thy little, wayward heart, that I, Rāvana, could not gratify? Power is dear to the heart of woman:—Come to my breast, O my Beloved, and I will set thy beauty on a throne, whither it shall draw to the light scorn of thy small feet the adoring homage of the universe! Sītā, my Love, —the life of man is scant:—There is an ardour in the pulse of youth that strains towards a sense more rich and large than any human mind can comprehend! Here I invite thee to this fuller Life, my Bride! Transcend the limits that narrow thy delight,—and, in the frenzy of a love like mine, drain utterly the draught that mortals barely sip, — and know the blaze and splendour of that Fire, of which all human passion is but the scantest spark!"

CHAP. XIII.

The clear untroubled gaze of Sītā seemed to look far on into the sunlit distance, and quite to lose the dark Rāvana, who, shaken by his strong emotion, stood before her with heaving breast and flashing eyes, and hands that clutched each other desperately.

"You speak to me of passion," she said, "and Fire; of throbbing pulses, and longings for more full delight: Love has another sense to me!—It is a Radiance, not a Flame, and kindles rather Light than Heat! Has it a Heat at all? It may be—yet, if it burn, it is that it may shine the more; and passion is only Love's minister! Love!—I have known its rapture,—O King of Rākshasas! I, your Captive, have known its rapture! Think you to waken unholy Fire in the breast where reigns a Star? to drag down to lust a heart that has been given wings? to tempt, by voluptuous heat,

Sītā's answer.

CHAP. XIII. one who has known the glory Brahm has made the Heaven of Life, where luminous souls flash out like suns, letting day in upon the gloom?"

Then, holding out both her arms, as though she beheld the Dasarathide standing before her in the path, she cried out loud:

"Rāma, my Lord! my Life! my Love! he thought this! This Rāvana thought to blow my passions to a flame by his impure desires! Rāma, my Lord! I who have held converse with thy high soul, and learnt to aspire in following thy thoughts,—he sought to beguile *me* by the unholy ardour of his words! O Rāma, O my Love! this Demon with a thousand crimes upon his head, a thousand vices in his soul, who has torn me from thy dear arms and brought this anguish into both our lives, comes to me and says: 'For all my guilt, and vice, and for the wrong I have done thee, and because there is not so vile a creature in the empires of water, earth, and air, *therefore* love me, Sītā!'—and, O my Lord, he stands there as though he doubted of my answer!"

Sītā defies Rāvana.

She finished with a little scornful laugh,—that died into a sob.

In her defiance and her scorn of him a new charm was given to her beauty:—this radiant creature, with the warm young arms outstretched, the quivering upper lip, and eyes that flashed through the mist of tears, had for him a more bewildering enticement, even, than the bashful Sītā, who had welcomed him in the hermitage of Panchavatī.

"Hear me!" he cried, in broken, passionate

RÁVANA ASKS SÍTÁ'S PITY.

tones: "revile, upbraid, taunt me,—yet be my Bride! *Chap. XIII.*
I do not ask thy love—only forbear to hate me. Oh, *Rávana asks for her pity.*
thou shouldst not hate me! They say the heart of
woman opens soon to pity; I, the Lord of Rákshasas,
would claim, at least, thy pity. Hearken—I suffer!
Thou art a torture to me! Fevered, maddened
almost in thy presence, away from thee I am wrung
by fiercer torments than any known in Tartarus! Is
my suffering nothing to thee? Wilt thou not have
mercy? Wilt thou not let me seek to conquer thee by
tenderness? Oh, if there be any womanly softness in
thy nature, show me, at least, this mercy!"

Flung on the earth, he dragged him to her feet,
and covered them with kisses.

Sítá answered:

"I belong to Ráma, as radiance to the sun:—Give *Sítá's reply.*
me back unto my Lord:—Repair this fresh guilt thou
hast taken on thy soul, and I will plead with my
Beloved, and say, 'Forgive him, Ráma, he is penitent.'
Thus will I show thee mercy!"

Then the Demon sprang upright and scowled
darkly on her.

"Thou shalt never see this Ráma more," he said; *Rávana's wrath.*
"on that score set thy mind at rest! Let me warn
thee, too, to make less frequent mention of a name I
hate!"

Then Sítá broke into disdainful laughter:

"Thou dost well to hate it!" she said; "the name *Sítá taunts Rávana.*
of my Avenger—Ráma! Ráma! Ráma! He will be
here anon,—a Lion among the sons of men! The
Gods are with him, and the hearts of all the living

CHAP. XIII.

creatures upon earth! Oh, there is a force in virtue that cannot fail; for this world is Brahm's, and Justice is His Law! Tremble, tremble, Rāvana, for Rāma is upon thy traces! Thou art a great Serpent, O King of Rākshasas! But he is like Garuda, the Sovereign Eagle, who rids the earth of vipers!"

Stung by her reproaches, the Rākshasa turned on her with a look of menace:

"Thou art a woman," he said. "Thy insults reach me not:—otherwise, thou shouldst die, here, and now! But mark me well, O Vaidehī; I have sought to stir thy ambition—the quality is not thine; to touch thy heart—thou hast closed it against me. There remains one other weapon—*fear!* I give thee one month to bend thee to my will; thou shalt yield then! I say thou shalt yield—if thou choose not rather *to die!*"

The Rākshasa threatens her with death.

And with that he turned him on his heel. Then Mandōdarī, the Diamond among beautiful Women, crept near, and smiled up into his face.

"Wherefore waste fire on ice, my Lord?" she said. "Love, unrequited, is all torture; but 'tis pleasant when flame rushes forth to meet flame!"

Her bewitching glance drew his down to her. As he put his arm round her the Dancing Girls broke out a-singing, and led the way back to the monarch's palace.

Now all this while the Listener in the sinsapā-tree had had much ado to restrain his indignation. It was fortunate that Rāvana had been too absorbed, and the Rākshasas too alarmed by their Sovereign's portentous countenance, to have thought for anything else;

otherwise they must have remarked how overhead a small Ape was for ever shifting his position and springing from bough to bough. As it was, Hanuman saw the hideous females once more gather round the Janakide, who, spent by her late excitement, and overpowered by Rāvana's parting threat, had sunk fainting on the grass.

Then Vinatā, or the Crooked One, leant over the half-conscious Sītā.

"My child," she said, "thou hast shown clearly thy fidelity to thy husband. Thou hast been very virtuous, and I commend thee; but it is an error to carry aught to an extreme; the moment for thee to yield has come, and such an excess of constancy resembles foolishness. Really, this Rāvana is a consort to be proud of. Is he not of colossal stature? Has he not ten heads? Not to speak of his wealth, and rank, and power! Come, be reasonable, and put this miserable Rāma out of thy head."

Here Vikatā, or the Bowlegged, interposed.

"What is the good of all this talking?" she shrieked. "If she still resist, let us tear her limb from limb, and devour her, to prove our loyalty to the King of Rākshasas!"

Then a third Rākshasī, Hayamukhī, or the Horse's head, approached the cowering Princess.

"Be not wilful, Sītā," she said. "Youth and beauty are capricious gifts! If even the Dasarathide discover thy hiding-place, who can say that he will care to take thee back to him, when grief and fasting have impaired thy charms? Respond to Rāvana's flame

CHAP. XIII.

The Rākshasīs consult together, and Trijatā warns them not to harm Sītā.

then, and enjoy some pleasure while there is yet time!"

Again the Bowlegged interrupted her.

"We have already shown too much forbearance," said this fury; "let us make our meal of her forthwith! When I first looked on this young Sītā—What round plump limbs, I thought; would she not make a delicious feast? It must have been a presentiment! Come, my Sisters, let us make everything ready for the repast!"

Weeping bitterly, the drooping Vaidehī cried, "Do what you will with me! Why should I care for death—I, who find life only in my Rāma's presence?"

The Rākshasīs, who had been strictly charged by Rāvana not to injure a hair of Sītā's head, though they might seek to intimidate her by the most dreadful threats they could think of, drew off a little, and began to consult in low voices how they might conquer their captive's resolution. Now amongst the company was an old Rākshasī, named Trijatā.

"Beware," she said, "how you illuse the Princess of Mithilā. Last night I dreamt that Rāma, the Dasarathide, slew all who had oppressed or tormented Sītā. Only the irreligious and the foolish disregard dreams! Besides, watch now her countenance; see with what intentness she is listening to the singing of some bird; the Immortals give the lower creatures power to converse with her; that is a proof they regard her with favour!"

At that, the Rākshasīs looked nervously at Sītā, who had raised herself to a sitting posture; and, pushing the heavy hair back from her brow with both hands, was listening with a rapt expression of countenance to a bird, who sang to her of Love, and Home, and Rāma! Alarmed,—her keepers retired out of earshot; sitting them down in a circle, they began to consult, putting their heads close together.

"Now," thought Hanuman, springing from bough to bough in his agitation, "is a favourable opportunity. If only this lovely Princess do not take me for an enemy, and, with the excitability natural to her sex, scream or faint ere I have time to explain my errand!"

The intelligent Ape bethought him that the name of Rāma would be the most efficacious method of assuring Sītā of his friendly intentions.

"Alas!" he exclaimed, in an audible voice, "there is a virtuous Prince, named Rāma, who is in sore affliction! An evil Demon has stolen the Bride that was the treasure of his soul! And, ever, this noble Prince laments in the hearing of all living creatures: 'Who is there that will bear a message to my Queen? Who is there that will bid her wait, and trust, and believe my love is strong to rescue her? Who is there that will tell my Darling I shall be with her soon, and hold her once more folded in my arms?'"

Then Sītā, a joyous wonder beaming on her face, looked up into the sinsapā-tree. But as she saw there only a little Ape, watching her with anxious eyes, her gaze fell mournfully.

"Ah me!" she sighed, "it was a dream!"

To attract Sītā's attention Hanuman tells aloud the grief of Rāma.

CHAP. XIII.
Sītā thinks her mind has failed her.

And then she sighed again, "Ah me! Yet it was not a dream! Too surely am I sitting within this Wood of the asokas; and the cruel Rākshasīs are still in sight! My brain is failing me! I am going mad!"

And so she clasped her temples with her hands, and seemed to be struggling to convince herself of somewhat.

"Now, here's an awkward thing!" said Hanuman, swaying him forward and back in his anxiety; "if she persuade herself that her senses are astray, she'll take me for a Phantom, and not credit a word I speak!"

But presently, to his surprise, Sītā clapped her little hands together, and broke into a low, wild laugh.

"Madness?" she cried. "So be it then! The great good Father has pity on me:—'I cannot stop the march of Destiny, my Child!' he says; 'but I will so wrap thy senses round, that they shall not be wounded by the rough edges of events.' Madness,—say men. Unconsciousness of pain,—say I. I joyously accept the pity of my generous God. Yes, since it brings me tidings of my Love,—since it tells me that Rāma goes a-mourning for his little Bride, and seeks, and soon, soon, will find, and rescue her, since it brings this comfort, in the dark,—gladly I put forth both my hands and snatch this blessed madness to my soul!"

Nevertheless she questions the Ape in the sinsapā-tree.

So, with a sweet, wild smile, she looked up once more into the tree.

"Who art thou, little Ape, with the eager eyes?"

she asked. "Did I not hear thee speak of Rāma a short while back?"

The Son of the Wind hastened to reply:

"I am Hanuman, the humble friend of Rāma. I have leapt across the sea to bear a message to his Queen. If, radiant Lady, you be this Sītā for whom the Dasarathide grieves, take comfort; for your Lord will soon snatch you from Rāvana's hand!"

Sītā, still scarcely crediting her ears, implored him to tell her of her Lord.

"How fares he?" she asked, eagerly; "and the gallant Lakshmana, the Warrior with the laughing eyes? What has chanced since Rāvana carried me off from Panchavatī?—Thou dear little Monkey with the brilliant eyes, tell me, I pray thee, all that has befallen!"

Then Hanuman related how the two Heroes had found the noble Vulture, Jatāyu, who, ere expiring, told them their enemy was the dreadful King of Rākshasas; further, he told of Rāma's alliance with Sugrīva, Monarch of Simians; and of how he, Hanuman, had been sent forth, together with a powerful company of Apes, under the direction of Angada, to scour the country of the south. Then he told of their despondency, and their meeting with the aged Vulture, Sampāti; and of how he had been chosen to traverse the sea, and explore the isle of Lankā.

"And doubt not, Princess, whose beauty is like the smile of Lakshmī," said the courteous Ape, in conclusion, "that Rāma and Lakshmana will fly to thy rescue: for joy has left them with thy presence.

CHAP. XIII.

Hanuman offers to carry Sītā back to Rāma.

Rāma no more delights in the beauty of woods, nor flowing rivers: when dawn crimsons the sky, he sighs, 'Alas, my Sītā!' And when night spreads her azure wings, he weeps, 'My Love! my Sītā!'"

Then the Princess of Mithilā exclaimed:

"O Hanuman, sweetly bitter are these tidings thou dost bring to me! I grieve to hear my Rāma suffers; yet scarcely could I wish his pain were less, since that were to desire him callous to my fate. Thou magnanimous little Ape, return swiftly, and bear my tender greeting to my dear Lord; salute the brave Lakshmana too from me, and charge them to lose no time—to lose no time! Rāvana has given me but one month to live!"

At that the impulsive Simian sprang down from the sinsapa-tree.

"You shall not stay an hour in this monster's power!" he cried. "Trust me, O Lady with the starlike eyes! Mount on my back: I will carry you across the sea, and bring you to your Rāma with no more delay!"

"Thou Pearl amongst Quadrumanous Creatures," answered the Vaidehī. "Though thy heart is mighty as the valiant Indra's, thy body is but as a slender cat's: how couldst thou bear my weight, good Hanuman?"

Straightway the puissant Orang-outang resumed his huge proportions.

"How think you, August Lady?" he cried; "am not I able to bear your slender weight?"

Then Sītā saluted the mighty Son of the Wind:

"O illustrious Simian," she said, "thy power equals thy courage! Yet—be not angry with me, friend—I will wait here for Rāma. Were it not almost a shame to him that another should save his Bride? Tell him his little Sitā awaits him in captivity, and will owe her rescue to none other than her Beloved!"

"Be it as your Highness wills!" returned Hanuman, a little sadly. "Only, I pray you give me some message to the noble Rāma, that he may be assured I have seen and talked with you."

Dropping her eyes, bashfully, she answered:

"Once, when our exile was young, and we dwelt on the Mount Chitrakūta, I lay in my Hero's arms, and looked up into his face with love. We were alone, on the hill-side—seated beneath some flowering shrubs. In sport, my Rāma plucked a branch, laden with many blossoms, and with their crimson sap traced a tilaka[1] on my brow. So, later, I rested my forehead on his breast; and when I raised it, lo! a red tilaka was stained there too! And we laughed greatly at that; for our hearts were full of love—and when that is so, a small thing gives happiness.

"There was none near; only the still blue overhead, and round us the fluttering leaves. Tell Rāma of the red tilaka; he will know that you have seen his Beloved."

So Hanuman performed a pradakshina round the Janakide; and bade her, respectfully, farewell. After-

---

[1] "*Tilaka*, a mark on the forehead and between the brows, either as an ornament or a sectarial distinction."—*Wilson's Sanscrit Dictionary.*

CHAP. XIII.

Hanuman tears up the asoka grove.

Ravana orders his guards to capture or slay Hanuman.

wards, he sprang up into the tree again, and prepared for his return. But there was hot indignation in his heart.

"Shall I quit this isle of Lankā, and do no damage to this Rāvana, who has dared to menace the peerless Bride of Rāma?" he said.

So he set about tearing up the trees in the asoka grove, and to defacing the monuments and grottoes it contained. In alarm, the Rākshasīs ran up to Sītā, round whom the impulsive Hanuman had left the trees still standing.

"Who is this destructive Ape?" they asked. "You would do well, O Princess, to answer us without disguise!"

Sītā answered:

"Since my captivity in this island I never know who any one may be: you Rākshasas change your forms at pleasure; how can people recognize you?"

When they saw she would tell them nothing, they ran to their monarch, crying:

"A monstrous Orang-outang has broken down the grove of asokas; but we are ignorant whether he has held any intercourse with Sītā."

"Capture or slay this mischievous Ape!" said Rāvana, negligently, to the Kinkaras, his guards of honour. So eight thousand warriors rushed forth against the noble Simian. The agile Son of the Wind sprang out of their reach, into a mighty nyagrōdha-tree; then bounding on to the roof of a lofty palace, he uprooted a huge column of marble, and swung it round his head with a shout:

"I am Hanuman, the Messenger of Rāma!" he cried. "Death to Rāvana, and this evil city of Lankā!" Then, hurling the pillar amongst them, he crushed the whole army of Rākshasas; so that the ground was covered with their mutilated corpses! Then the excellent Hanuman sprang up to an arch, that headed the doorway of the Palace, shouting: "Victory! victory! Live Rāma, and Lakshmana, and Sugrīva, the Monarch of Apes! I am Hanuman, the Marutide; a thousand Rāvanas could not conquer me!"

His cry of triumph reached Rāvana. Still somewhat negligently, the monarch turned to Jambumālin, the illustrious son of Prahasta.

"Do not return till thou hast slain this Boaster!" he said.

Rolling his eyes, that rage had crimsoned, the fierce Jambumālin rushed forth to the combat.

Hanuman quietly awaited him, perched above the doorway.

The Rākshasa aimed an arrow that struck the heroic Ape on the cheek; with a shriek of rage, the illustrious Orang-outang uprooted a sinsapā-tree, and hurled it at Jambumālin. But the Rākshasa shot it into splinters with his arrows! Then Hanuman tore up a sāla-tree, and flung that at his enemy; but again the Demon broke it into fragments, and with another arrow wounded the Marutide on the breast.

Seizing, again, his marble pillar, Hanuman made it

spin round his head, as he shrieked, in an ecstacy of rage; then, dashing it down on Jambumālin, the tiger amongst warriors, he crushed the gigantic Rākshasa into a formless mass—dreadful to look upon!

Chap. XIII.
Hanuman kills Jambumālin.

Having thus destroyed his enemy, the triumphant Orang-outang sprang up to his post above the doorway, shouting:

"Victory! victory! Long live Rāma, and Lakshmana, and Sugrīva, King of the Simian tribes! Who comes next to seek a greeting from Hanuman, Son of the Wind?"

When he heard the taunting shout, the mighty Lord of the Rākshasas sprang to his feet in wrath. "Who will slay me this insolent Ape?" he cried, with his eyes aflame.

At his summons bounded forth a hundred young warriors, the sons of the ministers, eager as coursers of war for the combat. Armed with numerous weapons, and mounted in splendid chariots, drawn by prancing steeds, impatient for the battle-shout, these young Heroes sallied forth against the gallant Simian.

Perched in the aperture above the door, Hanuman waited till they were within an easy distance. But, when they bent their bows, he disconcerted their aim, by springing, suddenly, into the air, far, far above the reach of their arrows;—then, with a hideous screech, that froze their hearts with terror, the dreadful Son of the Wind, pillar in hand, swooped down on them, like Garuda upon a nest of serpents; and, ere they

The sons of the ministers slain by Hanuman.

could break their serried ranks, or think of flight, he massacred them, as Indra's hailstones beat down the flowers!

When he beheld these young warriors stretched, lifeless, at his feet, the victorious Simian established himself, as before, on the summit of the doorway.

Then five Warriors of renown, Yupākhya, Virūpāksha, Durdharsha, Praghasa, and Bhāsakarna, implored the Monarch of Rākshasas to send them forth against Hanuman. Rāvana bade them go.

"But," said he, "beware of regarding disdainfully this Quadrumanous Creature! For my part, I am convinced he is a Being of a superior race, who has disguised him in the body of an Ape. I have encountered many heroic Simians; as, for example, Bālin, the Monarch of all Apes, whose vigour won my esteem in past days; but even that Elephant among monkeys was incapable of the daring shown by this insolent giant!"

Having obtained the Monarch's permission, the five Heroes leapt forth to the encounter, eagerly as the flames rush up to devour a sacrifice.

When they saw the colossal Orang-outang, calmly surveying them from his eminence, rage took possession of their hearts.

Durdharsha first aimed an arrow that struck Hanuman in the neck; then he lashed his steeds nearer, and as he advanced covered the undaunted Ape with showers of arrows. But when the Warrior was close to the doorway, Hanuman, with a sudden cry, let himself fall upon the chariot; it was shivered

Rāvana sends five of his best warriors against Hanuman.

Durdharsha slain by Hanuman.

CHAP. XIII.

Yupākhya and Virūpāksha slain.

Praghasa and Bhāsakarna meet the same fate.

Aksha, Heir to the throne, is sent next against Hanuman.

into fragments, and the Rākshasa hurled from it lifeless!

Then up rushed Yupākhya and Virūpāksha, with clubs and mallets upraised: but the gigantic Ape tore up a lofty palm-tree, and beat down first their weapons, then themselves; so that swiftly they joined Durdharsha in Yama's world.

Enraged at the spectacle of their comrades' fate, Praghasa and Bhāsakarna, armed, the one with an axe, the other with a lance, rushed at the intrepid Simian, uttering cries for vengeance. Hanuman, stained by blood, arrows everywhere quivering in his colossal frame, waited for them to come near; then, seizing a huge rock, all overgrown by large shrubs and plants, he hurled it at his adversaries with a shout of fury.

The two Warriors disappeared beneath the whelming mass.—Once more Hanuman was alone, but for the corpses of his foes.

Seated again in the aperture, the mighty and indomitable Ape seemed like the Death-god, reposing after the slaughter of worlds.[1]

Then Aksha, the Heir to the throne, a youth merely, but who had already made himself a name in the battle-field, flung him at the feet of Rāvana.

"If thou hast any love for me, Lord and Father," he cried, "grant me next to combat this Hero!"

Then Rāvana, smiling to see his ardour, motioned the youth to be gone. Seizing his bow, the gallant Aksha sprang into his golden chariot, and lashed

[1] This comparison is translated.

his milk-white coursers on, amid the bodies of the slaughtered Rākshasas. When the noble Son of the Wind saw this new opponent, his heart was filled with compassion.

"This Hero is still but a Child," he thought; "it were against my will to slay him in an hour when life seems filled with beauty!"

Hanuman is touched by Aksha's youth and seeks to spare his life.

Accordingly, wishing to spare Aksha, the gallant Orang-outang sprang to the ground, and struck the chariot a blow with his clenched fist, so that it was overturned, and the snow-white horses lay dead amongst its fragments.

But, nothing daunted, the gallant youth sprang up from amid the ruins, and, by virtue of his great self-macerations, bounded up through the air to meet Hanuman.

"Well done, O valiant Simian!" he shouted; "but as yet thou hast not triumphed! Come, let us measure our strength here, in Indra's world!"

When he saw that Aksha's daring only augmented with the combat:

"There is no help for it," said the magnanimous Ape, regretfully. "A fire that increases [1] cannot be despised; I cannot let pity for this hot-headed Boy imperil my mission!"

Aksha's valour makes Hanuman put forth his strength, and the youth is slain.

Thereupon he seized the young Warrior by the feet, and flung him down head foremost.—So Aksha, the lion-hearted young Warrior, the joy of the city of Lankā, lay cold and dead on the breast of the one earth-mother!

[1] This comparison is translated.

CHAP. XIII.

When he knew that, a cry of grief and rage mounted up to Rāvana's lips:

"Indrajit!" he shouted; "Pride of my heart! dost thou hear? Aksha, thy brother—the Boy with the sunny smile—is dead! Up, Warrior whose limbs are like young fir-trees! Avenge me thy brother's death; capture or slay this monster! Destiny has kept this triumph for thee, who hast already made the world quake by thy exploits! Indrajit, return not without this murderer!"

Indrajit goes forth against Hanuman.

Then, gravely Indrajit rose; and, when he had performed a pradakshina round Rāvana, he leapt into his chariot, drawn by three savage lions, whom he urged forward by dreadful shoutings.

Hanuman, leaping into the air, hovered above the chariot, taunting the fierce Indrajit, and making sport of his arrows.

But Indrajit, in compensation for long years of self-inflicted penance, had received a miraculous Arrow from the hands of the Immortals. Wounded by this supernatural Dart, the intrepid Son of the Wind, his strength paralysed, his vigorous limbs numbed by an icy chill, fell crashing down to earth, and lay, incapable of motion, on the ground.

He wounds Hanuman with a magic arrow and has him fettered.

Then, from every palace and hovel in Lankā rose up a shout of triumph. Forth rushed the Rākshasas and Rākshasīs, eager to jeer and deride an Enemy they no longer dreaded. A troop of officious Demons bound the gigantic Ape with cords, and fettered him with iron chains, so that his hands and feet were linked together.

Then the stern Indrajit, who had kept silence through the combat, as now, in this hour of triumph, drew forth the miraculous Arrow, and holding the end of the cord by which he was bound, motioned Hanuman to follow him.

Chap. XIII. Indrajit leads his captive before Rávana.

"If only he conduct me into the presence of Rávana!" thought the intelligent Ape. "When one is in the hands of Demons, it is better to have to deal with their King; who is at least *intelligently* malevolent, and cognisant of self-interest."

He soon perceived that his wish was about to be realized; for Indrajit paused before the splendid palace he had entered the preceding night. The Rákshasa, dragging Hanuman after him, entered the Assembly room, where sat Rávana amid his courtiers. The Monarch, robed in gorgeous raiment, was seated on a throne of crystal. On a daïs at his feet were his four principal ministers; and again, at their feet, sat the princes and first lords of the Rákshasas.

The mobile nature of the illustrious Ape was much impressed by the external splendour of the Rákshasa's court.

"Beyond a doubt, were he not a slave to injustice, this Rávana were a magnificent Prince," he thought. Rávana, sternly and in silence, bent his twenty terrible eyes upon the Orang-outang; then, turning to Prahasta, the most eminent among his ministers, he commanded him to question the Prisoner.

Then Prahasta, standing forth, demanded:
"Who art thou, Warrior? Assuredly thou art not what thou seemest, a simple Ape. Wherefore hast

The minister Prahasta questions Hanuman.

CHAP. XIII.

thou assumed this disguise? What cause has brought thee to this isle of Lankā? Art thou sent hither by Indra, or Kuvēra, or Yama? Wherefore didst thou destroy the asoka grove? and why hast thou slain the Servitors of the resplendent Lord of Rākshasas?"

Then Hanuman answered, courteously:

"Illustrious Rākshasa, I am that I seem. This Orang-outang's body is the wonted garment my spirit wears. I am called Hanuman, he of the broken Jaw: I come here on a mission from my Sovereign, Sugrīva, King of the Simian Tribes."

Then, bowing to Rāvana, he addressed himself to the Demon with the ten heads:

Hanuman tells his errand.

"Resplendent Lord of Rākshasas!" he said, "if I destroyed thy grove, it was to gain admittance to thy presence. As for thy Servitors, they assailed me—not I them; and if I slew them, it was in self-defence. My King—Sugrīva—greets thee, O Rāvana, and wishes thee prosperity and health. He has charged me to inform thee, that thou hast, unlawfully, in thy island, a daughter of the human race, the august Sītā, Princess of Mithilā, wife of Rāma, the Dasarathide—he who is known in the three worlds as the Friend of Living Creatures. My Lord, Sugrīva, doubts not this woman has been brought here by an error. 'Is not Rāvana a king?' he says; 'has he not much knowledge and science? Cannot he procure beautiful maidens to wife, if such be his pleasure? It is not possible that he has stooped to covet the wife of another!' Therefore he says—send back this illustrious Lady to her lawful spouse, and make, by presents and excuses, what amends lie in thy power, to the noble Rāma,—and he, Sugrīva, will intercede with the Prince for thee.

"On the other hand, my Sovereign says, if thou refuse to give back this Sitā, then know that there is war between the Simian tribe and thee! Know that, from all nooks and corners of the earth, monkeys, of every race and breed, will flock to the battle-cry of Rāma! Know that Lakshmana, the gallant brother of Rāma, has terrible renown; his enemies fall before him as the forest trees before the tempest! Know that men and animals, and the elementary forces of the universe, are with Rāma; that the Immortals are with him too; that his own great soul has the heroism and power of a God's, and that before its wrath this splendid town of Lankā and thou, its Lord, will vanish as foam before a gale!"

Maddened by the audacious words of Hanuman, Rāvana's eyes flushed a cruel red.

"Lead this insolent Ape forth from my presence," he shouted, "and let him die ere an hour have passed!"

But when Vibhīshana, the noble brother of Rāvana, whose nature revolted against the depravity of the Rākshasas, heard that Hanuman was condemned to death, he hasted to fling himself at the foot of the throne.

"O magnificent Rāvana!" he cried, "do not do thy fair fame this discredit! The life of an ambassador is sacred; be this Ape never so guilty, it were to harm thy reputation to slay him. For, Hanuman dead, what Rākshasa would dare take thy defiance to Rāma? And if he hear not from thee, will not the Prince attribute thy silence to fear of him?"

The Monarch was silent awhile, pondering with scowling brows. Then a cruel smile overspread his countenance.

Rāvana commands that Hanuman's tail shall be set on fire.

"Thou sayst well, Brother," he exclaimed; "to slay this vile Creature were an error. But he shall not go unpunished. Vanity is a characteristic of monkey nature; and his tail is ever a matter of fond satisfaction to a Simian's mind: let my Servitors, without delay, set fire to the tail of this Hanuman. So shall this precious Rāma behold his envoy become the laughing-stock of all living creatures!"

At these words of Rāvana, six vigorous Demons seized on the poor Hanuman. When they had dragged him out of the palace, they proceeded to envelope the beautiful appendant, in which he had always felt great pride, in cotton; then, having saturated it in oil, they applied to it a lighted torch.

Having been told what was going on, the malicious Rākshasīs, who had charge of Sītā, dragged her into the streets of the town.

"Thy Friend—that large Ape who broke down the asoka grove—is about to have his tail set on fire!" they said, jeeringly.

Then the tender-hearted Sītā, clasping her two soft palms together, whispered, under her breath:

Sītā's prayer to the Fire.

"O Fire! ruddy Fire! beside whose flame I vowed to be fond and true to Rāma—if I have kept my vow, be good to Hanuman!

"O Fire, that art so pure, and yet so warm! if Rāma's soul be clear and eager as thyself, pity his friend; be good to Hanuman!"

Then the Fire, leaping up in a bright golden flame, played round the tail, as though it were performing a pradakshina, and did not burn it! And thus it answered the gentle Princess:

"I am good to Hanuman!"

Presently the Marutide began to marvel.

"How is this? They have set fire to my tail; yet does it feel no ill, but only a soft warmth, which caresses its tip most pleasantly!"

When he understood that this was because of the intercession of Sītā, his courage and daring revived. He bethought him of a plan to be free of his bonds. Reducing his size to that of a grasshopper, he stepped out of them easily enough, and swiftly resuming his gigantic proportions, he shouted aloud:

"I am free once more :—Hanuman, the fearless Son of the Wind!"

Terrified by this miracle, the Rākshasas fled, screaming, before him; and soon the heroic Simian was left standing alone by the gateway of the town.

"Even so," he laughed, "I would fain do one more stroke of work ere taking my departure."

So saying, he sprang on to the roof of the nearest dwelling; and lashing his tail, round which the fire still played, from side to side, soon set the palace in a blaze. The kindly wind blew the conflagration into fury; so that soon all Lankā was wrapped in flames! Then a terrible apprehension flashed across the impetuous Monkey's brain.

"I have forgotten to warn Sītā!" he thought. "My Queen, the lovely Vaidehī, whose eyes are like the dreamy lotus flowers, will perish here!"

And, without more ado, he was about to fling him also into the angry fire.

But just then a second thought came:

"If, at her intercession, the flame respected even my worthless tail, how much less would it dare to injure the precious Bride of Rāma?"

So, much comforted, he rushed to the cluster of trees still standing, where once was the asoka grove; and there he found Sītā, safe and sound, with a dash of sunlight in her dreamy eyes; whilst the Rākshasīs crouched, shivering, round her. Once more Hanuman renewed his assurances of returning soon with Rāma; and having received more messages, for both the noble Dasarathides, he left the Princess sadly, often looking back, and often repeating: "We shall soon return!"

Then he climbed the Mount Arishta, and stretched out his arms towards the opposite shore. As he bounded forth, on his homeward journey, he gave one shout of triumph; and Angada and the other Apes, hearing it, said:

"Hanuman, the invincible Marutide, has succeeded in his mission, or he would never have this voice of thunder!"

CHAPTER XIV.

NALA BUILDS A MOLE ACROSS THE SEA.

"My loyal Wild Men of the Wood," said Rāma, the Dasarathide, to the faithful Simians who surrounded him, "ye have heard the story of this magnanimous Son of the Wind. Can ye not fancy how my impatient heart already rushes forth to where my Princess, with many longings, waits for me? Friends—if I have your love, let us delay our march no longer!"

Chap. XIV.
Rāma appeals to the Simians, and asks them to set forth without delay.

When he heard the tremor in Rāma's voice, Sugrīva, the affectionate Simian, knelt down to him.

"Thou hast our love, O dear Prince!" he said, "and we will march forthwith: do thou direct us. Because thou hast treated us as friends, it pleases us to be thy servants."

Sugrīva bids Rāma determine the order of their march.

As their Monarch spoke, the whole Band shouted for joy that the time for action was come, and Lakshmana handled his mighty bow, and laughed aloud. Then all gathered round the noble Dasarathide, to hear the order he would have them keep. Standing on a little hillock, his eyes surveying the host, Rāma issued his commands.

CHAP. XIV.

"Let Sugrīva be in the midst of the army," he said; "a King is the centre round which the people gather. Nīla, with a chosen band, shall precede the host; at its head shall march the giants Naya, Gaya, Gavaya, and Gavāksha; as in the prairie the large Buffaloes lead on the herd. Let the noble Simian named Rishabha, because he is a Bull amongst Apes, command the right wing; the left shall have for chief Gandhamādana, whose impetuous valour is like that of an elephant in the season of the rut. Mounted on Hanuman, as Indra on the celestial Airāvata, I will follow; and near me Lakshmana, borne by the illustrious Angada, shall seem a second Siva, carried by the supernal Bull! Jāmbavat, Sushēna, and Vēgadarsin shall protect the rear. Thus, if it seem good to thee, O magnanimous Lord of Quadrumanous Creatures! will we determine the order of our company."

"Let the noble Rāma be obeyed!" cried Sugrīva.

The enthusiasm of the Wild Men of the Woods.

But though the chiefs quickly assumed the posts assigned them, they had much ado to keep up any sort of discipline amongst the impetuous Wild Men of the Woods. Shouting and leaping, they made the forest tremble again, and wakened all quadrupeds and fowls, who had retired for the night, with their loud cries of:

"Long life to Rāma, the Beloved! Death to Rāvana, the Enemy of Living Creatures!"

Then the little Birds within their nests, and the blameless animals from out their dens and holes, answered:

"Oh that it may be so! Oh that the just may triumph!" *Chap. XIV.*

Amidst the turbulent Band, Rāma moved on, as it were, deaf to their loud shoutings; seemingly unconscious that he was the cause of their enthusiasm. Since the loss of his Beloved there was a vague sadness habitual to him; life had lost colour and distinctness—he told himself. Lakshmana, who alone ventured to break in upon this absorption, pointed upwards to the starlit sky.

"My Brother," he said, "mark how, through the night, the heavens smile down. Seems it not a promise that our expedition is pleasing to the stars? See the Maharshis,[1] whose light is kissing through the air; and Trisanku,[2] the Rishi among Kings, our Ancestor, who flames there aloft, and whose beams fall here upon my hands; and the pure and still Visākhās,[3] whose calm eyes rest on us with such a peace! Surely the stars are gentle? Would not there be a tremor in their gaze if evil threatened the fragile Sītā, whose beauty is as dreamy as their light? As a rule, night hangs grief upon the world; yet it seems as though to-night the fair earth smiled behind her veil of shadows! Note, too, how, as we pass, the trees shake away sleep, and open out their blossoms into the dim light, spilling the perfumes it is their wont to hoard up for the sun. Rāma, my dear Lord, amongst these genial signs canst not thou hold high

Lakshmana seeks to encourage Rāma.

[1] *Maharshis*—constellation of the Great Bear.
[2] *Trisanku*—*vide* chap. iv. p. 70.
[3] *Visākhās*—stars situated in the constellation of the Scales

CHAP. XIV. thy heart? Thou art marching now to conquer back the Radiance of thy life!"

"Ay," he answered;—"meanwhile I suffer in the dark."

On, through the winding pathways of the forest, and over the trackless steeps of the Mount Vindhya, marched the Simian host, taking no rest till the coast was reached. There they encamped, full of perplexity about the transport of this large company to the shores of Lanka. Followed by the faithful Lakshmana, Rama climbed the Mount Malaya, and looked far across to where a wall of blackness bounded the white, wrinkled sea. Presently his fortitude broke down.

Rama's lament.

"So long!" he cried, his two clasped arms held out. "So many Hours quite lost! So much of Fervour and of Beauty missed! How shall all this be given back to me—since Life itself is short,—too short for Love? Ye joyous Gods, look down—see, at the best, how transient is Man's lot. Each moment spends it; Time drives him ever on, and at each step—weeping—he leaves a fragment of his soul! Can he turn back to gather them? O deathless Gods! these joys that have thus fallen, fallen from my life, can I—the Slave of Yama—turn back to gather them? When the grey, dreadful Cloud sweeps on, with resolve to quench my heat of being, will the o'erwhelming mass be stayed awhile, because I have been mulcted of half my days? Shall it be counted me how many suns have failed to rise on me, because my soul was, oh!

so drenched with tears, it could not taste the flush and glory? Or shall the nights be given me, for rest, that I have paced the lonesome wood, fire eating through my heart, whilst dark-winged slumber overspread the earth, and held all else in peaceful trance? O just, large-hearted Gods, who meet men at a Moment, face to face—drawn down from highest Heaven ye—we raised from abjectness to the central air, to taste the Divine weakness, the human Apex, *Love!*—since that ye know the Ecstasy, have felt the Pain sublime, say, how shall all the treasures of my Sītā's love, her sweet caresses, and gentle whispered words, her smiles, that broke up my manhood's gravity, her tears, that held my heart back from growing stern, and that mysterious union of wedded love, which thrills sense through with spirit, and takes man into Nature's inner soul, showing him the Halo that dwells upon her Laws; how, how can this be compensated? If even I bear the burthen of my life, and all the slow, torturing delay a war involves, upheld by hope of winning thee again,—yet, yet, my Sītā, of these long hours of my youth, spent in the dark and chill for lack of thee, have I been robbed—and yet am I bereaved!"

Thus mourned he, and Lakshmana dared not essay to comfort him; there was a passion in his grief that warned off sympathy.

In a while his mood changed. He flung him, face downwards, on the cliff, and spoke so low, that through his voice was heard the sobbing of the waves.

CHAP. XIV.

Rāma calls to Sītā that he is near her, and a voice answers she is conscious that he is.

"My Love — my Child," he said; "my Little One with the large wistful eyes! '*thou dost wait for Rama,*' '*thou dost long sore for Rama*'—didst thou speak thus, O gentle One? Thy Rāma is not far—not far from thee, my Dove! And they did give thee but one month to live? Only one month—thou little frightened Bird? Beloved! Beloved! before the month be passed my arms shall be around thee. Be not afraid; let not the ugly Rākshasīs crush thy timid heart! Sītā—canst thou not *feel* thy Lord is near?"

He ceased. To Lakshmana was no sound, save the sobbing of the waters, and the low moaning of the wind; but to Rāma's ears came the words: "I feel my Lord is near!" And, comforted, he put his arm about his brother's neck; and the two came down the mountain side together.

Now, during their absence, the Monarch of Apes, accompanied by Hanuman and Angada, had gone down to the beach to watch how the waves, like unwieldy creatures at a boisterous game, rushed up, one after the other, their white, unkempt hair of foam streaming madly on the wind. The cold light of early morning was already stealing over sea and sky. Presently, sailing towards them overhead, they beheld a monstrous Cloud, that took form as it drew nearer, and appeared a colossal Rākshasa, from whose dusky wings fell sinister shadows. Hanuman recognized Vibhīshana, Brother of Rāvana, the Scourge of the Three Worlds. He was followed by four other Demons, armed like himself, with different sorts of weapons.

The arrival of Vibhīshana.

"These malignant Creatures thought doubtless to surprise us in our sleep!" exclaimed Sugrīva. "Let us at once alarm the camp."

But Vibhīshana called to them:

"Do not fear me, magnanimous Orang-outangs! I have come here to ally myself with Rāma. Often have I sought to persuade my cruel brother to restore Sītā to the noble Dasarathide. Thus have I earned his enmity; and Rāvana is vindictive and malicious. In peril of death, then, I have fled his court, and am come to implore the succour of this Prince, who is known as the Friend of Living Creatures!"

Now Sugrīva was far from being convinced of the sincerity of Vibhīshana's professions. However, he at once recounted to Rāma what had taken place.

"This Rākshasa requests an interview with thee, O Elephant among men!" he said; "but do not thou trust him, my Prince. It is more likely that Rāvana has sent him hither for our ruin, than that he seeks protection from his own brother! Give the word, noble Rāma, and we will forthwith slay this traitor!"

"Nay," interposed the noble Angada, "let us not slay him, ere we have proved his treachery. If the magnanimous Rāma permit, I will question this Vibhīshana, and discover the true motives of his coming."

"That were difficult," said Hanuman. "Thinkest thou, Prince among Simians, that one who would stoop to treachery would shrink from falsehood? For my part, I believe this Rākshasa has

Vibhīshana says he has come to ally himself with Rāma.

The Simians mistrust him.

CHAP. XIV

Rāma says it is not lawful to reject a suppliant.

heard how Bālin was slain, and the throne given to Sugrīva, and has thought, 'Who can say, but if I serve Rāma, the sovereignty of Lankā may be mine?'"

Then Rāma, who had listened to them all, spoke:

"There was, we are told in the Vedas, a Vulture pursued once by an Eagle. Seeing no refuge, he called to the Dove, and implored her to give him shelter. The gentle Bird did not hesitate, but concealed her natural enemy in her nest; and that was accounted right by the Gods. My Friends, it is not well to doubt another; the true heart trusts! Nor is it well to turn from any suppliant. He who allows his enemy to perish for want of succour, loses to him his merits of past virtue, and is burthened by the other's faults; this, too, is written in the Vedas. For me, the oath of the Kshatriya[1] has never released my memory. 'I promise,' said I, then, ' to make the security of all living creatures my care; and to spare in battle the Enemy who, imploring mercy, says: 'I yield me!' Bring, then, this Vibhīshana before me; were it Rāvana himself, I could not refuse him hospitality!"

Whilst the others hung their heads, Hanuman ran and fetched Vibhīshana; and when he was near to Rāma, the Rākshasa laid down one by one his weapons of warfare, and his followers did the same. Then they prostrated themselves before the noble Dasarathide, and Vibhīshana said:

"I have lost friends, and power, and country; but

[1] Oath of the Kshatriya—*vide* Note 1.

if the noble Rāma will let me serve him, I shall regret none of these."

At that, the Raghuide[1] raised him courteously, and embraced him on the brow; and when the impressionable Simians saw that, their enthusiasm was kindled, and they shouted:

"Long live Rāma, the Beloved, and his new Ally the mighty Vibhīshana!"

Sugrīva and the other chieftains now gathered round the Rākshasa, to consult how the passage of the army was to be effected.

"Is not the illustrious Rāma a descendant of Bhagīratha, by whom the beloved Gangā was led to the arms of the ocean?" asked Vibhīshana. "Let this heroic Prince claim a safe passage from the generous, though turbulent, Sea: she will not refuse it him."

"Nay," said Sugrīva, "Indra himself could not conduct so vast an army across this world of waters, unless it were spanned over by a bridge."

"If that be so," cried Lakshmana, "we will forthwith set to work, and fetter these restive billows with a bridge ere the day be done!"

"Thou dauntless Lakshmana!" returned Rāma, with a mournful smile, "the thing is not so easy! Without her leave, this boisterous Sea cannot be spanned; and even so, not one, but many days' toil will it take, to reach the shores of Lankā! Yet, as Vibhīshana says, this generous Ocean owes us a favour. I will down to her shores forthwith, and seek an interview."

[1] *Raghu*—son of the Sun-god, and ancestor of Rāma.

CHAP. XIV.

Rāma seeks an interview with the Spirit of the Sea.

So the sinless Prince went down to the beach of silvery sand, torn through, here and there, by dark and jagged rocks; and here he made a couch of sacred grass, and knelt there, taking neither food, nor drink, nor any sleep at night.

And ever he kept his gaze fixed on the shifting waters—until his eyeballs ached, and vision was a pain. The first day he saw nothing—nothing save the dark, vaulted waves, with ashen manes, who burst out of the Sea's profounds, and roaring ever on one note, rolled up to him dark matted coils of weed, that seemed the hair of drowned men! Night came on slowly, slowly; but the monotonous roar slept not. White Birds, like Phantoms, whirled round the Watcher's head; there were some stars on high, that seemed to shudder; out far upon the watery desert, a lambent, phosphorescent flame flickered and played fitfully amid its terrors. Then came the dawn—and with it the ocean's mood was hushed; blue grew its waters; the ripples there seemed but so many smiles; still no sign for Rāma. The sun sank down into the flushed wavelets, and night came on again. A fresh day dawned—still there was no sign!

On the third day there is still no answer

On the third day Lakshmana broke in on Rāma's solitude.

"No answer yet, Brother?" he asked.

The noble Raghuide sprang from his knees with flashing eyes!

"No answer, O Lakshmana!" he shouted. "Because I have been patient, and shown gentleness, I am a scorn to this ignoble Sea! There are on whom all just persuasions are thrown away, and to whom one must ever speak in words of menace. Give me my bow, Tiger amongst Warriors, and my arrows, like fiery serpents! My wrath shall overwhelm this ungrateful Sea, who forgets all she owes our race; my darts shall search the depths, and reach her active fish, with brilliant scales; her sharks, and whales, and lazy monsters, who love not motion; her coral reefs will I break down, and destroy her palaces of dazzling gems! Thus will I teach her I am powerful, though I stooped to speak of friendship."

Chap. XIV. Rāma losing patience threatens the Sea-spirit.

So saying, the wrathful Dasarathide shot an arrow into the deep heart of the main, and the Queen of flood and river flung up her arms of surge; and crocodiles and huge monsters, unknown before to air, were upheaved and hurled against the sky.

Then the small fish, whom she loved, came in shoals to their Queen, imploring her not to provoke the Dasarathide further. The Sea comforted her children, and putting on one side the waves, rose, beautiful and wild, attended by four dolphins with breath of flame. Robed in nacreous azure, that had the pearly lustre one finds in shells, garlands of scarlet flowers amid her heavy hair, soaked through, and dashed with spray,—she with the lustrous eyes, the Sea-spirit—stood on the darkling waters, her hands raised to her smooth brow, to pay the Heroes the reverence of an anjali.

The Spirit of the Sea appears to Rāma.

"Rāma," she said—it seemed the song of waters on sultry nights when the moon's kisses ruffle the som-

CHAP. XIV.

The Sea-spirit bids them construct a mole.

brous blue—" it is not well to loose thine anger thus. The Earth, the Air, the Light, have each their province; I, too, have mine. We gods are but the eldest-born of God; in the beginning He laid a Law on us, by some called Nature—we obey; man only chooses to assert that he is free—*to err;* for us, the Will of Brahm is our necessity. I cannot quit the order laid on me in the early days; my billows may not be fettered by any bridge : but build a mole across to Lankā, and I will give thy Simians a safe passage to Rāvana's Isle. Let Nala, son of Visvakarman,[1] who has inherited his father's skill, construct this mole. I will prevent my sharks, and crocodiles, and other monsters from interfering with the work; my impetuous waves, too, will I hold back. This will I, Rāma, for love of thee, and gratitude to those who gave thee life. Let not this bring me dishonour in the world of men. Not from cupidity nor cowardice do I give thus a pathway through my kingdom, the home of dangerous monsters and innocent bright-scaled fish ; if, for love's sake, I let thee ford my depths, do not despise me, O Hero with the sinless soul !"

Rāma and Lakshmana bowed them low before the beautiful Goddess of the Sea; when they rose, the fair Spirit had sunk back into her unfathomable world.

Without delay the Dasarathides told the Simians of the promise of the Sea. Then turning to the colossal Ape, Nala, Lakshmana asked :

[1] Visvakarman—*vide* Note 2.

"Whose son art thou, Bull amongst Quadrumanous Creatures?"

Nala laughed.

"Once, up in the hill country," he replied, "Visvakarman, the celestial architect, met my mother, the beautiful Ape, on the mountain of Mahēndra. Her unusual charms won his favour; I, noble Raghuide, am the issue of their union, and my father's skill is mine!"

"Also, it is to thee we will confide this structure," returned Rāma.

So all the company of Apes, shouting in their eager joy, spread them over the face of the country, uprooting sālas, and bamboos, and asvakarnas, and huge trees of every description; breaking off rocks, and rolling up mighty stones for the building of this mole, which was to chain Rāvana's Isle. Sugrīva, leaping from brow to brow, flung down crashing mass after mass he had torn from the mountains; Angada broke the summit of the Mount Dardura, and hurled it into the abyss! Under the direction of Nala, a hundred thousand Apes leapt into the passive waters, laden with shrubs and stones; and in the liquid waste, as though by miracle, surged up a solid path, that grew ever, like some huge serpent, stretching it slowly towards Lankā.

The Rishis, the Siddhas, the Gandharvas, and Garuda the Monarch of Fowls, hung overhead, held in admiring wonder by this stupendous spectacle. Indra sent fleecy clouds, to refresh the toiling Simians with bright rains, and the good Marut gave them fresh

Nala tells his parentage.

To him is entrusted the direction of the builders.

The construction of the mole.

CHAP. XIV.
The mole is finished.

breezes, that they might not faint beneath the great fatigue.

At length the mole was done; and a mole of ten yojanas' width parted the vast ocean-field, and bound fast the evil isle of Lankā to the southern coast.

"Who has bound with a chain these coasts together?" asked the Charanas and Vidyādharas in amaze.

"Rāma!" shouted the Simian band. "He is marching at our head to rescue Sītā with the starlike eyes."

CHAPTER XV.

RĀMA AND LAKSHMANA, WOUNDED BY INDRAJIT, ARE RELEASED FROM THEIR TRANCE BY GARUDA, KING OF BIRDS.

NIGHT. Rāvana, the Scourge of the Three Worlds, stood alone upon the ramparts of the pleasant town of Lankā. When they had told him that his enemy had made a pathway through the trackless sea, and in a few hours, at most, would reach the island he had thought impregnable—he had laughed.

*CHAP. XV.
Rāvana, learning that his enemies have traversed the sea, knows that his time has come.

That was when he stood surrounded by his courtiers; now that he was alone, shadows round him, and in his soul dense blackness, there was yet a sneer upon his lips, and bitter mockery in his eyes. Scorn for the Gods, for man, for nature, for himself, had swayed his life ; Scorn, *the master-passion of the Fiend*, now reached its triumph hour, and, in a burst of evil exaltation, mocked at despair itself !

For he was not deceived ; he knew his Hour had come.

Standing there, with folded arms, he watched the Simian army coming ashore in serried companies, and ranging themselves along the beach. The distance and the dimness lent a weird terror to the sight.

CHAP. XV.

Ravana in his despair shows no repentance.

He consults the Magician Vidyujjihva.

The Rākshasa enters Sītā's prison.

No sound was heard; the shore was too far off for any tramp of feet to reach that solitary Watcher.

At length the Rākshasa spoke :

"It is near," he said. " The more reason that I should be swift : Love first—then Revenge ! After, if needs must, Death !"

And so he left the ramparts.

When he reached his palace, he sent for the Magician Vidyujjihva, and the two spent the night in close consultation. At first hint of dawn, the Monarch of Rākshasas, followed by the Wizard, sought the clump of trees which Hanuman had spared out of the asoka grove ; and where, in a cavern, hidden away by oleanders, rich in blossoms, the Vaidehī was kept a prisoner.

Motioning Vidyujjihva to await him without, Rāvana pushed on one side the flowering boughs, stepped lightly by the slumbering Rākshasīs, and entered the inner cavern. The pale morning had not penetrated here ; yet a strange light irradiated the crypt. Lustrous stalactites hung from the roof, and their liquid radiance touched with sheen the leaves of the twining plants that clung to the rocky walls ;— there, too, gleamed a spray of crystals, that looked like dewdrops, through which light smiled.

This tearful splendour seemed to concentrate itself about the youthful Princess.

Darkness upon him, the Rākshasa paused on the threshold, watching her. She sat, wrapped in her sombrous hair, the soft silk amber of her garment peeping through its heavy waves : one arm, bare save for its golden bracelets, was thrown across her lap :—the beauty and the roundness of this arm troubled the enamoured Demon. Sitā did not stir, yet she slept not; her large, mournful eyes watched the cavern wall, with a fixed, hopeless stare, which proved that the long captivity had broken her young spirit down. Even when she saw Rāvana standing there, his fiery gaze bent on her, she only shuddered, and turned her lovely face away; to reproach him now, or to seek to escape from him, was beyond her power.

Sitā in her prison.

The Rākshasa knelt down beside her on the cavern floor.

"Sitā," he prayed, and the consciousness of approaching death lent a wild pathos to his voice, "the time has come for thee to yield! Must I have risked my all in vain? Nay,—thou SHALT listen to me! What did thy Boy-Love, Rāma, to win thy childish heart? 'Tis certain he sought it not; chance led him to the country of Vaidēha: and if he snapt the Bow of Siva, it was not love for thee which lent him ardour. Janaka gave thee to him as one gives a warrior a chariot, or a horse, in recompense for valour. But I,—my life itself have I not spared to purchase thee! For thee, have I provoked the enmity of all living things; for thee, have I defied the Gods, and outraged man; for thee, have I fought, and sinned, and suffered,—ay, and do suffer now! Thou art mine, Sitā—mine, by right of guilt, and sacrifice, and loss! Mine,—my own sweet Conquest! Into one deep abyss have I flung wealth, and power, and life. Time filters

Rāvana enumerates the risks he has incurred for her sake.

CHAP. XV.

Sītā calls on Rāma, and Rāvana says he has been slain.

The Magician throws down a Head like Rāma's.

through my fingers ;—by Heavens ! I will be paid the Price !"

As he approached still nearer, Sītā sprang to her feet.

" Rāma ! " she cried, " my dear Lord—help ! " .

" Look not to him for help," said the other, sternly. " Call on him no more, O Vaidēhī ! Thy Rāma is dead ! "

A passion of terror swept her against the rocky wall : she dragged the hair back from her face, and stood looking at him, with wild, dilated eyes.

" Dead... " was shuddered between her paling lips.

Rāvana broke into a cruel laugh.

" He crossed the seas," he said, " to murder me, and to destroy this town of Lankā. But, ere he had the time, my young warriors surrounded him, and slew him. So, ho ! Vidyujjihva, bring me here the head of the Dasarathide thou thyself didst sever on the battle-field ! "

Then the Magician rushed into the cavern, and flung on the floor a Head, soiled with blood, and gashed by many wounds; but which yet bore a resemblance to the noble countenance of Rāma. He threw down, too, a mighty Bow, which seemed the one Visvāmitra had given to the Boy-Warrior long ago.

Powerless to scream, or faint, or die, held motionless by horror, Sītā remained, staring at the hideous sight.

" What can a Dead Man for thee, Pearl of Beauty ? " asked the Demon. " Mourn for him ;—waste thy youth away ;—weep thine eyes dull ;—moan thy sweet voice harsh;—beat thy fond breast with passionate hands:— what then? Will he or know, or care? My Sītā, life is more transient than a dream, since those who waken from it, or enter on another vision, forget the past has ever been. It is well to bury grief for those who have put off memory; Rāma is lost; there is no Rāma! Wilt thou weep for the Non-existent? Do men sing to the Deaf, or show colours to the Blind? That were less folly than to mourn the Dead! Since there is none to share thy grief, nor to be grateful for it, take pleasure to thy heart; divert thee with the living whilst thou mayst; brim thy days full with joy—for time is passing—each moment is somewhat lost: O large-eyed Queen, Life is not long enough to waste an hour on grief!"

His words were meaningless to her. At this moment she flung up her hands: "Dead!" she shrieked; and fell, rigid, to the earth.

Rāvana sought vainly to restore her to consciousness. In desperation, he called in the Rākshasīs;— whilst he stood there, muttering curses on the feeble wits of women, a Messenger came to summon him to the Council, to hear the fortunes of the army he had ordered to march at dawn against the invaders.

Now, amongst her guardians was an elderly Rākshasī, named Saramā, whom the beauty and misfortunes of the gentle Princess had touched with pity. When the Demon had departed, she took the fainting Sītā in her arms, and, bending tenderly over her, whispered comforting words in her ears.

"He is not dead, my gentle Singing-Bird," she

Saramā comforts Sītā.

said; "thy Hero is not dead. It was a cruel trick of magic, meant to conquer thee by robbery of hope. Open thine eyes, be not afraid, oh, fragile as the lotus-flower! See, see! the ugly thing has vanished; it was but a lying vision. Rāma lives, and is near thee even now!"

The Head vanishes.

At that the fluttering heart of Sītā took courage; she dared, once more, to look around; and sure enough the pale Head, with its cruel crimson streaks, had vanished.

Then Saramā told how she had heard Rāvana and the Wizard plan this scheme for persuading Sītā her Hero was no more. Further, the kindly Rākshasī narrated the landing of a vast army, that seemed to have sprung from the bosom of the sea.

"And," added she, "there is among them a warrior whose limbs are like young fir-trees, and in whose glance is sunlight; surely it is the fearless youth, Lakshmana? And near him moves One with strange majesty of bearing, whose countenance has a sad, godlike beauty. This must be Rāma, for there is not his like among mortal men!"

"It must be Rāma," repeated Sītā; and a smile irradiated her sweet face as she flung her arms round the neck of the good old Rākshasī.

The tidings of Prahasta.

Meanwhile, those were ill tidings the Minister Prahasta had brought Rāvana. The Rākshasas had been utterly routed by the gallant Wild Men of the Woods, and only a few stragglers had returned to tell the tale. With them the Raghuide had sent the noble Orangoutang Angada to speak a warning in the ears of the inhabitants of Lankā. The fearless son of Bālin now stood forth in the midst of the town, and shouted so that in every palace and hut his voice was heard.

"Rāma, the Friend of Living Creatures," he cried, "the lion-hearted Warrior Lakshmana, and Sugrīva, King of the Simian tribes, salute the citizens of Lankā. Let those who love justice, and to whom Rāvana's sin is odious, quit this evil city, or hold them safe within their dwellings, for it is not the pleasure of my Lords to slay the innocent. To Rāvana, he who is called the Scourge of the Three Worlds, the noble Rāma sends this message. 'Thou hast made an ill use of the gift of life,' says the Beloved of Gods and mortals; 'thou hast turned thy powers of mind and body against the Law of Justice, and set thy pleasure in opposition to the Eternal Will of Brahm. This last crime has summed up thy guilt; thou hast transgressed the limits—and must die! Thou hast caused too many tears to be shed to look for mercy. Yet,' says the blameless Hero, 'would I spare thee shame and suffering! Send back the august Princess of Mithilā forthwith; and thou, build thee a funeral pyre, and cleanse thee of thy guilty life within the purifying Flame. So may thy soul find mercy with the Gods, and thy death at least be worthy of a King!' This done, the noble Raghuide pledges him to quit these shores; and thus thy servants' lives, and the wealth and prosperity of this fair city of Lankā, may be spared!"

Then rose up a mocking laugh from the courtiers of Rāvana.

CHAP. XV.

Angada proclaims in the names of Rāma and Sugrīva that no terms will be made with Rāvana.

CHAP. XV.

Rávana orders Angada to be scourged; but he escapes, and returns to the camp.

"On my word," said the Monarch, "this precious Rāma, the chosen associate of Apes, has a valorous tongue! We shall see if blows be as easy to him as words ere long. Meanwhile, to show our appreciation of his generous counsels, let us instruct this envoy of his in courteous bearing. Seize him, and let him be scourged forthwith!"

But the doughty Angada broke easily from those who essayed to tether him; and springing on to the roof of the palace, clapped his hands, and shouted aloud:

"Long life to the gallant Dasarathides, and their chosen ally, Sugrīva! Death to Rāvana, who has filled the world with tears!"

Afterwards, with a few bounds, he returned to the Simian camp.

The war begins.

Then the war began in earnest. Armed with shoreas, palms, and huge trees of every description, the Wild Men of the Woods marched against Lankā. The colossal gōlāngūla,[1] Kumuda, with a hundred thousand Apes, blockaded the eastern gate; the western was attacked by Sushena, the magnanimous parent of Tārā; Satabali, with his hosts, assaulted the southern barrier; whilst Rāma, Lakshmana, and Sugrīva assailed, unaided, the northern portal. The Rākshasas, in serried bands, charged forth from each gateway on the invaders. Then ensued a fearful struggle,—the Demons brandishing clubs and pikes—the Simians wielding their gigantic trees, and rending their enemies with their teeth and claws, in a frenzy of ferocious rage!

[1] *Gōlāngūla*—ape with a cow's tail.—Note by Fauche.

All day they battled thus; night came on: and then the fight grew hideous. It seemed the stars refused to shine on such a scene of carnage. The adversaries could barely discern each other's forms; and such shouts as, "Art thou a Rākshasa?" "Art thou a Simian?" were frequent, ere two dusky giants rushed at each other, and grappled in mortal combat. The Bears, who had followed in troops Sugrīva's army, stalked about—their swarthy forms hidden by the night—devouring the Rākshasas in the midst of the battle-field! The sound of drums and trumpets blended hideously with the shrieks and groans of the wounded, and served to keep up the delirious fury, which had half its source in terror.

Chap. XV.
The battle by night.

All through that night, the noble youths Rāma and Lakshmana moved calmly from post to post; the rage and evil excitement of the others had no place with them; they seemed, too, to bear charmed lives, for no arrows reached them, nor were they soiled by blood.

In the grey of morning, Indrajit, Rāvana's eldest-born, and the most dreadful among the Rākshasas, withdrew a space from the battle. In a lonely field, whence was heard the tumult of the fight, he built him an altar, and adorned it with blossoms, crimson, as though soaked in blood. Then, kindling a fire there, he stabbed a struggling Ram he had dragged thither by the horns, and poured its blood upon the altar. A moment the sacred Fire hissed, and seemed about to die in smoke;—then sprang up a little Flame of a

Indrajit builds an altar.

cruel red, and the fierce Indrajit, falling on his knees, caught the flush and heat of it upon his face, whilst round him gloomed the pale shades of morning.

Indrajit invokes the Fire.

"Fire, eager for destruction," chanted he, "who hast been fed on blood, and learned the lust of slaughter,—Fire, whose burning passion knows no check, whose appetite is never sated,—Fire, pitiless and fiercely cruel as myself, lend me thine aid! Help me to slay mine adversary!"

Suddenly the crimson Flame blazed up, and stained, through and through, the air with red; no floating smoke hung round, nor any golden Halo such as

A chariot rises out from the Fire.

plays above the Brahman's sacrifices; but from the midst rose slowly a resplendent Car, drawn by six fiery steeds, and streaming from it was a serpent with golden scales, and cold gleaming eyes, the same device Indrajit carried on his flag. By that he knew this came in answer to his prayer,—and with a fierce laugh sprang into the chariot, and it upbore him into the dawning light.

Indrajit, invisible to his enemies, hangs over the Simian army, distressing it with his magic arrows.

Wafted on by these miraculous Steeds, the Rākshasa soon hung suspended over the Simian host, invisible to all eyes, save those gifted with the sense of magic. The followers of Sugrīva were mown down on all sides by this unseen adversary; it was as though the skies rained death on them!

"This is the work of magic, Brother!" cried Lakshmana, in grievous wrath at the slaughter of the faithful Simians. "Hast not thou also weapons of miraculous power? Shoot off, I pray thee, the Dart of Brahma, that there may be an end of these Rākshasas, and this foul city of Lankā! It is vain to ply honest warfare against a nest of traitors."

"Nay," returned the Raghuide; "even among the Rākshasas may be many guiltless creatures undeserving of death. Shall I use the arm Brahma gave to me in trust in a fit of heedless passion?"

Whilst he spoke, a shower of poisoned arrows covered Lakshmana and himself,—and, pierced by a hundred darts, the noble Brothers fell, like two large palm-trees blasted by the storm!

Then the fight stayed;—simultaneously, a shout of triumph and a wail of anguish rang out upon the air!

"Behold!" shouted Indrajit, flashing into sight, standing erect in his flaming car; "behold these mighty Heroes, these godlike allies of the monkey tribes! Was it worth while to build a mole across the sea for this? Pick up your dead, ye poor deluded Apes; get ye back from whence ye came, and hide your wounds and shame in the deepest, darkest glens within your forests."

When he heard the Dasarathides were slain indeed, Rāvana sprang from his throne and embraced his son in joy.

"My presentiments were false!" he cried. "Life, —warm, bright, voluptuous Life, shall still be mine! And still shall I conquer the high spirit of my lovely Vaidēhī."

Meanwhile, Sugriva and Vibhishana rushed to the spot where the Brothers lay stretched side by side.

The faithful Orang-outang wrung his hands and sobbed aloud.

"Rāma!" he cried, "thou King of Men! My Benefactor; my Friend; my Lord;—O Heavens, that I should live to see thee thus! Would I were still an exile in the wood of Rishyamūka. Of what avail is wealth and power to me since thou art gone? I will die with thee here, my Lord! Thy poor Sugriva will stretch him by thy side! Angada shall lead the Simians back to the sweet quiet forests; I will return no more; I will not see again the pleasant cave Kishkindhyā, nor Tārā, the gentlest of she Apes. Bear her my greetings, Simians, and say I perished with the gallant Rāma!"

But Vibhīshana reproved the afflicted Ape.

"This is no moment to give way to senseless grief," he said, sternly; "if dejection spread amid thy followers, the Rākshasas will exterminate them; and not thou alone, but all this army will die on these shores of Lankā. For my part, I do not believe that death has clutched these Heroes. Mark the beauty of their countenances, and the still grace with which they lie; it has not the rigid stiffness of those on whom the Icy Hand is laid. Indrajit deals much in magic; if these youths be but held in trance, by some subtle poison, it may yet be possible to release them from the charm."

As he spoke, Rāma feebly opened his eyes, and raised him a little on his arm. The watchers round held their breath in anxious hope. But when the Hero's eyes fell on the senseless Lakshmana stretched beside him, he sank back to the earth, his face turned to the dust.

"It is well that death is near!" he groaned. "Alas, Lakshmana! alas, my Brother! my beautiful large-hearted Brother! Could I meet Sumitrā without thee? Could I return to Ayōdhyā, the palace we both loved—and the groves—and the wood that is near, where flows the river Sarayu? It is for me, for my sake, thou didst choose exile—and hast found death! Have I sometimes thought Heaven loved me? It is well that I must die: I should lose trust in Brahm himself had I to carry in my heart the sight of thee, thus lying dead! Forgive me, Vibhīshana. I had kept my promise to thee, save that I must die. And thou, O dear Sugrīva, lead back thy Wild Men of the Woods. I thank thee for thy loyalty; but all is vain now, since I must die!"

Again his eyes closed, and his nether jaw fell; it seemed that all was over. Then Sugrīva sprang up and tossed his long arms wildly above his head.

"Do what ye will," he said; "for me, I swear I will not quit these shores! Alone, I will drag Rāvana from his throne; alone, I will tear out the false traitor's heart, who by fraud has robbed the world of Rāma; alone, will I rescue Sītā, and then set fire to this vile town of Lankā, that there be none left who dare exult, because this godlike man has died."

But at that moment Marut, the kindly Wind, whispered in the faint hearing of the dying Warrior:

"Rāma, Rāma with the strong arms. Remember thy great heart; be true to thyself. Bethink thee how

CHAP. XV.

Rāma thinks of Garuda.

The King of Birds arrives, and Rāma and Lakshmana are released from the enchantment.

the world is grieved with sin. Was it not thy mission to cleanse it of Rākshasas, and by thy life to put evil to a shame? Call then to mind Garuda, the brave son of Vinatā, charged, like thee, to rid the earth of Vipers!"

Struggling hard against the languor and the chill, the Raghuide, by a mighty effort, formed through the mists of dimness a thought of the divine Bird, whom evil creatures dread.

Then sprang up a gusty wind, so that the trees and mountains danced again; and in a rush, darkening the sky with his large wings, came Garuda, the celestial King of Birds. At sight of him the malignant Serpents, who in the form of arrows had thrust their venomous tongues into the Heroes' bodies, dropped writhing from their victims, and sought to hide them in the earth!

Then Rāma and Lakshmana leapt to their feet and shouted loud with joy—and the whole Simian army shouted back again; and that Rāvana heard and paled, as he sat among his courtiers.

CHAPTER XVI.

THE DEATH OF KUMBHAKARNA.

Now Rāvana had a younger Brother, by name Kumbhakarna. He was a Giant of a terrible aspect, and of baneful force of nerve and limb. Not that his nature was so very vicious, but his large body required much sustenance; therefore, to appease his hunger, he devoured most beings whom he lighted on. Many, too, he crushed quite unintentionally, because of the hugeness of his feet, and the weight of his monstrous hands.

Thus, without much malice, the mischief he did was quite incalculable.

In the early days, his children of every race had appealed to the Universal-Father.

"Bind, we pray Thee, this monstrous Kumbhakarna!" they had cried; "otherwise his insatiable appetite and formidable vigour will unpeople the realms of ocean, earth, and air."

Then the magnanimous Ancestor of Worlds had summoned the lusty Rākshasa to his presence.

"What is this I hear of thy inordinate gluttony and uncontrolled force of limb?" He had asked.

*Chap. XVI.

Kumbhakarna's destructiveness.

Brahma summons him to his presence.

CHAP. XVI.

Kumbha-karna is condemned to sleep.

He is allowed to awake once in six months.

The burly Giant, whose share of wit was small, could find no excuse to make for himself; but whilst he stood sore embarrassed in the august presence, Brahma had duly examined his vast proportions and astounding muscular force.

"Surely," the resplendent God had exclaimed, "it was for the destruction of the world that thou wast engendered by the Son of Pulastya! Thy monstrous bulk and proportional vigour have rendered thee the bane of thy fellow-creatures! I will not judge thee as a criminal:—that thou mayst do no more harm, —sleep, O Kumbhakarna! Thus only canst thou lead a blameless life."

At these words, the mighty son of Visravas had fallen down before the august Brahma, deeply slumbering.

But his kindred and acquaintance had implored the Supreme Father to mitigate the sentence.

"Dost thou condemn the tree whose nature it is to bear poisonous fruit?" they asked. "How has this innocent Kumbhakarna deserved punishment? Shall he know nothing of the joys of life?"

In answer to their petition, the most ancient of Gods accorded a day's grace to Kumbhakarna after six months of slumber. Thus twice every year the Colossus woke, and for the space of one day was free to provide himself with nourishment, and to roam over the face of the earth.

All this while that war had raged without the gates of Lankā, Kumbhakarna had slumbered in bland unconsciousness, both of the tumult and the peril.

To seek to awaken him had not, as yet, occurred to
Rāvana's mind. But ever, day by day, the situation grew more desperate. There seemed no diminution of the Simian host; yet at each battle the
Lord of Rākshasas lost the noblest and most valued
of his warriors: each setting of the sun signalized
fresh loss for him—fresh triumph for his adversaries!
Nearer and nearer drew the Doom; he, of all others,
beheld it looming overhead. Yet as the circle round
him narrowed, and hope receded, his defiant valour
grew, with the savage heroism of despair.

The fresh losses of Rāvana.

One day in the Council-chamber he let his blood-shot eyes roam round, counting how many were missing there; and, in a burst of savage grief, he cried:

"How is it that I stand alone? Have I not a
Brother, who should share my griefs? Whilst this
Vermin, Rāma, has cleared off from the woods,
threatens to overthrow my fair town of Lanka,
Kumbhakarna, glutted with the bestial pleasures
in which he alone delights, enjoys the heavy content of sleep! Of what use to me is this Giant's
prodigious strength, if at so critical a juncture it
does not serve me?"

The Rākshasa asks why Kumbhakarna is allowed to sleep through such troubled times.

When they heard that, his principal ministers rose
and left the Council-chamber. Calling together many
musicians, they loaded them with divers instruments,
with rich apparel, and caskets of rich perfumes;
themselves were charged with all manner of savoury
viands, such as Kumbhakarna loved; and thus they
set off for the palace of the slumberous Giant.

The ministers set off for the Giant's palace.

As they reached the portal, they were all thrown

CHAP. XVI.

The ministers are nearly thrown by Kumbhakarna's mighty snoring.

backwards by the tempestuous breathings of the mighty Kumbhakarna! Holding to each other firmly, they succeeded, not, however, without difficulty, in keeping on their legs, and finally in entering the apartment where lay the stupendous Son of Visravas,—supine, head thrown back, mouth open, snoring, so that the building trembled!

They heap viands round his couch.

Then these intrepid Warriors, holding hard to the wall and to one another—for all that, thrown often by the tornadoes that issued from the Giant's gaping jaws—piled up round his couch mountains of buffalo flesh, whole gazelles, boars, and all manner of meats tasty to a carnivorous appetite. Golden vases they brimmed full with blood and fiery liquors, and placed near, so that the odours streaming from them might caress pleasantly the Slumberer's nostrils.

Then, exchanging congratulatory glances, they retired a little out of the too gusty atmosphere of Kumbhakarna's immediate vicinity,—and awaited the result.

But no sensible effect was produced; perhaps a slight smile irradiated the Monster's countenance; but, if even their fancy did not mislead them here, it was only in sleep that the savoury odours gave him pleasurable sensations; for evidently his stupor was not shaken, nor were even his boisterous snorings abated.

They anoint his limbs with perfumes.

Nothing daunted, the servants of Rávana proceeded to anoint the Giant's limbs with oil of sandal-wood; they laid rich garments on him; afterwards they sounded brazen trumpets; they shouted simultaneously, and clapped their hands, and leapt, until the mighty couch on which he lay was shaken! Still Kumbhakarna slept.

Then they fetched camels, and asses, and elephants, and, shouting the while, they lashed them till the frightened creatures galloped round and round the vast chamber, with a din and tumult that was heard through all the town of Lanka!

But, even so, Kumbhakarna wakened not.

Out of patience with this opiniative Sleeper, they took to maltreating him. Some laid hold of his shaggy, unkempt hair, and swung by it to and fro; others pinched or pummelled him;—one fastened his teeth viciously on the helpless Kumbhakarna's thumb;—more again belaboured him with mallets, clubs, and hammers. But nothing of all this disturbed the heavy Son of Visravas! Nay,—even when they leapt on to his prostrate body, and ran races on him from head to heel, and back again, his slumbers appeared not a whit the less serene!

Then they tried a fresh expedient. They brought thither the most lovely damsels in all the town of Lanka. Their footsteps were very light; but as they fluttered forward, the purling of their silver nūpuras rang out, sweetly and clearly. Fragrance floated on with them; and sunshine streamed from their beauty: they joined hands round the couch of the torpid Giant, and, laughing aloud, sprang into graceful dances; bending down near to him; calling to him in song,—in song, telling him of all the delights of love, and wooing him to regard them.

T

"We are daughters of Ananga, the amorous God!" they sang; "do not close thine eyes against us; O Kumbhakarna, do not close thine heart against us!"

In the mists round Kumbhakarna, a shower of stars were flashing;—in the breast of Kumbhakarna, a host of flowers were springing;—in the heart of Kumbhakarna, a singing-bird was laughing;—in the ears of Kumbhakarna, sighed, sighed a zephyr—that grew into a song—that broke into the ringing of nūpuras—that merged into the laughter of young maidens!

Kumbhakarna awakes.

The Rākshasa flung up his large arms; a yawn, strenuous as the heaving of some submarine volcano, distorted his cavernous mouth; then with a mighty sigh that shook the walls' foundations, his eyes rolled back their lids, and he lay staring round him in stupid amaze.

Seeing they had roused the dull-brained Giant, the Dancing Girls, still laughing and singing, vanished one by one through the doorway;—then his eyes rested on the row of timorous courtiers, who clung to each other, cowed by the return to consciousness of him whom they had lately outraged. With another hideous yawn, the Demon sat upright.

He demands why they have disturbed him.

"For what cause have ye disturbed me?" he roared. "One does not lightly break the slumber of a Prince of royal race!"

The obsequious Rākshasas bowed them to the earth, and Yūpāksha, the noblest in the company, answered, reverently:

"We are the servants of thy Brother, the great Ravana. The Sovereign of Gods and Rakshasas has need of thee, O resplendent Kumbhakarna; therefore have we broken in on thy repose."

When he heard that, the brawny Demon leapt to his feet at once. Ravenous after his long fast, he flung him on the food prepared for him, and soon the great piles of meat disappeared between his monstrous jaws; then seizing one by one the golden vases, he drained each at a draught.

Drunk with blood and fiery liquor—his riotous strength alive to the full once more—Kumbhakarna, with a dreadful laugh, glowed on the ministers of Ravana.

"I am ready!" he cried. "Who is my Brother's enemy? Be he from Mount Meru, or from Tartarus, he shall hardly stand before me now."

Mahodara, the wisest counsellor among the Rakshasas, answered:

"The noble Ravana's life is put in peril, not by the rivalry of Demons, nor the indignation of the Celestial Armies, but by a multitude of ferocious Apes, led on by a Prince among Men, one Rama, son of Dasaratha. Already Aksha, the hereditary Prince, has perished, and the noblest warriors of our tribe have shared his fate; nay, Ravana, the Victor of the Deathless Gods, has more than once been driven from the field! In earth, nor heaven, is none capable of mastering these savage Men of the Woods, save thou, O Kumbhakarna! Deign then to follow us, and reassure thy Brother and our Lord."

CHAP. XVI.

Ravana is rejoiced at sight of his brother.

He gives Kumbhakarna an account of the cause of this war.

So, accompanied by the Yātavas, the colossal Rākshasa started for the palace. As he passed through the streets of Lankā, the confidence of the citizens revived; flowers were showered on him, and shouts of triumph rose on every side.

"Among the Simians, is there a warrior like to this?" they cried. "Will Rāma, or Lakshmana, or Sugrīva match them against our Kumbhakarna?"

At sight of the lusty Giant, Rāvana, with a cry of joy, sprang forward to greet him; he flung his own necklace round him, and embraced him affectionately; then he drew him to a throne beside his own, and, still holding his hand, exclaimed:

"Lankā and myself are saved! Since the disabling hand of sleep has released thee, O my hero, the case is changed:—Rāma's life, not mine, is now the one in peril!"

"Ay," returned the other, "the danger is to thine enemy's life—not thine: but who is this Rāma? and wherefore does he battle with thee, Rāvana?"

Then, with an evil sneer, the Fiend replied:

"Rāma is very noble! They call him 'the Friend of Living Creatures,' which means that he chooses for associate never mind how vile and low a being. He gave up his crown through dread of his stepdame's tongue, as though it were a merit to be a paltry chicken-hearted fool; this has gained him great credit with the Gods, who love to keep men humble. After his exile he built a hermitage in our wood of Dandaka, with no more reason than right; for what does a would-be saint in the domains of the Lord of

Rākshasas? There, because Sūrpanakhā, our Sister, presumed to look with too much favour on his smooth false face, he and his brother fell on her and hewed off her nose, and hacked her hideously. Then Khara and Dūshana, furious at the story of her wrongs, arrayed them in battle against this Rāma; but he slew them with some magic arms, bestowed on him by Brahma. When I learnt this, knowing that this paltry, malignant Rāma was wedded to a Princess of more beauty than Lakshmī, Queen of Heaven, I resolved, as most efficient vengeance, to carry off this bright young Bride of his. This plan I consummated, and it is because I hold his Sītā a prisoner here that Rāma has allied him with these Wild Men of the Woods, and brought them to defile my fair town of Lankā!"

Now, as has been said before, Kumbhakarna's disposition was not naturally an evil one.

"It had been better to dare this truculent Prince to combat, than to carry off his Wife," he said. "My counsel, Brother, is that we send back this Sītā, ere we defy the Warrior in battle. A bad deed weakens the arms, and spoils one for honest warfare."

At that, Rāvana's brow grew dark.

"I do not need thy counsels, Brother," he said; "nor is this the moment to discuss the merits of my past actions. If I troubled thy repose, it was that thou mightest help to extricate me from my present strait."

Then Kumbhakarna fixed his eyes mildly on the angry Monarch.

Kumbhakarna counsels to send back Sītā.

CHAP. XVI.
Kumbhakarna tells of his meeting with Nārada.

Of the council on Mount Meru, and the decision that Vishnu shall become man for the destruction of Rāvana.

"One day that I sprang from my six months' slumber," he said, "tormented sore by hunger, I ravaged the glens and forests, and devoured an incalculable number of living creatures. At length, my craving appeased, I sat me down on a rock, and Nārada passed me there. So, making room beside me, I called to the Messenger of the Gods, and invited him to sit by me, and to chat awhile. 'Whence comest thou?' I asked him, seeing he was in a great sweat, and looked fatigued. 'From Mount Meru,' he answered; 'there were assembled Brahma, and Vishnu, and Siva, and Mahēndra, with the lower Gods, and Garuda the enemy of Vipers, and the Stars who battle against shade.'

"'For what cause was this large gathering?' I asked.

"'To consult how Rāvana, the Lord of Rākshasas, and all his evil brood might be destroyed!' replied the God. Struggling hard to conceal the dismay I felt, I asked again:

"'And was there a plan decided on?'

"'Many and many a scheme was suggested,' returned Nārada; 'but Brahma refused to listen to them. "An Immortal's word is sacred," he said, "and I have guaranteed this Rāvana against Gods and Demons; against the venom of serpents, and the fury of beasts of prey; only at the hands of man can he receive death, for from man only he claimed no exemption." Then Brihaspati, the Guru of the Immortals, turned to Vishnu, in whose sight life is precious: "Let thy Divinity put on the Human Cloak!" he said. "Long enough has the short life of mortals been filled with tears. Take the form of man, and cleanse the world of Demons!"

"'So be it!' shouted the Gods; and thus the matter was decided.'

"As I sat there, aghast, the Celestial Envoy rose, and, bidding me farewell, returned to Paradise.

"Now, Brother, if this Rāma be he of whom Nārada spake, that is, Vishnu hidden in a human shape, it were not well to provoke him more to wrath."

At that Rāvana laughed aloud.

"It is well said of thee, O Kumbhakarna," he cried in scorn, "that what thou hast in bulk more than other mortals, thou hast the less in wit! Tell me, thou blatant Simpleton, would Vishnu, thinkest thou, choose for ally Sugrīva, King of Apes? Or again, if this Divinity had taken so much scorn on him, solely for my destruction, though I sent back Sītā twenty times, should I disarm his wrath? Besides, what matter? If Rāma be this Vishnu, and Lakshmana Siva; if the Orang-outang, Sugrīva, be Brahma, and Hanuman the Sun-god Indra; I, Rāvana, can face them all, and die, if needs be—but not yield! Go, get thee to thy couch again! Sleep, eat, drink, lead thy bestial life:—I myself will face these foes, since in all thy monstrous frame there is not heart enough!"

Rāvana mocks his Brother, and taunts him with lack of courage.

Only the last words struck Kumbhakarna; it was true, he was but shallow-brained. His interview with Nārada, and all his misgivings, escaped his memory; —he only knew he was accused of want of daring.

Drawing himself up, he looked down on Rāvana and his courtiers.

"Where are thine enemies?" he asked. "Who says I have not heart to face them?"

Swiftly changing his tone, the wily Lord of Rākshasas loaded the Giant with flatteries. He put into his hand a pike of gleaming silver, and gave him his own cuirass of gold.

"Go forth," he cried, "and lead on my young Warriors to triumph!"

At that, Kumbhakarna, who had reached the doorway, paused.

"I need not thy young Warriors!" he said, doggedly; "I will go alone."

But Rāvana soon overpersuaded the simple Giant.

"It is not meet thy Grandeur should contend with Apes," he urged. "Wrestle thou with Rāma and Lakshmana; thy followers will hold the Simians employed."

So the monstrous Son of Visravas, in a chariot drawn by a hundred asses, led on a gallant company to the battle-field. At sight of the dreadful Giant, Gavāksha, Sarabha, Nīla, and Kumuda, who were in advance of the others, flung down their weapons and fled. But Angada recalled them with wrathful shoutings.

"Whither would ye go, Poltroons?" he cried. "Behind you lies the sea, and around you are those who will slay all traitors to the cause of Rāma. In front are the Rākshasas. Fling at them, then ;—there is your only chance of life; and if ye perish, is not a hero's death better than a dastard's?"

At his voice the fugitives returned, and seizing once

more their clubs and trunks of trees, awaited the onslaught of the colossal Rākshasa.

As he neared, the valiant Angada hurled a mighty rock at him; the asses were overturned, and the charioteer fell dead. With a savage roar the Demon leapt from his car, and brandishing his mighty pike, rushed on the Simian ranks, mowing down his foes by hundreds, and trampling them under his feet. He seemed impervious to all blows, and even to poisoned arrows; nothing checked him in his work of slaughter; and though he was soaked in the blood of his victims, he had not himself a single wound.

Presently, bounding over the corpses of his loyal servitors, came the furious Sugrīva, armed with a mighty shorea-tree.

"Hola, thou savage Monster!" he cried, "leave my Men of the Woods awhile, and try thy strength with mine!"

Kumbhakarna held his sides for laughter.

Beside himself with rage, the Simian Chief rushed at the lusty Demon; but his great tree snapped into bits as it smote Kumbhakarna, who only laughed the more. But as Sugrīva was about to renew the attack, the Colossus snatched up a rock that had been thrown at him, and flung it easily at Sugrīva; and, stunned by the blow, the Monarch of Simians fell fainting to the earth.

Then Kumbhakarna picked up the senseless Orangoutang, and held him above his head between his finger and thumb.

"Your Chief is dead, illustrious Apes!" he shouted.

Kumbhakarna having slaughtered many Apes is defied by Sugrīva.

Having stunned Sugrīva, the Giant holds his body up in sight of the Simian army.

CHAP. XVI.
Having insulted the Apes, Kumbhakarna marches off carrying Sugrīva.

Recovering consciousness Sugrīva makes his escape, and the Giant rushes back to the field.

He is wounded by Rāma.

"I give you one hour to decamp and fly; afterwards, ye shall be whipped from off these shores of Lankā."

So saying, he strode from the field, bearing the Monarch of Apes in his arms. But ere he reached the ramparts of the town, Sugrīva revived. With a sudden spring the fierce Orang-outang leapt up into the Demon's face, and tore it down with his nails till the Monster howled again from rage and pain.

Obeying his first impulse, Kumbhakarna flung the Ape from him with all his might. In no wise injured, the gallant Sugrīva picked himself up again, and in a few bounds was soon once more amid his loyal servitors.

The furious Giant, blinded with rage and blood, rushed back to the field. All whom he encountered, Rākshasas and Simians alike, he trampled under foot, or crushed between the palms of his hands, and devoured in sight of the two camps.

Meanwhile Rāma and Lakshmana, who had been assaulting the western gate, now first heard of Kumbhakarna's onslaught, and rushed to the scene of action.

"So ho, Rāma!" shouted the Giant to him from afar, "dost thou dare to match thy strength with mine? Thy gallant ally, the Ape, can scratch like an angry woman; hast thou more warlike modes of battle?"

In answer to the scornful defiance, an arrow from Rāma's bow shot through the Giant's arm. As a withered leaf falls off in winter, the shattered limb

THE DEATH OF KUMBHAKARNA.

dropped down; and—the quivering muscles working still—the hand yet clutched a club, and pounded it upon the ground, as though a Will still guided it!

But Kumbhakarna, in a frenzy, tore hither and thither in the battle-field; falling on the Simians with his teeth; tearing, kicking, and crushing them till the earth was strewn with corpses! Gaya, Gavaya, Gavāksha, Nīla, and Angada flung them on him, and sought to hold him down; but he shook them off from him as easily as a wild boar tosses away the dogs.

He was rushing straight at Rāma, when a second arrow from the Hero's bow struck him in the side. The only hand now left him clutched down to drag forth the dart;—but ere it reached it, it dropped down by his side. With a crash like a mountain hurled down from its height, the Giant fell; as his head smote the ground, his heart broke—and he died.

Kumbhakarna's frenzy.

He is slain by Rāma.

CHAPTER XVII.

THE LAST COMBAT—LAKSHMANA WOUNDED.

Chap. XVII.

NIKUMBHA, Makarāksha, Matta, Unmatta, and Virūpāksha had found a like fate with Kumbhakarna; most dire misfortune of all, Indrajit, whose fierce, wild nature had endeared him to Rāvana, fell also, slain by the unerring shafts of the brave Lakshmana. The Monarch of Rākshasas, surveying the army, and the court, and the streets of his beloved City, and everywhere beholding tears, and on all sides hearing wails of mourning, swore a mighty oath that this state of things should end.

In sight of the Widows, Mothers, and Orphans, weeping before his throne, he clenched his hand, and hurled his large fist aloft.

Rávana's oath.

"By Yama's Soul, I swear," he shouted, "that ere nightfall this Dasarathide, or myself, shall bite the dust!"

On that, he decked him in his most splendid robes, set on him his tiara, and his jewelled necklace, and girdle studded with pearls; and, like a guest bound to some festival, sprang into his chariot, and rushed forth—eager to brave his fate!

At sight of him, the Simians set up a yell of hate and rage;—he yelled back at them—but his blood-red eyes took in naught in all that battle-field, save the figure of his enemy; who leant upon his bow, not joining in the shout of execration, but with his stern, grave eyes fixed on the desperate Rāvana.

"Rāma! Rāma!" roared the Fiend, "the hour has come! There is not force enough in Life to bear the stress of Hate between us two;—or thou, or I must die! Be thou God, or Man, or Devil, step forth, —and let us wrestle, each for life."

The Rākshasa challenges Rāma.

Rāma, still with his calm gaze on the Demon, prepared his bow, and answered the defiance only by his arrows. The Rākshasa tossed the winged shafts away with one hand, as though they had been drops of rain! But a dart from Lakshmana's bolt struck the Demon's charioteer; and, at the same moment, Vibhīshana brought his club smashing down on the skulls of the two foaming coursers, and stretched them bleeding heaps upon the field!

Rāvana's charioteer slain by Lakshmana, and his coursers by Vibhīshana.

With a low roar, like that of a lion roused from his lair, the Lord of Rākshasas leapt from his car, and rushed at Vibhīshana.

Rāvana turns on Vibhīshana, but Lakshmana interposes.

"For the kindred there is between us, I owe thee a debt," he cried. "Brother, I will rid thee of thy vile and treacherous life!"

But ere he could reach Vibhīshana, Lakshmana stepped in front of the furious Demon and caught his raised lance between his hands—snapping it off into two fragments. Then Rāvana turned upon the

CHAP. XVII.

Ravana turns on Lakshmana, and wounds him with a magic spear.

Sumitride; in a moment he had the young warrior by the throat.

"Who shields a traitor, incurs his doom," he said, sternly; "think on thy wife, or child, or mother, or on whom thou holdest dear—for thou art about to die!"

And with that, he plunged into the Hero's side the fatal spear of Maya; and, bound by its baneful enchantment, Lakshmana sank senseless to the earth.

From afar, Rāma saw him fall. The first shock of so terrible an apprehension struck him numb; but soon hot indignation lent him unusual fury; and bounding over the bodies strewn about the field, he flung him, madly, on Rāvana, and drove the Fiend before him, as a leaf is carried by the wind! Long

Rama drives Ravana from the field.

the two Warriors battled;—at the last, feeling himself spent by the Dasarathide's eager attack, Rāvana retreated behind the walls of Lankā, for a breathing space; whilst Rāma, anxious for his brother, was glad to seize the momentary truce, that he might learn how it fared with him.

Angada, Hanuman, and Sugrīva surrounded the unconscious Hero. Vainly had they striven to withdraw the fatal spear; Rāma now joined his efforts to theirs, but the cruel weapon resisted even his energy

Rama grieves for Laksh- mana.

and strength! Seeing this—and that Lakshmana gave no sign of life—Rāma covered his face with his two hands, and wept aloud.

But Sushēna, the father of Tāra, and the most skilful leech among the Wild Men of the Woods, strove to comfort the noble Dasarathide.

"Thy Brother is not dead, magnanimous Prince!" he said. "The smile of life has not yet left his countenance. He is held thus motionless, and cold, by the power of magic. Alas that we should be at such a distance from our native forests! There grows on the slopes of the Mount Gandhamādana a plant of sufficient virtue to heal this warrior forthwith; but it should be applied without delay: and who were able to take so long a journey, and to return here in a few hours, at the most?"

Chap. XVII. — Sushēna tells of the miraculous plant that grows on Mount Gandhamādana.

"That am I," said Hanuman, Son of the Wind.

Rāma turned, and wrung the hand of the faithful Marutide.

Hanuman proposes to fetch it.

"If Lakshmana be restored to me," he said, "I will see again Ayōdhyā, the pleasant town where reigned my fathers:—otherwise, I will leave my bones upon these shores of Lankā."

Then Sushēna took the valorous Hanuman apart, and gave him many instructions.

"The plant is of a yellowish hue," he said; "the fruit is green; the flower of a light gold, with a scent of sandal-wood. It creeps along the earth, and loves to hide it in the grasses. Dost thou note me well, Hanuman?"

Sushēna describes the plant.

"Ay, ay!" returned the impatient Marutide, in too great haste to be gone to heed much Sushēna's wise directions.

Now as this Hero amongst Quadrumanous Creatures sprang upwards to pursue his journey through the pathway of the air, his large form attracted the notice of Rāvana.

Rāvana sees Hanuman fly off, and suspects his errand.

"That is Hanuman, the audacious Ape who destroyed my asoka grove, and burnt so many houses," he thought. "Doubtless they have sent him to fetch the panacea, which grows on Gandhamādana."

So the crafty Rākshasa called to him Kālanēmi, a Demon well-learned in magic.

"Prevent the return of this truculent Marutide," he said; "and thou shalt have half my kingdom!"

Then, by virtue of past macerations, Kālanēmi transported himself in a moment to the side of Gandhamādana, and, in the garb of a Hermit, awaited the coming of Hanuman.

The direction followed by the loyal Ape soon brought him above Ayōdhyā. It chanced that Bharata, absorbed in many thoughts of Rāma, was standing in the street beneath.

"That is a marvellous Creature I perceive above me!" he exclaimed; "let me arrest his flight with this arrow, that I may discover to what race he belongs."

Then he prepared his bow. Hanuman, noting that, became uneasy.

"For," reflected he, "this Prince has doubtless some of his brother's skill in archery!"

So he called to him:

"Hola! hola! noble Bharata, lay aside thy bow. I am an Envoy from the illustrious Rāma, who is now besieging the town of Lankā."

Delighted to hear his brother's name, Bharata questioned him of the Hero's health and fortunes. Then the Marutide told of the rape of Sītā, of the passage of the Sea, the Siege, and now this grievous wound of Lakshmana's, the sunny-hearted Warrior.

"I must quickly return with this healing plant," said the Orang-outang, in conclusion; "therefore, O Prince, grant me permission to pursue my road."

With many praises of his loyalty and devotion, Bharata wished the indefatigable Simian good speed, and watched him continue his journey with redoubled haste. He did not pause again till he reached the Mount Gandhamādana. As he alighted on firm ground, the fictitious Hermit, Kālanēmi, approached him, and invited him to rest awhile in his hut hard by.

Bharata wishes him good speed.

Kālanēmi invites Hanuman to rest in his hermitage.

"The wayfarer is ever a cherished guest to the lonely Anchorite!" said the Demon, adopting the humble tones of a penitent. Hanuman thanked him courteously, but declined his hospitality, pleading the pressing nature of his mission.

"At least," urged Kālanēmi, "drink, and lave thy face in the clear waters of yon crystal lake. It grieves me to see a fellow-creature in such a heat and sweat!"

Not to appear ungrateful, the Orang-outang walked down to the limpid lake, where lotus flowers and red nympheas wove them into garlands. But as he stooped to drink, a Crocodile, springing up from the treacherous blue waters, clutched him by the throat.— That was not a great matter to our indomitable Ape. He dragged the monster off, as though it had been some leech merely: and, that it might entrap no more thirsty travellers, tore it in twain.

The Ape is seized by a Crocodile; but he destroys the monster.

CHAP. XVII.

From the crocodile rises a lovely Apsara.

What was his amaze to see, rising from the slaughtered crocodile, a lovely female form. Just above him the fair Vision paused.

"Hail to thee, Marutide, and thanks!" she cried; "thou hast released me from a cruel enchantment. A holy Penitent, whose staid reflections my beauty once disturbed, condemned me to this hideous form. 'But,' said he, 'when Hanuman, that Bull amongst Quadrumanous Creatures, shall come to Gandhamādana, thou shalt cast off the Crocodile, and be once more the lovely Apsara, Gandhakālī.' Therefore did I take thee by the throat, Simian; forgive me—that I may return joyous to the palace of Kuvera."

So Hanuman, wondering much at the Apsara's beauty, said:

"I am glad to have done thee this service, enchanting Gandhakālī: thou didst me no injury; go in peace, O Flower of Beauty!"

When the Apsara had vanished, Hanuman thought:

"I will go tell the holy man what strange Creatures dwell within his crystal lake."

Hanuman suspects Kālanēmi's treachery.

But the Anchorite seemed so much disturbed by the appearance of Hanuman, safe and sound, that the wily Simian's suspicions were aroused.

"Holy Father," said he to the false Hermit, "it is strange how marked a resemblance thou bearest to the Demon Kālanēmi!"

Then the Rākshasa, seeing he was discovered, cast by his hermit's garb.

Kālanēmi avows himself to be a Rākshasa,

"Yes," shouted he, "I am that Kālanēmi, the favoured servant of Rāvana! And half his king-

THE INHABITANTS OF GANDHAMĀDANA.

dom shall be mine when thou, Ape, hast entered the realms of Yama!"

So they rushed at each other, and battled fiercely there. This time it was no easy struggle, for the Demon was strong and subtle; but even so he was no match for Hanuman! After a savage tussle, the Simian crushed the Demon between the cable of his arms, and wrung the breath from him—so he died.

and is killed in a battle with Hanuman.

Now, what with this encounter and his too impulsive haste, Hanuman had forgotten every word of the minute description of Sushēna.

Hanuman forgets the description of the plant.

"Something there was of green and yellow and gold," he reflected; "but what the flower was like, or what the fruit of this miraculous plant, I have no notion!"

In his perplexity, he sought counsel from the Gandharvas, who made this mountain their home.

"Show me this precious Antidote, I pray," he said. "Is not this Gandhamādana within the domain of Rāma? And do not ye owe him love and service as loyal subjects?"

He questions the Gandharvas, who refuse to answer.

But at that the Gandharvas flew into a pet.

"Subjects of Rāma's?" they shrieked. "We—the genii of this mountain, governed by a *man?* Know thou, Insolent Ape, that the great Princes, Hūhū and Hāhā, are our lawful sovereigns:—As for thee and thy Rāma, get thee gone; thou shalt not pluck our healing plants!"

Then one and all set on him; so Hanuman, uprooting a palm-tree, slew these cantankerous Gandharvas.

He slays the Gandharvas.

CHAP. XVII.

Hanuman breaks off the mountain and carries it away.

He brings it to Rāma, and bids him find the healing plant.

Rāma's gratitude.

But when that was done, he was no nearer to a means of recognizing the miraculous plant.

"There is no time for me to return and consult Sushēna," meditated the Ape, taking his chin in his hand; "one course alone is open to me."

So, calling to mind his valiant father the Wind, who lets no obstacle arrest his will, Hanuman snapped the great mountain off from its base! Large drops fell from its ruptured veins of metal; the living creatures who dwelt in its caverns, and the birds whose nests were amid its forest trees, quaked for terror as the doughty Simian shouldered Gandhamādana, and, without more ado, bounded back into the air's pathway!

When, thus laden, the valorous Orang-outang appeared in sight, the Simian army shouted in mad triumph.—Rāvana bit his nether lip, and said:

"It were a pity I should die ere I have put that Kālanēmi, traitor or dolt, to divers sorts of torture!"

Hanuman, alighting, laid down the mountain at Rāma's feet.

"Thou Prince of men!" he said, "my Master and dear Lord, see, here is this Gandhamādana. The nature of the plant dripped through my memory. I have brought thee the mount itself. Seek thou for it!"

Then Rāma fell on his neck, and embraced him before them all! As for Angada and Sugriva, they each held one of the brave Marutide's hands, and shook them till his colossal frame swayed to and fro.

Sushēna meanwhile had plucked the healing plant.

One leaf he laid across Lakshmana's brow, a second on his heart; he bruised the fruit, and with its luscious juice moistened the young warrior's lips.

Lakshmana opened his eyes. He seemed dazed awhile, like one awakened from a deep sleep. But, of a sudden, he sprang to his feet, tossed back his hair that the fresh wind might reach his brow, and, looking round on them, laughed—half in wonder, half in joy—to feel himself so strong!

"Brother!" he cried to Rāma, "did I dream, or didst thou swear to slay this Rākshasa ere nightfall?"

"I swear it now!" said Rāma, seizing the young warrior's hand, still cold after that chill trance.

Sushēna lays the plant on his wound, and Lakshmana revives.

CHAPTER XVIII.

THE LAST COMBAT (CONTINUED).—DEATH OF RĀVANA.

Ravana's miraculous Chariot.

*RĀVANA, by means of magic, constructed a fresh Chariot of War. It was of more dreadful aspect even than the renowned Pushpaka. The car of ebony, unrelieved by any golden chasings, was drawn by two coal-black steeds, with faces that strangely resembled the countenance of man. So nearly was this dark chariot an emanation from his soul, that his thoughts alone set the wheels gyrating, and he was borne along silently, as in a sombre cloud, swiftly, as his eagerness for the combat was fierce and strong!

The Immortals appeal to Indra, and he consents to lend his own Chariot to Rāma.

When the lower Gods saw the Rākshasa sweeping on thus against the tall, slight Rāma, they hastened to the Palace of Mahēndra.

"This is no fair struggle!" they said. "Behold, O God of Light and Storm! Rāvana sits aloft in this strong chariot, whilst Rāma is on foot."

Then the Lord of the Firmament sent down his own Chariot for the Dasarathide's use. It was a shell of softest, palest blue; and above it, a banner of rosy purple fought with the gusty air; four tawny coursers were harnessed to it. They had manes bristling with gold, and golden plumes nodded over their brows, and golden bells tinkled merrily from round their necks.

Chap. XVIII.
The Car of Indra.

As the radiant Car touched the earth, a cry of admiration broke from all the Wild Men of the Wood;—but Sugrīva, Hanuman, and Angada called out at once:

"Rāma, beware! This is some wile of the crafty Rākshasa's!"

The Simians fear treachery.

"Nay," said Vibhīshana; "I know the secrets of magic possessed by the learned of my people. So bright a thing as this cannot spring from their enchantments!"

Whilst Rāma hesitated, the celestial Charioteer, Mātali, called to him:

"Hail, Sun amongst the Princes of Men!" he cried; "Indra himself has sent thee this Car of Victory, that thou mayest triumph over this cruel Fiend, and deliver the oppressed races of the earth!"

Mātali reassures Rāma, and he enters the chariot.

Then Rāma, having described a pradakshina round Mahēndra's Charioteer, leapt gladly into the resplendent Car, and Mātali urged the tawny coursers into speed.

When Rāma and Rāvana met, it seemed the battle between Light and Shade.

The meeting of Rāvana and Rāma.

The darts of the Rākshasa were so many venomous serpents; but Rāma, with arrows formed of the plumes of Garuda, King of Birds, drove them off from him. Soon there was darkness round the two warriors, because of the myriads of arrows that wrapped them as in a seething cloud:—through this gloom the calm, clear voice of Rāma rang out over all the battle-field.

"Rāvana," he said, "thou Lord of evil creatures, death is so near, it is well, for once, thy soul should have clear vision of itself! Because thou hast seen living creatures tremble at sight of thee, pride has swollen thy heart, and thou hast thought, 'Am not I mighty?' Know that it is a shameful indigence to lack the trust of the innocent!—Because to gratify thy lusts thou hast defied the law of Brahm, thou hast cried, 'I am more powerful than the gods!' Thou poor Rāvana! Thou hast been the most abject of all slaves; the toy of those low instincts the very brutes hold in some government!—Because now thou wouldst meet death with scornful arrogance, thou thinkest, 'Am not I a Hero?' Nay, Demon —for scorn is the dastard's quality, narrowing all things to fit his soul. Life is a godlike power; the *true* Hero reverences it in others and himself!"

Maddened by the sweet strong voice, and the words whose truth he recognized, yet loathed, spent by fatigue and rage, the dark of arrows hissing round working him into wild excitement—the Rākshasa's nervous grasp failed him; the string of his bow was slack, and his shafts went wide astray. Seeing that, his Charioteer of a sudden wheeled the car round, and, dashing in by the northern gate, sheltered his Master by the wall.

Then Rāvana hurled down his weapon, and turning his tearless, despairing eyes on the Charioteer in fierce reproach, asked:

"Because fortune abandons me, hast thou too turned traitor? Is it not enough for thee that these foes will slaughter me? Wouldst thou shame me in my death?"

Then his servant flung him at the Rākshasa's feet.

"I love thee, great Rāvana," he cried; "thy high renown is dear as my own life! Because I saw that passion and fatigue had marred thy skill, I risked thy wrath, and brought thee from the field."

Rāvana let his large hand fall on the other's head.

"I thank thee for thy love," he said; "yet resume thy post,—drive me back once more."

As he was borne swiftly to the field, a flock of vultures hung over him. Where he went, they followed;—moving slowly, as it seemed, though the faithful Charioteer lashed frantically his steeds to escape from the shadow of these birds of evil omen!

"Thine hour has come, Rākshasa!" cried Rāma; and with a hissing dart, tore off one of the Demon's heads. But at once another sprang up in its place. Again and again the Dasarathide severed the Rākshasa's heads; but they were always replaced directly, and Rāvana appeared in no way injured!

"Why dost thou aim at the Demon's heads?" asked Mātali, the celestial driver; "that is not the seat of the evil which makes him vulnerable."

Obeying this hint, Rāma adjusted in his bow the terrible Dart of Brahma, and aimed at Rāvana's heart.
As the celestial Shaft struck him, the Lord of Rāk-

shasas flung his clenched fist above, as though even then defying Heaven—tottered to the edge of his chariot, and—like a ruptured mountain—crashed to earth!

At first was no shout of triumph;—a deep long breath hushed through the army—whilst from afar were heard the muffled throbbings of the Drum of Victory, sounded by the Celestial Hosts!

Then down from heaven fluttered a rain of flowers; a fresh soft breeze sprang up; all there heard the Gandharvas singing: and round Rāma a troop of bright Apsaras joined hands, and danced for joy!

"Hail to Rāma, the Friend of Living Creatures!" cried the Simians then. "The Evil power is broken, the reign of Justice has commenced!"

Meanwhile, the Rākshasis, weeping and lamenting, had flung them on the earth beside the body of Rāvana. Vibhīshana, too, stood near, and looked on the noble frame of his dead Brother with tearful eyes.

One alone amongst the widowed consorts of Rāvana wept not, nor smote her breast, nor threw her on the earth—Mandōdari, the Diamond amongst beautiful Women. She stood erect—her two hands held across her breast—a strange, fierce passion paling her—scorn on her lips, and in her large eyes—agony!

"Dost thou lie thus low?" she said. "Thou—Victor of the Deathless Gods—there in the dust, whilst all these watch the blood trickling away from thy great heart? Where is the power of thy large limbs—the fire of thy glance—thy majesty of mien—the thunder of thy voice? All dead?—all in the dust there? Ay, so it ends: so ends thy amorous Folly, O my Lord! Thou didst not heed me; how shouldst thou heed me, when eye, and ear, and heart,—once *mine*, all mine,—had gone from me? This Sītā... Was there no woman in all the world but Sītā,—no charms like hers,—no beauty more than hers? Was I—Mandōdarī—foul of favour? Or was I cold to thee? Or did I keep back beauty of soul or body? All Demon though thou wert,—did I not *love* thee, O Rāvana? But her tears were dearer to thee than any smiles of mine! Nay, her very scorn and loathing of thee won more passion than all my ardour! Well—thou didst choose between us, and—thou liest there. Why should I mourn,—*I?* Since thou didst unclasp my arms in life, shall I cling to thee in death? Thou gavest me scant love; shall I be lavish of my grief?...Yet—yet —a Giant, O Rāvana!—and hadst thou loved me as in the early days, I had not looked upon thee thus— and lived!"

She stood a moment, still; then, with a strange wild cry, "My Lord!" she said:—she said "My Love—" and fell beside the corpse!

They sought to raise her; they called to her, "Mandōdarī, Diamond amongst beautiful Women!" But she did not answer.—Then they put their hands upon her heart—and found that it had ceased to beat; so they laid her down tenderly beside her Lord.[1]

Then Rāma, approaching Vibhīshana, said: "See, Friend, that these two have royal obsequies." But Vibhīshana hesitated.

[1] *Vide* Note.

Mandōdarī dies of grief.

Rāma commands that they have funeral honours.

CHAP. XVIII.

Vibhīshana's objections are answered by Rāma.

"Were it well," he asked, "to give funeral honours to Rāvana, who made so ill an use of life?"

The Dasarathide answered:

"Death has removed Rāvana beyond *our* judgment; see on his brow the still calm seal which proves the supreme acquittal! It is *in mercy* Brahm has quenched out the evil from this soul, that failed to earn a noble immortality: shall man use harsher justice than Eternal Brahm?"

The funeral pyre.

So, at his command, they raised a noble funeral pile, and adorned it with wreaths of flowers and costly jewels. Then on Rāvana's breast they laid the mighty bow he had never cast aside in terror; and kindling the sacred fire, they stood round in silence,—watching the flame spring up and wrap the great Rāvana and his impassioned Bride in their last shroud of fire.

CHAPTER XIX.

THE REUNION OF SĪTĀ AND RĀMA.

IN the low-roofed cavern, where pale, weird light steeped through the flowering creepers, lay the Captive, her head upon her arm—asleep.

This had been a day of terrors. From afar, the tumult of the battle had seemed the confused mutterings of the wrathful God of Storm; then, the shout the Rākshasas gave when Lakshmana fell had reached her ears; and later, on, another shout—then stillness, so utter and deep, that she had almost preferred the stormy sound of fight, to which these last days had accustomed her; for there at least was sign of life.

There was no one she might question as to what had chanced. The Rākshasīs had thrown up their post of gaolers; her cavern was unguarded; but she feared this might be some snare of Rāvana's, so remained in her rocky prison, wondering sore, till sleep came and eased her of anxiety.

She was roused from tranquil dreams by the consciousness that some one stood there, gazing on her. With a shudder, she opened her eyes, thinking to meet the hateful gaze of the Lord of Rākshasas; but when

*CHAP. XIX.

Sītā's apprehensions.

She falls asleep.

CHAP. XIX.
Sītā's Visitor.

she recognized her Visitor, she gave a little scream of joy, and, springing to her feet, seized his hand affectionately.

"Thou Pearl amongst Quadrumanous Creatures!" she cried, between laughing and weeping, "thou hast come with tidings from my Rāma?" Tears conquered then, and fell in a glistening shower on the hand of the faithful Hanuman.

Hanuman tells her the good news.

"Nay, nay, my Princess!" pleaded the tender-hearted Marutide, sore distressed to see her weep, "the hour of tears is past. Rāma has triumphed, Lady with the radiant eyes! Thine enemy, the cruel Rāvana, is slain! Henceforth is joy for thee and thy Beloved. Oh, wherefore dost thou weep?"

"For happiness!" she laughed back through her tears. "And my Lord is here? And I shall see my Lord?"

"Right soon," returned the other, embarrassed seemingly. "Doubtless he had sent for thee to-night, but that the Field is strewn with corpses, and our Warriors stained with blood. At sunrise he will send;

He says Rāma will send for her at sunrise.

—because of this delay, doubt not thy Rāma's love, august Lady!"

He had not needed to say that: to doubt her Lord's love had never yet chanced to Sītā.

"At sunrise he will send," she repeated; "at sunrise—in a few short hours! How I love thee, thou most comely and kind of Apes!"

And there was such a light in the smile she turned on him, that the faithful Simian's heart bounded with pride and pleasure.

SITĀ GOES TO MEET RĀMA.

"Grant me one favour, august Princess!" he cried. "I am in a heat of joy and devotion to thee, hard to bear! Let me avenge the insults thou hast received from the hideous Rākshasīs; it were a relief to tear them with my claws, to knock them down, and trample on them! Have I thy leave, O star-eyed Queen?"

Chap. XIX
Hanuman asks if he may punish the Rākshasīs.

Then, because her great happiness strove to find an outlet, Sītā laughed merrily at that.

"Fie on thee, thou vindictive Hanuman!" she said, and shook her finger at him. "Nay, thou shalt not touch those poor old Rākshasīs; I would not for all the world ill should chance to them; I would not any creature should be in grief to-morrow!"

Sītā forbids him to harm them.

It seemed a long time waiting for the dawn; yet Sītā never thought, "Why is not Rāma here? Since Hanuman could reach me in my prison-house, why could not he?"

Her great love made her trustful.

At first blush of dawn, Vibhīshana, the new Lord of Rākshasas, came laden with rich apparel and jewels, and caskets filled with rare perfumes.

Vibhīshana comes to fetch Sītā, and brings her jewels and raiment.

"Array thyself, gracious Princess, in these robes befitting thy rank," he said; "then we will conduct thee to thy noble spouse."

"Nay, courteous Demon," returned Sītā; "but I will first go to my Lord in these mean garments; then if it please him, I will deck me in this splendid apparel."

But Vibhīshana, thinking to do Rāma a pleasure, said:

CHAP. XIX.
Vibhīshana bids Sītā put on this bright apparel.

"Thy Lord desires thou shouldst return to him in the full splendour of thy beauty."

Hearing it was her husband's will, Sītā put on the queenly robes the Rākshasa had brought her, and stepped into the gorgeous palanquin, whose draperies and fringes were of gold, interspersed with brilliant gems.

Sītā is carried in a palanquin, and the Simians press round her to Vibhīshana's wrath.

As the lovely Bride of Rāma, carried by four of the noblest Warriors among the Rākshasas, approached the late field of battle, the inquisitive Simians pressed round the palanquin, seeking to get a view of this Princess, whose beauty was a marvel in the three worlds.

Vibhīshana drove them back, chiding them angrily for their ill-bred audacity.

Then the gentle Vaidēhi heard her Rāma's voice, and it sounded strangely cold and stern to her.

"Why dost thou vex these Warriors, Vibhīshana?" he asked. "I see no wrong that they should look on this Princess—who comes from the harem of the Rākshasa! Long ere this, the radiant Sītā has no doubt laid by her coyness; let them gaze their fill.—The eyes of my honest Wild Men of the Wood will not work her harm."

Rāma says their gaze cannot confuse Sītā now.

At the cold displeasure of his voice, Sītā's heart failed her. She sprang from the palanquin, and had rushed forward to him, but astonishment and wounded love, combined with the joy of seeing him again, held her there unconscious of all else, seeking to read his averted countenance.

Sītā marvels at her Lord's coldness.

The enthusiastic Simians could not refrain from a

cry of wondering admiration as they looked at her. The bloom of her youth had not faded, but fresh majesty and warmth were added to it:—never in her sunniest days had she this resplendence and glow of beauty. Rāma recognized this at once,—and it was a torture to him!

Rāma is grieved to find Sītā so little changed.

"Am not I a worn and broken man?" he asked. "Have not sleepless nights weakened my frame, and given fever to my blood? has not the incessant torment of regret hollowed out my eyes, and driven the healthful glow from either cheek? But *she?* What trace of sorrow have these long cruel months left on her? She comes to me more brightly lovely than before, and decked in the raiment of a Queen. Ah, if for all these charms there were one line of care—one wrinkle on her brow—a little dimness of the eyes, speaking of tears,—the faintest cloud upon her youth,—how gladly had I gathered her in my arms! But now, where in this radiant Sītā shall I find my Love?"

Meanwhile she stood there, her large eyes imploring him; but because they were so bright, he heeded not. There was a murmur of surprise and discontent among the Wild Men of the Wood. Lakshmana, in spite of his great reverence for Rāma, was wroth to see the lovely Princess thus slighted in the sight of this vast company.

"Brother," he urged, "thy Beloved stands there waiting; hast thou naught to say to her,—no word for this dear, gentle Sītā, whom thou hast so often wept?"

Lakshmana remonstrates with Rāma.

CHAP. XIX.

Rāma says that grief has made him unfit for such a radiant bride.

"Have I wept for her?" answered the pale, stern Rāma. "That was my folly—*She* had more wisdom than to spend her days in tears! What should I say to this enchanting Princess, O Lakshmana? Speak to her rather thou; for thou art young and happy yet, and shouldst be better able to use pleasant flatteries. Tell her she is of rare loveliness, and that this rich apparel becomes her marvellously well:—Say, too, that this Rāma, to whom she once was pledged, has in a few short months outlived his youth—there is not enough amorous heat left in his blood to be stirred at sight of all her charms—yet bid her take heart; doubtless there are many willing to replace Rāvana at her side, and, for the sweetness of her glances, to forget her sojourn in the harem of the Rākshasa. Tell her that Rāma forbears to claim her—that she is free of Rāma! He has laved his shame, and that suffices; he is sick of love!"

At this, Sītā, casting by pride and resentment, came and fell down at his feet.

Sītā appeals to Rāma.

"Alas!" she said, "I dreamed another greeting from my Lord than this! Why, if thy heart had turned from me, didst not thou send word by thy messenger—this Hanuman? I had died then, and so had thy shame been laved, and all the fatigue of this great army, and the loss of innocent life, been spared. But thine Envoy brought me messages of love, and therefore I lived on. Thou speakest of suffering and torment of regret, my Love! I am a woman—timid, frail of health and frame—was not the burthen harder to support for me? And then—I fain would think my ears deceived me,—but I heard thee name the harem of the Rākshasa? Rāma, this Hanuman can say how I was lodged : a captive in a lonely cavern, where came no sunlight, tormented by the menaces of hideous Rākshasīs, and threatened by Rāvana with instant death !—But I am still beautiful,—sayest thou? Since it offends thee, I would that I had no charm left! I take no pride nor pleasure in being comely for myself. When the Saint Anasūyā gave me the gift of unfading loveliness, I was happy only because I thought of thee! But since thou hatest my beauty, I hate it too! Take from me all grace of face and form, ye puissant Gods, and only give me Rāma's love !"

And so she fell a-sobbing, and kissed her Lord's feet, and bathed them with her tears.

Rāma, pale, and struggling hard against his grief at seeing her thus, still put her from him.

Rāma still turns away from Sītā.

"There is no beauty to be compared to thine in the three worlds!" he said. "Wouldst thou have me think Rāvana was dead to all these charms, and kept thee prisoner merely out of hate to me? Nay; though thy heart be innocent, his love has tainted thee !"

Then, with sad dignity, the Vaidēhī dashed away her tears, and rose from the dust at his feet.

"Son of Sumitrā," she said, turning to Lakshmanā, "in thine eyes I see pity and trust of me ! Build me a funeral pyre, Brother; since I am tainted in Rāma's sight, it is time that I should die !"

Sītā bids Lakshmana build her a funeral pile.

Indignantly the Sumitride collected a vast pile of

boughs and trunks of trees scattered about the field.

"When he sees his innocent Sītā ascend the pyre, Rāma's heart will relent," he thought.

Sita ascends the pyre.

But, with eyes sad with unshed tears, the Dasarathide watched the gentle Princess mount the funeral pile; and, even when the sacred Fire sprang up round her, gave no sign, nor spake one pitying word. Then Lakshmana, Sugrīva, Angada, and Hanuman rushed forward to drag Sītā from the pyre:—But, with a gesture of command, Rāma waved them back. Their reverence for him made them obey; but an angry murmur spread round, and indignant eyes glared on him from all sides.

She prays to the God of Fire to prove her innocence.

"Agni, God of Purity and Light!" prayed Sītā, amid the flames, "if I am true, and clean, and bright of soul as thou, then prove my innocence to Rāma and all this host!"

Agni appears, and carries her to Rāma's arms.

A golden Flame, smokeless, and of clear radiance as the sun, swam round her. Then from the midst sprang Agni, the resplendent God, who, bearing the Princess from the pyre, placed her in Rāma's arms.

Then was broken up the Hero's forced restraint.

"I hold thee!" he cried, "my Own—my Love!" and wept for joy.

Sītā, lying on his breast, asked:

"Yet didst thou doubt me, Rāma?"

He answered:

Rāma explains that he chose she should be justified.

"Nay: or I had not trusted thee to the pure God of Fire! But it was needful there should be no speck on thy soul's whiteness:—for thy own sake first; then, for the sake of all these here—that they might learn that loveliness of outward form cannot make vice more tolerable; and that where is not utter reverence, is no true love! Dost thou forgive me, O my Queen?"

She answered not in words, but clung more close to him.

Above the two, as they stood thus embraced, appeared a Cloud-chariot, gilded by the sun, and within it, behold Dasaratha, the aged King of Ayōdhyā!

He smiled on his children there.

"Rāma," he cried, "the fourteen years of thine exile have elapsed. Well hast thou served thy fellows, and done honour to the Soul entrusted thee during thy wanderings; return now to the pleasant Town where reigned thy fathers. When thou hast given to mankind the example of a just governor, and hast shown moderation in prosperity, as thou hast already displayed patience in affliction, thou shalt join me in the Restful World. Thou, too, Lakshmana, and thou, my large-eyed Daughter, shall enter Paradise with this Hero ye have loved and followed through his days of trouble!"

Raising his hands to his brow, Rāma cried to the ancient Monarch, reverently:

"Father! if thy love and favour be mine indeed, grant me a pleasure ere thou depart. Thou didst quit life in wrath against Kaikēyī and the innocent Bharata. 'I abandon thee and thy son!' didst thou say to thy once favoured Consort. Deign to remit thine anger. Empower me to say to the repentant

CHAP. XIX.

Dasaratha grants the request.

He blesses his children and returns to Paradise.

Kaikēyī, 'Dasaratha pardons;' and to the just Bharata, 'Thy Father's love is thine.' Thus, O Magnanimous King, shall disunion and ill-feeling cease!"

Dasaratha answered:

"At thy request, Rāma, I pardon Kaikēyī, and restore my favour to her son.—Have ye aught else to ask, my children? for I may not linger."

"Thy Benediction!" cried they all—and fell upon their knees.

Then the ancient King spread his hands out above the two Heroes, and Sītā, the Vaidēhī. And as he ascended slowly, still he looked on them—and blessed them still.

At length the blue of Heaven opened, and wrapt him from their sight—till the time should come, as he had promised, when all three should join him in the Restful World.

NOTES.

CHAPTER I.

NOTE 1, p. 1. "*Eighteen hundred years before the Christian era.*"— This is the date given in the introductory chapter of Fauche's French translation of the Rāmāyana. Monsieur Michelet, in the "Bible de l'Humanité," attributes the Poem to a still earlier period, mentioning 2000 B.C. as the latest epoch admissible. There seems, however, to be little unanimity of opinion amongst Sanskrit scholars about even the approximate date of the Rāmāyana. Weber, in his Academical Lectures on Indian Literature, concludes, from the silence of Megasthenes, that there existed in his day no record of Indian Poetry; whence he infers that the compilation of the *Mahā-Bhārata*, generally supposed posterior to the Rāmāyana, took place at some time between the year 300 B.C. and 50 A.D., when it is mentioned by a Greek Historian.

CHAPTER II.

NOTE 1, pp. 13, 14. "*Eternal Spirit,*" &c. "*Brahm,*" &c.—"Strictly speaking, the Religion of the Hindus is *Monotheism*. They worship God in unity; and express their conceptions of the Divine Being in the most awful and sublime terms. God thus adored is called Brahm, the One Eternal Mind, the Self-existing Eternal Spirit, &c. The Will of God that the world should exist and continue is personified; and His preservative power appear in *Brahma* and *Vishnu*; while *Siva* is the creative and emblem of his destructive energy : not, however, of absolute annihilation, but rather of reproduction in another form." (*Vide* Moor's "Hindu Pantheon.")

NOTE 2, p. 24. "*The eight things of the Arghya.*"—Presents offered in a basket to a newly-arrived guest; amongst these offerings were rice, darbha-grass, flowers, water, and honey, all of which had their emblematic significance.

NOTE 3, p. 24. The story of the *Hundred Daughters of Kusanābha* scarcely admits of translation into English. At the same time it contains so much *naïveté* and humour, that I have no hesitation in recommending it to the notice of my readers, as it stands in M. Fauche's French translation, chap. xxxv. vol. i. French is an easier medium than our own language for the transmission of this primitive candour, which is free from all impurity; and only seems coarse to our modern taste, because we are less simple and single-minded than men were in those early days.

CHAPTER III.

NOTE 1, p. 36. "*Tiger of Men.*"—"Expressions in frequent use are. Lion among Kings, Tiger of Men, Bull among Solitaries, &c., when one would say : the most excellent of anchorites, the most eminent of men, the noblest of kings, &c. We have at times translated in this somewhat timorous manner, but have ceased to do so, seeing at once that it was to efface the individual, primitive, and local colouring." Thus speaks Monsieur Fauche. I, too, would ask my readers to pardon the first strangeness and apparent extravagance of these expressions in consideration of the covert fun glancing through them; which, I do not doubt, will conquer in the end the objections they are pretty sure to be disposed to make in the commencement. I was myself inclined to call out on these characteristic phrases as barbarisms, unworthy of conversion; until the humorous significance of the term, "*Bull among Penitents*," as applied to the persistent Anchorite Visvāmitra, won me over to the same opinion as Monsieur Fauche.

NOTE 2, p. 36. "*Pradakshina.*"—A method of salutation, consisting of turning round the person to be greeted, taking pains always to have him to the right of one.

NOTES. 313

NOTE 3, p. 42. "*Rahu.*"—A headless monster, who in times of eclipse was supposed to devour the sun or moon, as the case might be. How he managed this little matter, lacking a head, and consequently one would suppose a mouth, I cannot undertake to say; nor do any of the Mythological Works I have searched throw light on the subject.

CHAPTER XI.

The occurrence of this chapter in the midst of the history of Rāma's wanderings is somewhat unfortunate. I should have preferred placing it among the earlier chapters, where there was no continuous thread running through the narrative. But in so doing I should have seemed to interpolate a sketch of my own among the stories purporting to draw at least their subject-matter from the Rāmāyana. All I can suggest is that the Reader good enough to feel an interest in the fortunes of the bereaved Dasarathide should return to this chapter only after having seen the Hero well through his troubles.

It is probable, too, that I may be accused of having given a significance to this Legend, unwarranted by aught in the original Poem. To a certain extent, I plead guilty to the charge. That is to say, I admit that Valmīki relates the story of the false Brides of Indra without revealing any allegorical sense, nor intentionally suggesting any. But what then? I do not profess to be *translating* the Rāmāyana; merely, I am striving to put into readable form the leading incidents therein related. It is simply unavoidable that, to a certain extent, these stories should have a colouring of detail, and a purport more or less personal; otherwise how could I hope to make them more than meaningless fragments of the great Poem, which dawdles languidly through seven formidable volumes, at a pace ill-suited to the impatient intellects of our busy age?

At the same time, as far as the facts or leading points of the tale go, I have not, in any instance, departed from the original Work. That the Reader may judge for himself how far I am justified in lending an allegorical sense to this fable, I will quote the passage as given by Monsieur Fauche, in the forty-fourth chapter of the fifth volume.

Sugrīva is giving a detailed description of the country he is sending certain of his envoys to explore. Having told them how they may reach the country of the Uttarakurus, he says:

"Il est défendu par un fleuve noir, grandement épouvantable et de qui le torrent impétueux entraine toute chose avec lui. Vous le traversez à grande peine, vous en fouillez habilement les deux rives, et vous entrez nobles Singes, chez les Uttarakurus, grands, magnifiques, qui vivent toujours dans la joie et de qui l'âme est inaccessible aux soucis. On ne connait là ni l'hiver ni l'été, ni la vieillesse, ni la maladie, ni la crainte, ni le chagrin, ni les pluies furieuses, ni les ardeurs brûlantes du soleil. . . . Là cachées sous des arbres d'or, coulent sur un sable d'or, les rivières à lotus d'or, où les montagnes d'or vont baigner leurs pieds ; les nympheas d'or bruni couvrent de riches moissons les étangs. . . . On ceuille sur les arbres des fruits qui sont de merveilleux bijoux, or au chaton de pierreries, et modelés suivant la forme que chacun désire. Ils produisent à leurs branches et des lits, et des hausses brodés, et divers compositions de parfums. . . . Là, fières de leur jeunesse et de leur beauté, vivent des femmes comblées des plus séduisantes qualités. . . . . Les hommes de la plus haute noblesse, bien faits, vigoureux, de qui la bouche ne sait dire que des choses agréables ou flatteuses, tous devoués à la volupté, exempts de fatigue, de faim, de peril, et d'inquiétude habitent là avec leurs épouses au sein d'une grande fortune et dans la satisfaction de tous les désirs. . . . On voit des femmes d'une incomparable distinction, aux yeux de lotus, aux visages de nelumbos. . . La jeunesse de toutes ces femmes s'écoule dans un seul jour ; elles naissent au lever du soleil et la nuit à son retour les voit déjà vieilles ! On sait que jadis elles furent des Apsaras, qui sans plus songer au Monarque des Immortels passaient le temps à s'amuser dans ces lieux aimables. . . . Le grand Indra les maudit toutes. . . Tous les jours naissent et meurent ces femmes qui furent des Apsaras, et la malédiction du grand Indra les roule ainsi de la naissance à la mort."

CHAPTER XIII.

NOTE 1, p. 203. "*Hanuman's tail.*"—I was much startled by the announcement, that this illustrious Orang-outang was so far favoured beyond his species. In fact I confess to having had some design of suppressing the tail altogether ; but as the Reader will perceive, later on, that would have involved passing over many memorable events in silence. Now not being myself a Sanskrit scholar, I cannot tell whether my authority, Mons. Fauche, may have erred in calling Hanuman an Orang-outang. He certainly does so speak of him : for example, in the first chapter of the fifth volume, and in other instances. But after all there may be no mistake; Hanuman was altogether an extraordinary Ape; might he not have possessed a tail, together with his other exceptional qualities,—or have obtained one in recompense for a few thousand years of self-maceration?

CHAPTER XIV.

NOTE 1, p. 248. "*The Oath of the Kshatriya.*"—"The oath on admission into the military order or caste of the Kshatriya, was the origin of the vows of Knighthood in the Middle Ages." (Note of M. Fauche.)

NOTE 2, p. 252. "*Visvakarman.*"—"The Architect of the Universe, and the fabricator of arms for the Gods, is the Son of Brahma, and the Vulcan of the Hindus. He is also called 'Sootar,' or carpenter, and presides over arts and manufactures." (*Vide* Coleman's "Mythology of Hindus.")

CHAPTER XVIII.

I should, perhaps, state that Valmīki does not mention the death of Mandōdarī; yet her fate, as related in this chapter, appears to me quite in keeping with the impassioned though jealous character of the "Diamond among Beautiful Women."

THE END.

www.ingramcontent.com/pod-product-compliance
Lightning Source LLC
Chambersburg PA
CBHW021158230426
43667CB00006B/454